A Country Called Prison

A COUNTRY CALLED PRISON

Mass Incarceration and the Making of a New Nation

Mary D. Looman

John D. Carl

OXFORD
UNIVERSITY PRESS

OXFORD
UNIVERSITY PRESS

Oxford University Press is a department of the University of
Oxford. It furthers the University's objective of excellence in research,
scholarship, and education by publishing worldwide.

Oxford   New York
Auckland   Cape Town   Dar es Salaam   Hong Kong   Karachi
Kuala Lumpur   Madrid   Melbourne   Mexico City   Nairobi
New Delhi   Shanghai   Taipei   Toronto

With offices in
Argentina   Austria   Brazil   Chile   Czech Republic   France   Greece
Guatemala   Hungary   Italy   Japan   Poland   Portugal   Singapore
South Korea   Switzerland   Thailand   Turkey   Ukraine   Vietnam

Oxford is a registered trademark of Oxford University Press
in the UK and certain other countries.

Published in the United States of America by
Oxford University Press
198 Madison Avenue, New York, NY 10016

Library of Congress Cataloging-in-Publication Data
Mary D. Looman
A Country Called Prison : Mass Incarceration and the Making of a New Nation / Mary D. Looman,
John D. Carl.
    pages cm
ISBN 978-0-19-021103-5 (hardback)
1. Imprisonment—United States—History.   2. Prisons—United States—
History.   3. Prisoners—United States—History.   I. Carl, John D.   II. Title.
HV9466.L66 2015
365'.973—dc23
2014039670

9 8 7 6 5 4 3 2 1
Printed in the United States of America
on acid-free paper

In memory of my brothers—Nick & Jim Schuman.
If only I knew then what I know now.
Your loving sister, Mary Dale

To my loving wife, Keven,
who shows her inner strength every day.
Love, John

CONTENTS

PREFACE

Change is the law of life. And those who look only to the past or the present are certain to miss the future.

John F. Kennedy

The first thing that you need to know is that this book is about change—big change. We have studied and taught about crime, criminology, and criminal justice for years. We have also worked in the industry. Mary, in particular, has more than 30 years of experience in the criminal justice system. She has been a prison psychologist for many years and is a college professor; John is a college professor but always a social worker and sociologist. We look at the reality of the criminal justice system through our respective backgrounds.

This book is the result of years of study, thought, and concern for the current state of America as well as its citizens: not just the citizens who have been caught committing a criminal act but also those who have broken the law and not been caught. We believe that the United States has unintentionally built a country within its own borders, a country we call "Prison." Prisons are found far and wide. And for the most part they are filled with people who have broken the law. No one denies this fact.

Most of us have broken the law at some point in our lives, even if it is just driving at an excessive speed. Frequently the difference between criminals and noncriminals is the act of getting caught. We know many noncriminals who have done the same thing as criminals but who have not been caught, and no one is the wiser.

Data show that many people have used an illegal drug. A report from the Centers for Disease Control and Prevention shows that approximately 40% of high school seniors have tried marijuana by the end of their senior year (Centers for Disease Control [CDC], 2011.). The U.S. Department of Health and Human Services reports that over 20% of Americans between the ages of 18 to 25 have used an illegal substance in the past month. These reports indicate that most of us either have or know someone who has done something illegal in the last month (Substance Abuse and Mental Health Services Administration [SAMHSA], 2012). If the something is using illegal drugs, it could very well be a ticket to the Country Called Prison.

The difference between the 20-year-old who lights up a joint at a fraternity party and the 20-year-old who lights up in a public park and is arrested is less about the act and more about the person's status. The college student is protected by a perception that getting high is just a social "rite of passage." He will have a funny memory to tell on the golf course in years to come. Meanwhile, the poor young man smoking pot in the park may end up in jail because he has nowhere to hide.

Since the 1980s, the United States has been experimenting with an interesting method of social control. The country hopes that sending millions of wrongdoers to prison will somehow change their behavior. Such a policy is not only expensive but also has made the United States the world leader in prison populations. Don't believe it? Review the data that follow.

Table P.1 shows the top-10 countries in prison populations worldwide according to the World Prison Brief, as well as the population-size ranking of those countries according to the U.S. Census. These data show that the United States incarcerates more of its own citizens than any other nation on earth. The high prison population numbers in the United States dwarf many of its similarly sized counterparts. In addition, the United States, which is approximately one-eighth the size of India and China combined, has more prisoners than those two countries put together. At the same time, the United States, which is only slightly larger than Indonesia in total population, incarcerates 14 times more people than that country. So does population size necessarily influence the incarceration rate? Perhaps. But one thing is clear: Incarceration is a priority in the United States.

Table P.1. TOP-10 PRISON POPULATIONS

Prison Population Rank	Country	Total Prison Population	World Population Rank
1	United States	2,228,424	4
2	China	1,701,344	1
3	Russia	675,000	10
4	Brazil	548,003	6
5	India	385,135	2
6	Thailand	307,924	21
7	Mexico	254,108	12
8	Iran	217,851	19
9	South Africa	157,394	28
10	Indonesia	154,000	5

Sources: U.S. Census, 2010; World Prison Brief, 2013.

Of course, total numbers only tell part of the story. The total number of inmates in a country could certainly be affected by its size. Total numbers can also be misleading because some countries may not have the same level of economic development and quality of law enforcement that the United States does. For example, if a country has few high-value, lightweight items, like laptop computers, there is less to steal. In this particular country, because everyone is poor, then it seems unlikely that such a nation would have high crime rates. A more important question is, "How does the United States compare to other countries of all sizes?"

Using rates of incarceration allows for a fair comparison. Rates in Table P.2 represent the number of incarcerated people per every 100,000 of the population. Table P.2 shows the top-10 prison population rates according to the World Prison Brief and the population-size ranking of those countries according to the U.S. Census.

According to these data, the United States ranks second in the rate of incarceration for every 100,000 people of population. The winner in the incarceration rate competition is the tiny Indian Ocean island of Seychelles, with a rate of more than 860 prisoners for every 100,000 people. The United States, in second place, imprisons 707 people out of every 100,000 (World Prison Brief, 2013).

Table P.2. PRISON POPULATIONS PER 100,000 PEOPLE

Prison Population Rank	Country	Prison Populations Rate per 100,000	World Population Ranking
1	Seychelles	868	198
2	United States	707	4
3	St. Kitts and Nevis	611	209
4	Anguilla (U.K.)	543	221
5	Virgin Islands (U.S.)	535	195
6	Barbados	529	181
7	Cuba	510	78
8	Belize	495	178
9	Rwanda	492	74
10	Russia	470	10

Source: U.S. Census, 2010; World Prison Brief, 2013.

Table P.2 also provides the rank of the country by the size of its population. Note that the United States is the most populated country on the list. Most of the countries listed are small, and none of them, except Russia, would meet the criteria for a developed nation. Thus, the data appears to demonstrate that with the exception of Russia and the United States, most countries with high incarceration rates are small and poor.

Comparing the United States to these nations may seem unfair and perhaps misleading because we are not similar to most of them. Nearly all of them are underdeveloped. Except for Russia, most of their populations are small, and some, like Cuba and Russia, are known for repressive leadership regimes that incarcerate people who disagree with government policies (but these types of prisoners are probably not reported).

Since the countries that report high rates of incarceration are so different from the United States, another question comes to mind. How does the U.S. incarceration rate stack up against similarly wealthy countries? The ten largest economies in the world in gross domestic product (GDP), according to the International Monetary Fund, are listed in Table P.3. It ranks the countries by size of GDP and shows their value in trillions of dollars. The table also ranks the

Table P.3. RICHEST COUNTRIES' INCARCERATION RATES

GDP Rank	Country	GDP in Trillions of Dollars	Prison Population Rate Rank	Prison Population Rate
1	United States	17.50	2	707
2	China	10.00	124	124
3	Japan	4.80	198	51
4	Germany	3.90	164	81
5	France	2.90	146	102
6	United Kingdom	2.80	97	149
7	Brazil	2.20	41	274
8	Italy	2.20	90	90
9	Russia	2.10	10	470
10	India	2.00	216	30

Sources: World Economic Outlook Database, n.d.; World Prison Brief, 2013.

countries by prison population per 100,000 people, as well as their rate of incarceration.

As is commonly known, the United States is the largest economy on the planet. What you'll notice is that, with the exception of Russia and the United States, there seems to be almost an inverse relationship between wealth and incarceration rates. Wealthy countries, except the United States and Russia, generally have low rates of incarceration. These data suggest that for most of the countries that are similar to the United States in economic standing, wealth does not increase incarceration rates. So, the claim that somehow because the United States is wealthy it has high crime does not seem to fit international comparisons.

To illustrate this point further, as you consider these data, you will notice some interesting facts. Japan, the third-richest country in the world, is about a quarter of the economic size of the United States but has an incarceration rate approximately 13 times lower than ours. Germany's incarceration rate is about 9 times lower, while that of France is about 7 times lower.

These data seem to raise more questions than they answer. Wealth and incarceration rates do not seem to be obviously related. Perhaps the answer is that the United States simply has more crime. After all, if we incarcerate more of our citizens than our wealthy, industrialized counterparts, perhaps it is because our citizens are more criminal than theirs. Just as with incarceration rates, international data tell the story.

Table P.4 provides comparison data for the United States and a few other wealthy, industrialized democracies. Like the rates in the other tables, these rates are per 100,000 people of the population of the country. Additionally, these countries were chosen because most criminologists would trust the data from these nations. In other words, their reporting is believed to be as accurate as that of the United States, and so a fair comparison can be made.

It is important to note that many of the countries listed in these tables are likely to keep good records and openly report all their incarcerated citizens. This is especially true for the modern, industrial democracies that are listed in Table P.4. For other nations that might not be in that category, or that might be wealthy but not democratic, we should accept that the data they report may not be accurate. However, when we consider modern, industrial, wealthy democracies, comparisons likely are fair.

These data show some surprising results. You will see that contrary to what many think, the United States does not have the highest crime rates in the world. In fact, its total crime rate is less than that of the United Kingdom and almost the same as Germany's. The United States does have significantly higher rates of homicide. Yet the rates are not higher when it comes to other types of crime such as theft, robbery,

Table P.4. INTERNATIONAL CRIME RATES PER 100,000 PEOPLE

	United Kingdom	France	Germany	Japan	United States
Robbery	159.95	35.94	74.81	3.34	147.36
Homicide	1.5	1.6	1.2	0.5	5.0
Rape	16	14	9	1	32
Assault	834	163	139	22	805
Theft	3,358	3,844	3,891	1,279	2,503
Motor Vehicle Theft	711	507	114	225	412
Drug offenses	231	176	276	21	560
All crime	10,061	6,088	7,676	1,705	8,517

Source: Kesteren, Mayhew, & Nieuwbeerta, 2000.

and assault. The data do not support the claim that the United States has significantly higher crime rates.

Another important category in which the United States has the highest rates of crime is drug offenses. The U.S. decision to criminalize illegal drug use and punish harshly anyone associated with it is, in our estimation, the main reason that we have now created a country within our nation that we call Prison.

While criminality may be part of high U.S. incarceration rates, it is also important to note that the rates of certain crimes do not match the ratio of those incarcerated for them. For example, the United States incarcerates at a rate of 707 per 100,000 people, while France incarcerates at a rate of 102. But France's crime rate is not 7 times lower than that of the United States.

In fact, France's crime rate is only slightly lower. A simple review of these nations' data and total crime rates show clearly one thing. While some of these nations may have lower total crime rates, the rates seem to be minimally related to their incarceration rates. Therefore, proclaiming that "the U.S. must incarcerate more people because there are more criminals" is not supported by the data.

If these countries have similar rates of crime, why do they have lower rates of incarceration? The simple answer is that these countries have different social policies and cultural attitudes about incarceration. The United States decided that prison is the best and, frequently, the only way to control people who do things the majority of citizens don't like.

Put another way, the United States incarcerates those who frighten society, as well as those at whom society is mad. No one questions the wisdom of incarcerating violent offenders—those we fear. Most of the nations listed in the tables do just that. The difference in incarceration rates between the United States and other countries is often in the way that these other countries punish people who do things that their societies don't like. For example, no one likes to see someone drunk or high on drugs in public. It is unpleasant to view an addict in the subway. However, should we really spend millions of dollars incarcerating these people?

Prisons are ubiquitous in the United States. They have become a part of life for many. Almost everyone knows someone who has either been to prison or works in one. Prisons are not just centers for punishment; they are also places to work.

The Federal Bureau of Labor Statistics (BLS) reports that prisons always need workers (BLS, 2012). If you have a high school diploma and desire to take a bit of risk, you too can be a "prison guard." The BLS reports that the median annual salary for a correctional officer is $38,970, or $749 per week. Compare that to the current minimum hourly wage of $7.25, which adds up to $290 per week. You can see that guarding the incarcerated is a relatively well-paying job. It requires no advanced training or certification, since on-the-job training is provided. No wonder that in 2012 more than 400,000 people in the United States worked correctional jobs (Bureau of Justice Statistics [BJS]).

Of course, correctional officers are the tip of the proverbial prison employment iceberg. There are more than 90,000 probation officers and correctional treatment specialists (BJS). In addition, literally millions of people work in prison-related businesses. Criminal justice has become not only a way of life for many in the United States but also a way to make money.

A report on prisons by the Pew Trusts identifies that, from 1977 to 2003, state and local expenditures on prisons increased by over 1,100%. Meanwhile, spending for education and health care grew by less than 600% and public welfare expenditures grew by a little over 700% (Pew Charitable Trusts, 2013). Spending on prisons has continued to grow at significantly higher rates than other important human services. This diversion of money from the public or social good to prisons raises an interesting question. Are we spending tax money wisely when we spend it on prisons?

The government funds social services or the public good in order to improve the lives of the country's citizens. Generally, this spending is intended to benefit large numbers of people. If your town is building a new park, then the government is spending that money on the justification that the park will be a public good. Defining what is and is not a public good is the source of great political debate. Those on the far Left suggest that almost all public services should be deemed as public goods, while those on the far Right suggest that almost nothing, other than military protection, should be viewed as such. We cannot hope to resolve this debate in our book, but we do raise the question: Is spending money on prisons really a social good or are we inadvertently developing a new nation inside U.S. borders?

As you read this book, we hope to take you on a journey of understanding that will provide you with up-to-date facts, figures, theories, and research, as well as human stories of life in the Country Called Prison.

Max Weber challenged researchers to practice *Verstehen*, to attempt to understand the actions of an actor from the actor's point of view (Weber, 1968). This is what we attempt to do in this book. We want to move you, the reader, beyond the mere facts and figures that you can find in a textbook. Through the anecdotes in this book, we want you to see the lives behind the data.

ABOUT THIS BOOK

This book is filled with stories that were created from our memories working in criminal justice organizations and social service agencies. The names and descriptions of people depicted in our stories are representative of those we have met in our professional experience. In every case, names, genders, ages, races, offenses, and towns were changed so that no one specifically could be recognized. The stories are representative of real criminals, prison workers, and politicians we have encountered. We believe these stories strengthen our thesis and help you, the reader, to better understand the human faces behind the data. We stand on the shoulders of Max Weber as we strive to move beyond facts and figures of this social phenomenon.

In chapter one, we introduce the ways prisons became a country. We discuss the history of punishment both in the United States and the Western world as a whole. We also investigate theories that have guided the types of punishment that have been used over the centuries. These theories guide governments as they try to exert social control over their citizens. We will address some of the policy decisions that have led to the mass incarceration of U.S. citizens and eventually the unintended consequence of the creation of the Country Called Prison.

In chapter two, "What Makes Prisons a Country," we review the elements that characterize a country: unified people, geography, history, language, and culture. Then we identify ways that mass incarceration fits those elements. We discuss the ways offenders must assimilate to prison culture in order to survive. The culture of prison shows them ways to behave and interact with others and gives meaning to their lives behind the razor-wire fences. Inmates must adapt to a culture that includes values and beliefs that do not exist anywhere else in the world except prison. Over time, prison inmates learn to live in their new world and, when released, return to a land they no longer understand.

In chapter three, "Who Are the People of the Country Called Prison?," we begin by debunking the pervasive myth, popular in the United States, that all people in prison are violent and scary. We then examine the very different way that most people from the Country Called Prison grew up. As children, they frequently experienced a very different psychosocial development process than children in traditional American families. Our examination demonstrates that the majority of prison inmates are not violent and scary but are often poorly educated, poorly socialized, often addicted, and frequently mentally ill. We suggest that the reason for the continued high recidivism rate of former prison inmates is that we base solutions and programs on the erroneous assumption that it is only the offender's fault.

We believe that the root of the problem lies in an impeded normal childhood development process, as well as social and cultural components that encourage criminality. Therefore, in order to make the current culture of the Country Called Prison more pro-social, we propose solutions that focus on restoring the psychosocial development process of its citizens.

In chapter four, "Living in the Country Called Prison," we deliberate the reasons that prison environments have changed so little since the infamous Stanford Prison Experiment conducted by Phillip Zimbardo in 1970. In our discussion, we bring to light the four different subcultural groups that coexist within the prison geographic region: inmates, security personnel, administrative staff, and licensed professionals. Each group has its own language, customs and values, perceptions of power, and relationship patterns. Since adults learn new cultural behaviors through observation, instruction, imitation, and reinforcement, we propose strategies that rely on these principles in order to shift the prison environment toward a milieu that encourages human development and growth rather than human degradation.

In chapter five, "Visiting America from the Country Called Prison," we state that most former inmates return to prison within five years after their release. Then we ask, "Why?" All over the world, people successfully transition from one country to another, from one culture to another. How does this happen? What can we do differently that will make the homecoming of former inmates permanent and beneficial to society? Through Mary's experiences of helping former inmates during their first year of release, we reveal a constellation of obstacles that former inmates face when they return to the "free world," which for many is a misnomer. However, by understanding these obstacles, we can help explain the steadfast recidivism rate of the last twenty years. With our new insights, we use Abraham Maslow's Hierarchy of Needs model of human motivation to discuss strategic proposals that aid successful assimilation of citizens from the Country Called Prison into U.S. culture.

In chapter six, "Emigrating from the Country Called Prison," we pose the question, "What can be done for the long haul?" We point out that there is a difference between crime control and punishment. Crime control involves either setting up situations that make crime more difficult to commit or creating citizens who don't want to commit crimes. Prison and punishment are something totally different.

All social systems are designed by people and, therefore, can be changed by people. We acknowledge, however, that the status quo has evolved over time and will naturally take time to change. We use theories and models from sociology and macro social work to orchestrate legitimate changes in order to reinvent the criminal justice system. These are the big changes we warned you about at the beginning of the book. These are the changes that will require legislation, long-term policy and procedure changes, and long-range visions that focus and measure success rather than failures.

In chapter seven, "Assimilating the Country Called Prison," we summarize the main reasons that the United States now has a huge problem and the primary justifications for solving it now.

At the end of the text, we provide an appendix that summarizes our proposals along with a list of strategies and measurable goals for each proposal. It is our hope that policy makers and interested parties will take these proposals and strategies and use them as a road map for decreasing the size of this growing nation within U.S. borders.

We conclude that the United States has, through deliberate policy decisions, disenfranchised millions of its own citizens, citizens who could pay taxes, support local schools, and care for their children. Instead, these citizens have become residents of this country we call Prison. As you read the book, we hope that you will better understand the reasons we steadfastly believe that within the United States there is a Country Called Prison and that we must transform the criminal justice system now to regain these lost citizens.

WHO CAN BENEFIT FROM THIS BOOK

This book is intended for criminal justice and correctional leadership, policy makers, reformists, interested parties, and the academic community. Since this is such a broad audience, we want readers to first explore and become familiar with universal cultural concepts that are superimposed over the harsh realities of poverty, crime, incarceration, and social alienation. We hope then that policy makers and reformists will close the book with new insights into the vastness of the problem, which goes beyond razor-wire fences. We hope that criminal justice and correctional leaders will realize that they inhabit a brave new world where a century of traditional policies and procedures will no longer be sufficient. We hope academics will be introduced to a perspective of corrections that is humanistic and pro-social rather than regulatory, pejorative, and detrimental. We hope students will become passionate about the possibility of change and bring their fresh insights to an antiquated system.

ACKNOWLEDGMENTS

MARY D. LOOMAN, MAJ, PhD

To those who made this journey worthwhile I give my affection and thanks: my daughters, Calypso Gilstrap and Adrianna Cherry, who give me unequivocal love and support; their endearing husbands, Rob and Jeremy; and my unique, wonderful grandchildren—Cynthia, Alexandra, Veronica, Ian, and Aspen.

I am grateful for all the people, past and present, who have listened to me wonder about all sorts of things, some of which evolved into the concepts found in this book. In particular, I thank Kevin McAndrew, LaDeana Cummins, Joyce Lopez, Sharon Neasbitt, and Mary Ellen Million.

Who would have guessed that when my coauthor agreed to combine our experiences and wisdom in writing this book I would discover that I now have a buddy who completely understands the value of playing in a sandbox.

JOHN D. CARL, MSW, PhD

I cannot overstate my gratitude for the support I receive from my wife, Keven. Your unwavering support for me is the greatest blessing in my life. I also send all my love and appreciation to my father, who continues to show me how to age with dignity. To my daughters, Caroline and Sara, as well as Gray, I'm lucky to call you all my family!

I also appreciate the support of many friends, too numerous to list here, as well as colleagues who have served as an "ear" for ideas in this book. I especially thank Aaron Bachhofer, Michael Copeland, Jim Goins, Bill Ross, and Arnold Waggoner.

Last but certainly *not* least, I thank my coauthor and friend, Mary D. Looman. When Mary came to me and suggested we collaborate on a book, I had no idea where that would end. Her insight, dedication, and effervescent personality have made working on this project a pleasure. Thank you!

MARY D. LOOMAN AND JOHN D. CARL

Of course, no book of any kind is solely constructed by its authors. The process of writing involves many talented people who use their talents to support and improve the book you see before you. Throughout the process of writing this book, the staff and editors at Oxford University Press have been exceptional. They are quite simply the best we have had the privilege with which to work. Thanks to the whole team! We thank in particular Dana Bliss and Brianna Marron for their enthusiasm, professionalism, and trust. Special thanks go to LaDeana Cummins, for her willingness to proofread the book and provide us with valuable feedback from a fresh perspective.

ABOUT THE AUTHORS

Mary D. Looman holds a master's degree in administration of justice from Wichita State University and a PhD in clinical psychology from the Fielding Graduate Institute. She spent her early childhood in Virginia and most of her life in Kansas. She now lives in Norman, Oklahoma, near her two daughters' families, including five grandchildren who keep her nights and weekends full of activities. Dr. Looman is a psychologist with the Oklahoma Department of Corrections, serves as an adjunct professor for the master's degree program in criminal justice at the University of Oklahoma, and has a part-time private practice conducting evaluations and equine-assisted growth and learning programs. Her clinical practice experiences include rural mental health, child and adolescent inpatient services, and forensics.

Dr. Looman always maintains a list of new things to learn and experience alongside the joy she experiences being with her family. In her free time, she enjoys writing, art projects, learning to play the piano, and gardening.

John D. Carl holds a master's degree in social work and a PhD in sociology, both from the University of Oklahoma. He lives in Norman, Oklahoma, with his wife and family. Dr. Carl is an assistant professor at the University of Oklahoma, where he teaches criminology and criminal justice–related course work. He has spent most of his life in Oklahoma, living for brief periods of time in Texas, Indiana, and Mexico. His social work practice experiences include mental health, prisons, disabilities, and hospital- and hospice-related work.

Dr. Carl continues to enjoy his life as it unfolds, striving always to be curious. In particular, he finds support from family and friends who enrich his life. In his free time, he gardens, throws pottery, plays his guitar, and occasionally finds a golf course on which he loses a few balls.

A Country Called Prison

CHAPTER 1

Introduction to the Country Called Prison

> Being unwanted, unloved, uncared for, forgotten by everybody, I think that is a much greater hunger, a much greater poverty, than the person who has nothing to eat.
>
> *Mother Teresa*

What to do with "wrongdoers" is a problem as old as humanity itself. No matter the size, shape, or demographic makeup of an area, there have always been people who break the rules. In preliterate societies the problem might have been rather simple to solve. First, most population groups were small; therefore, social control was relatively easy. Anyone who has more than one child understands that more people in any social system increases its complexity. Preliterate societies generally handled disputes by assent to an authority figure who made decisions.

As societies became more complex, however, so too did questions of laws and fairness. The first legal code with any precision is known as the Code of Hammurabi. Named after the 6th Babylonian king, the code dates from around 1770 BCE and provides more than 280 laws and punishments. Many of these laws concern legal matters of contract, issues of inheritance, divorce, and family issues. The code also deals with criminality, including appropriate punishments for certain acts. It paints a picture of a society struggling with the meaning of justice. The code attempts to define the tenet of *lex talionis*, better known as the "eye for an eye, tooth for a tooth" standard, by providing precise limits on punishments for certain crimes. Some acts that are determined to be "acts of God" can exonerate the individual from responsibility. For example, if a person owes a debt and a storm ruins the grain that he planned to use to pay the debt, then he can avoid paying his debt that year because it is an act of God. If, on the other hand, you merely try to welsh on your debt, then punishment can occur (Code of Hammurabi, 1770 BCE).

Early Greek and Roman societies laid the foundation for much of the Western world and our ideas about justice and punishment. These two societies frequently used slavery, banishment, and death as punishments for illegal activities. During that time banishment could be a fate worse than death as the offender lost the protection of the city and had to fend for him- or herself. Romans also crucified thousands in an effort to control enemies of the state. Overall, punishment in these societies was quite harsh.

Later, in Europe, this view of punishment persisted. Throughout Europe's history, harsh punishment abounded. Notably, harsh punishments did not seem to curb criminality. In fact, severe punishments, such as those listed in Table 1.1, had little effect on the actions of those they were intended to rehabilitate. The table provides a list of punishments used in the Western world throughout the Middle Ages and even into the Reformation. These punishments are only a few of the ways that those in power throughout history have tried to control the behavior of others.

Whenever we take an action to control an entity, whether a person or a dog, some thought process is behind it. If, for example, you housebreak your pet, you do so because you believe that animals should go to the bathroom outside. But you would never expect a human houseguest to use the lawn as their toilet. You have an idea about how each situation should be handled. Decisions about the way to deal with rule breakers are not that much different. Frequently, we decide that punishment is necessary and take for granted the manner in which we do it. Although some of the punishments listed in Table 1.1 seem archaic and inhumane, the people who enforced those punishments thought that they were doing a public good. We are not that much different today in the way we decide who goes to prison and who does not.

Table 1.1. PUNISHMENTS

Form of Punishment	Description
Banishment	Forcing the offender to leave his or her home permanently or for a set time period.
Beheading	Often carried out with a sword or ax and eventually with the guillotine.
Cane & Flogging	Hitting the offender with sticks or a whip. Used on slaves and soldiers to maintain control. Also used in reform schools of the early 17th, 18th, and 19th centuries.
Dunking Stool	Involves tying the offender to a seat on a long wooden arm and dunking the seat into the river. Usually used against women.
Flogging	Flogging involves whipping the person. Common throughout history; frequently used in the United States against slaves.
Hard Labor	Hard physical work, including rowing in the galleys of military ships.
Mutilation	Blinding or cutting off parts of the body, including hands, feet, tongue, among others. Used throughout history.
Pillory and Stocks	Placing a person's hands and head through a wooden frame attached to a pole. Usually used for public shaming.
Slavery	Enslavement of losers in battle and conquered people. In ancient Rome certain crimes could result in the person becoming a slave.
Transportation	Transporting criminals to colonies by European governments.

Sources: Farrington, 2000; Lyons, 2004.

Throughout history, people have been punished for a number of reasons that seemed valid at the time. Today we try to justify the reasons for punishment as well. Why? In reality, no one likes punishment. We don't like it when we are punished, and we feel uncomfortable punishing others. So let's look at some theories regarding punishment and see how they fit into the background of this Country Called Prison.

The theory of *retribution* or *retaliation* is as old as life on earth. Retribution allows the wronged party to impose a suitable punishment on the person who hurt them. When you were a toddler and someone hit you on the playground, you most likely hit them back. This is retaliation. The "eye-for-an-eye" standard is often quoted as the benchmark for retribution theorists.

Contrary to what many people believe, the "eye-for-an-eye" standard actually aimed to prevent people from taking *excessive* private vengeance for wrongs committed against them. As we have already discussed, the Code of Hammurabi was an effort to create a system of equitable justice. Our modern notion that the punishment should fit the crime follows this logic. There needs to be a reasonable consequence for the wrong action. Therefore, at least in the United States, we do not put burglars to death because such a punishment does not seem to fit that crime.

Expiation suggests that the criminal has committed a moral wrong. This theory holds to the idea that the guilty party must atone for his or her crime. Historically, crime and sin were linked in the minds of Europeans, and so it was logical that the wrongdoer should "make up" for the offense. If you have read Nathaniel Hawthorne's novel *The Scarlet Letter*, you might recall that it is a tale of expiation. In the story, an adulterous woman must atone for her sins by wearing a scarlet "A" on her clothing so that the community knows she has committed a transgression and that she suffers the shame and indignity of her "wrongdoing."

Today we do not force people in the general population to wear letters on their clothing indicating that they are criminals. In prison, however, "inmate" or "corrections" is printed on the back of shirts prisoners wear every day, even those in minimum security who are allowed to work outside the prison must wear these. We do believe that people who have wronged society should show remorse for their actions. When society assigns community service to a person who has driven under the influence, we are in some respects forcing them to atone for their crime by, for instance, picking up trash in a park. Their community service sentence is imposed to expiate or compensate for their crime.

Deterrence is perhaps the best known theory of punishment. Many parents instinctively use deterrence methods to socialize their children. If your 4-year-old son takes a cookie when he or she is not supposed to and you put him or her in "time-out," you are practicing deterrence. You believe that restricting your child's activities to the "time-out chair" will somehow teach him or her a lesson and deter him or her from taking the action again. Deterrence, like all theories of punishment, does nothing to prevent the initial action; it is designed to prevent future crime.

There are two types of deterrence: general and specific. General deterrence aims to prevent crime by teaching people that breaking the law brings punishment. When your 3-year-old daughter sees your 4-year-old son in time-out and therefore decides not to try to steal a cookie without permission, she has been generally deterred. Prison works as a general deterrent for most people. When John asks students whether they would be willing to risk incarceration, he always gets a resounding "NO." He then follows up that question with, "What personal experiences have you had that would cause you to feel so strongly about not wanting to go there?" Few in the room can adequately answer the second question. Yet they know they do not want to end up in prison. They are generally deterred by the mere thought of losing their freedom.

Specific deterrence is believed to have its effect on the offender. In theory, it is supposed to limit the likelihood that the lawbreaker will commit future crimes. When your 4-year-old son cries because he has been placed in time-out, he is supposedly "learning his lesson." When former inmates re-offend, society doesn't understand why they did not "learn their lesson." We believe that specific deterrence will correct behavior. When it does not work, society is troubled and often thinks that harsher punishment is needed. In this book, we will identify some reasons that prison does not deter crime, no matter how long the sentence or how harsh the conditions.

It is possible that through punishment your 4-year-old will learn how to be a better thief rather than learn to obey you. Consider your own actions. Were you ever punished for doing something wrong, but then did it again later? Have you ever received a speeding ticket and then exceeded the speed limit again? If the answer is yes, then you see that deterrence efforts are not always effective.

The British philosopher Jeremy Bentham (1748–1832) suggested that deterrence will usually work when three clear criteria are met ([1789] 1970). First, the action taken against the actor must be swift. When the mother sees the little boy reaching for the cookie jar, she must act immediately. Warning him to "wait till your father gets home" will do little to deter his behavior.

Second, there must be certainty. In other words, the boy must know for certain that if he goes for the illicit cookie, his mother will catch him and punish him. A lack of certainty is why people continue to exceed the speed limit, even after they have received a ticket. If you tend to drive fast frequently, you have learned that most of the time you will not be caught and punished. The efficacy of deterrence is limited to how certain the person is that she or he will get caught (see Figure 1.1).

Third, and finally, Bentham suggests that deterrence will work only if the punishment is severe enough that someone would not want to risk getting caught. If all the mother does is scold her son, he will likely get used to the tongue-lashings and not be deterred by them. Conversely, if the punishment is too severe, the person is unlikely to learn from that either. The child who is put in time-out for an entire day would likely see the punishment as unjust and therefore not accept its moral message. In other words, people who believe they have been singled out and harmed for no good reason are unlikely to learn deterrence from their punishment.

Because punishment rarely meets these three criteria, a person's ability to make a purely rational choice related to the potential risks of his or her behavior seems unlikely (Beccaria, [1764] 1963). Although punishment may be one of the few tools we have to deter bad behavior, it is, according to Bentham, an evil to be used cautiously ([1789] 1970).

Another reason for punishing individuals is grounded in moral reformation. Many early punishments in Europe had their roots in the Judaic-Christian tradition. The belief was that crime is a moral problem and therefore moral training is essential. Simply put, if people learn right from wrong, then they will make good choices and avoid crime. Hard labor was frequently the tool of moral training.

Hard labor as a method to teach values might seem odd. However, the current boot-camp prison movement is not really that different.

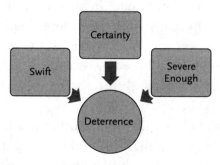

Figure 1.1: Components Necessary for Effective Deterrence.
Source: Bentham, (1789) 1970.

Inmates, usually young, are sent to quasi-military style prisons where their heads are shaved, they exercise regularly, and correctional officers act like drill sergeants. They work long hours under the rationale that these wrongdoers will learn from iron discipline and carry this discipline out into the world upon their release.

Perhaps the most important reason for incarceration is to protect society. By protecting innocent people from those who would harm them, prisons serve society well. When a serial killer or rapist is sent to prison, everyone is safer. As we will show, however, truly dangerous people make up a small percentage of those in prison in the United States.

As we will discuss, modern societies have determined that incapacitating those whom we fear is the best way to keep society safe. If we simply lock offenders up, we will all be more secure. In our work, we both have met people in prisons who should in fact be incarcerated. They are dangerous people. However, our experiences have shown that these offenders are the minority of prisoners.

The United States, at one point or another in its history, has used virtually all of the theories of punishment we just discussed. Frequently the religious, political, and economic forces of the nation have influenced our history of prisons and punishment.

Early settlers from Great Britain brought to the colonies attitudes toward punishment that were similar to those they had left behind in England. Begging and theft had become a problem in England, and so workhouses were instituted to keep potential troublemakers off the streets. Workhouses were essentially factory-style prisons that produced a source of cheap labor for the emerging capitalist class. Exploitation of these workers was common. It was hoped that through work these criminally minded people would be taught the importance of "proper" living.

Troublemakers might also become indentured servants. Rather than be sent to filthy dungeons, offenders would sign on to work for a craftsman. Their contract typically would last seven years. In exchange for their labor, they received housing and vocational training. Many chose this path to escape the poverty and overcrowding of England and make passage to the New World. However, indentured servitude was often as bad as slavery.

Slavery was instituted in the New World almost from the colonies' inception. Africans were taken from their homeland and forced to work, enriching the landed classes, particularly in the South. Until the Civil War, it was a criminal act if a slave endeavored to extricate him- or herself from slavery. In the midst of the Civil War, the U.S. Congress passed the Confiscation Act of 1862, which declared that all slaves who took refuge behind Union lines were free.

The slaves' new liberty was not long enjoyed, as homeless ex-slaves fleeing from their southern masters found themselves in poverty and frequently dependent on the federal government for sustenance (Freedmen, 2013). Many ex-slaves, then referred to as "freedmen," were sent to refugee camps where they were hired out to loyal Unionist plantation owners for low wages. Many died in the deplorable conditions of the camps. Some freedmen voluntarily returned to their former masters after the war as sharecroppers.

Racial inequality is clearly a part of U.S. history. As it applies to incarceration, we see a link between the way we treated slaves and former slaves, as well as Native Americans, and the disproportionate rates of incarceration of these two groups. Table 1.2 shows the rate of incarceration by race and ethnicity as reported by the Federal Bureau of Prisons. It also provides the percentage of each racial and ethnic group in the U.S. population.

The numbers are staggering. Although mass incarceration is detrimental to the American way of life for all citizens, many researchers believe it to be catastrophic for ethnic minority populations (Alexander & West, 2012; Wilson, 1987). Asian Americans and Caucasians are underrepresented in prison in proportion to their

Table 1.2. PERCENTAGE OF INMATES BY ETHNICITY

Ethnicity	Percentage of Inmates	Percentage of U.S. Population
Asian	1.6%	5.3%
Black	37.1%	13.2%
Native American	1.9%	1.2%
White (non-Hispanic)	24.9%	62.6%
Hispanic	34.5%	17.1%

Sources: Federal Bureau of Prisons, 2014; U.S. Census Quick Facts.

population, but African Americans are overrepresented by a factor of almost three while Hispanics are overrepresented by a factor of two.

This reality has led some to think of the prison system as a new form of slavery. Once again in the United States people are making money at the expense of African Americans, which prompted civil rights lawyer, advocate, and legal scholar Michelle Alexander to suggest that we are living in a new Jim Crow era. Her well-researched book *New Jim Crow* points to this hypothesis and the damage that it inflicts on families and communities (Alexander & West, 2012). This injustice is one of the reasons we decided to write this book.

We have considered the justifications for imprisonment, as well as some who are more likely than others to be put into unjust restrictive situations, so now let us turn to prisons themselves. They have changed a great deal over time. Prisons have existed at least since the first millennium BC, as evidenced by archeologists digging up ruins in Mesopotamia (www.prisonhistory.net). Societies have always needed to isolate those who are truly dangerous and destructive. The Country Called Prison did not appear overnight, with its citizens sneaking across the border like many undocumented immigrants today. Historical factors have influenced the current situation America finds herself in.

As soon as explorers began arriving on the shores of the newly discovered America, prisoners, providing a source of cheap labor, arrived as well. By 1650, many immigrants to America were indentured servants who had sold themselves into bondage for a trip to the New World. During this time prisons were essentially holding cells for people either awaiting trial or preparing for punishment. One of the most widely used punishments of this time was "transportation."

Nearly 50,000 British prisoners were transported to America between 1717 and 1775, with the number of prisoners from France and Spain following close behind. Not surprisingly, as cities came to life in America, jails were among the first structures erected. At one point, the colonies had more jails than public schools or hospitals. From its beginnings, America, which was founded on "freedom," has had a long history of limiting that freedom to certain groups, such as indentured servants, slaves, and Native Americas (Christian, 1998).

By the 1800s, prisons were being built in eleven states; most were called penitentiaries. These penitentiaries were named as such because crime was considered a sin and the criminal should learn to be penitent. In short, these centers of punishment did little to rehabilitate offenders.

Prison architecture changed a great deal over the years (Johnston, 2000). Initially, prisons were like the dungeons that you have seen in television shows and movies. They were large group holding cells filled with filth. People frequently died, not from the punishment, but from diseases contracted in the squalor.

In the early 1800s, Pennsylvania built one of the first prisons designed to isolate individuals. It did so because people believed that large group prisons were becoming training grounds for crime, so inmates needed to be isolated from one another. Isolating prisoners would keep the disease of criminality from spreading as well as physical diseases. While individual cells seemed plush compared to the dungeon-like conditions of earlier eras, the Pennsylvania prisons did little more than house and incapacitate individuals.

In the late 1800s and early 1900s, the United States transitioned into the Progressive Era, during which social reform took center stage. New ideas emerged about the role of government and way it should deal with social problems. Many reforms we take for granted today came about during the Progressive Era, for example, child labor laws. During this period, for the first time, the United States passed laws to criminalize certain substances. Previously, people were free to put whatever they wished into their bodies based on their right to privacy. The expansion of government control of people's daily lives changed our view of the purpose of prisons.

In the 1900s, the reform movement was in full bloom. Cities grew even larger, and as people moved to them, crime rose. During this time of intense immigration, squabbles often turned into violent altercations. Policy makers thought crime was a disease and charged prison administrators to "cure it." In addition, the rehabilitation movement grew on the premise that prisons should help eradicate crime by giving criminals the skills they need to avoid future offenses (Blomberg & Lucken, 2010).

The theory of rehabilitation was built on the belief that the criminal was a sick person. The job of the prison was similar to the job of a doctor. It was supposed to make the criminal "well." Therefore, if the inmate came into prison with deficits, the prison was supposed to fix those deficits. Prisons began to offer job training and occupation-related assistance. Prisons began to function less as houses of punishment and more like school; they began to "reform" the criminal (Blomberg & Lucken, 2010).

Offering different types of vocational training in an attempt to rehabilitate offenders became quite popular. Efforts to rehabilitate youthful offenders fell to reform schools. In theory, reform schools were supposed to prevent young people from becoming hardened criminals. In the case of Daniel O'Connell (1870), the Illinois Supreme Court ruled that young people could not be held against their will unless they had committed a serious offense. O'Connell was a vagrant teen who was caught and placed in the reform school. The ruling called into question the manner in which reform schools were being used and whether or not they were actually reforming anyone. In releasing O'Connell, the Court asserted that setting up prison-like facilities for teenagers didn't work well in preventing criminality and that the process of sending young people to them violated due-process standards (Champion, Merlo, & Benekos, 2013).

In the mid-1950s another phenomenon added citizens to the Country Called Prison. During this period U.S. psychiatric hospitals reached a population of about 550,000 (Lamb & Weinberger, 2005). About this time, the advent of antipsychotic medication initiated a drive to deinstitutionalize psychiatric hospital patients. Community-based treatment led to the reduction of long-term psychiatric inpatients to only 130,000 by 1980. While on paper community mental health appeared to be a humanitarian way to care for individuals with mental illness, funding for community centers never seemed sufficient.

As inpatient hospitals closed, a flood of people suffering from mental illness began living on the streets and in the homeless shelters of America's cities. Many eventually broke the law and were sent to prison because inpatient mental health care institutions had been closed (Jencks, 1994). Conservative estimates suggest that 56.2% of people in prison have a mental illness, 5 times greater than the general adult population (Humans Rights Watch, 2006).

Current research indicates that psychiatric deinstitutionalization has merely become "transinstitutionalization." Transinstitutionalization refers to the phenomenon where the inadequate and underfunded community-based mental health care programs are no longer able to care for mentally ill individuals. These people often commit crimes, and the criminal justice system is forced to accept them. Ironically, prison provides the structured environment that many mentally ill people need and that is no longer available in the community. Essentially, the mentally ill have moved from one institution to another. Of course, prisons are not meant for mental health treatment. They are designed for security (Prins, 2011).

After the end of World War II, crime rates rose as did the use of illegal substances. Public outcry over the inability of prisons to deal with crime led many to accept the claim by Robert Martinson that "nothing works" (1974). He and his followers claimed that rehabilitation had failed, and therefore there was no reason to spend money on prisons. Warehousing inmates and isolating them from society should be the new model. With a desire to cut spending, Martinson's proposal took root in America and remains the dominate paradigm for incarceration today. The logic of the warehousing model boils down to the belief that there is no need to spend money rehabilitating criminals. As our earlier example about a mother putting her child into all-day time-out showed, the problem with warehousing criminals is that eventually most get out of prison and they may emerge as angry or angrier as they were when they were sentenced.

In the 1980s, crime rates continued to rise. Ronald Reagan's "War on Drugs" was an attempt to punish drug dealers and users and solve the problem of drug abuse. At the same time, many states instituted "get tough" legislation to deal with crime. "Three-strikes" laws, aimed at habitual offenders, became popular. These laws put a person in prison for life for a third felony conviction. Sentencing laws created mandatory minimum sentences that limited judicial discretion and required convicted offenders to serve a greater portion of their sentence before being eligible for parole. Since the 1980s, the theory behind get tough laws has been incapacitation: If you lock up the *bad* people, we'll all be safer.

From 1980 to 1998, the number of people incarcerated rose 295%, from 329,821 to 1,302,019 (Austin & Irwin, 2001). Of those incarcerated, less than 20% were jailed for serious or very serious crimes, with 53% for petty crimes and 30% for moderate crimes. For Austin and Irwin, serious crimes included all violent crimes as well as theft over $10,000 and the smuggling of narcotics. Moderate crimes included acts that involved minor injury, such as assault, crimes that involved the use of a weapon, theft over $1,000, and sale of Marijuana. Petty crimes were everything else. By 2008, more than 2.3 million Americans were in prison or jail, 1 of every 48 working-age adults, but there was little evidence that mass incarceration reduced the crime rate (Schmitt, 2010). We consider this time period to be the point at which the Country Called Prison came into existence.

In the past, researchers focused on those incarcerated, those released from prison, and those who returned to prison. However, over the past 10 years, researchers have begun to look at the collateral effects of incarceration—the cost to society due to loss of wage earners and the disruption to families and communities caused by incarcerated members.

Imprisonment of nearly three-quarters of a million parents disrupts family life, which is the critical foundation of any society. It also affects the network of familial support and places new burdens on government services, such as schools, foster care, adoption agencies, and youth-serving organizations (Travis, 2005; Wakefield & Wildeman, 2014).

Although recidivism of over half a million offenders annually has been the primary concern, an equally important focus should be on preventing disruption to social networks. This disruption results when a significant number of offenders in concentrated areas, such as inner-city neighborhoods. There is almost a revolving door of people in many of these neighborhoods, with some leaving for prison just as others are returning. This cycle leaves family and neighborhood life significantly disrupted and economically devastated (Rose & Clear, 2001).

Few citizens think about criminals as people. It is easier to think about them as statistics. However, they are people, people with families and human needs and desires. After all, they were not born in prison. They usually had jobs before they became inmates. Most have families, children, and friends. Once released from prison, former inmates need food, clothing, and shelter, which they often cannot pay for. Jobs are hard to get, and bills are hard to pay. They need medical care, which they definitely cannot pay for. They also get old with all the extra needs that come with being elderly. Since many have not worked steadily over their lifetimes, their social security retirement income will be low, if it exists at all.

Very few researchers have studied the tsunami of children who are likely to head to adult prisons. In 2006, nearly 300 juvenile detention and correctional facilities housed about 93,000 teens, many of whom will eventually find their way to adult prisons (Davis, 2008). In 2000, 14,500 minors were in adult jails and prisons (Austin, 2000), and in 2013 3,000 were serving life sentences (Equal Justice Initiative, 2013).

According to the National Center for Children in Poverty (NCCP), about 16 million U.S. children, or 1 in 5, live below the poverty level, and 32.4 million are part of low-income families. These are important statistics, as research has shown that many people in prison were raised in poverty (Clear, 2007). Impoverished children are 7 times more likely to be abused and neglected (Payne, 2005), which can lead to the development of serious mental disorders (American Psychiatric Association, 2013). If left untreated, these disorders could eventually develop into severe, chronic mental disorders in adulthood, thereby increasing the likelihood that those affected will end up in prison, since community mental health resources are inadequate.

The bottom line is that we have a huge problem that costs states in excess of $50 billion a year, with budget increases for prisons over the past 20 years outpacing increases in other essential government services such as transportation, education, and public assistance (Petersilia, 2011). Figure 1.2 shows the elements that make up this mountain of a problem. Throughout our history, we have built this mountain based on values and beliefs about punishment and morality. Even if we stopped incarcerating people tomorrow, millions of prisoners will be discharged from correctional facilities over the next ten years. Many will leave with untreated substance addictions, post-traumatic stress, limited work skills, medical problems, and poor social skills. How many of them will be able to productively contribute to U.S. society?

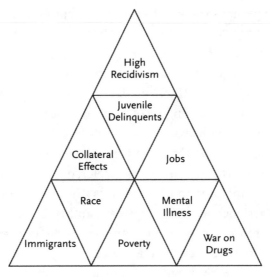

Figure 1.2: The Mass Incarceration Mountain.

The millions of U.S. children now growing up in poverty will reach adulthood over the next twenty years, and a portion of them will not function well as adults or productively contribute to society. Certainly not all impoverished children will end up in prison. In fact, most will turn out to be hard-working Americans. But enough of them will cross the border into the Country Called Prison that poverty should be a major concern of anyone interested in shrinking the prison population.

And what will we do with all the people suffering from mental illness who will overburden an already inadequate community mental health system, if prisons no longer provide a place for them? The incarceration mountain is not about prison. It is about the Country Called Prison, which exists both inside the fences of correctional facilities and in neighborhoods throughout America.

We are not the first researchers to argue that prisons function like a community. Nearly 80 years ago, Donald Clemmer (1940) studied various prison communities and identified something called the "convict code," which existed alongside, and sometimes in opposition to, prison policy and procedures. He outlined a process by which prisoners were socialized into the prison community that he referred to as "prisonization."

But we are perhaps the first to take the theory further: that prison culture is no longer contained within the walls of correctional facilities but now exhibits the characteristics of a country with provinces both inside and outside the razor-wire fences. Citizens of the Country Called Prison live all over the United States, adversely influencing the next generation and draining resources that could be spent on more socially progressive endeavors.

How did we arrive at this new perspective? We are both mental health professionals and university professors with education and training in criminology and business. With more than 30 years of combined experience working in prisons and with marginalized citizens in the community, we have witnessed some of the history that you just read about. As social science researchers, we are curious about the ways humans interact with each other and are interested in the ways people excel and, at the same time, the way they fail. So we view human problems from a wide angle.

We are also of course not the first to suggest that the U.S. criminal justice system is in need of reform. Over the last decade or so there have been attempts to reform the system, and yet little has changed. Good books with good ideas on ways to improve the system have been written, not only on prisons and reentry programs, but also on crime and sentencing policies and educational programs in poor communities.

In 2007, President George W. Bush signed into law the $330 million Second Chance Act, which gives government and community service agencies funds to initiate best-practice reentry strategies for people being released from prison. These programs may be part of the reason the incarceration rate is slowing. Additionally, more and more states are experimenting with prison diversion programs like drug courts and alternative sentencing. These too could decrease the rate of incarceration. The U.S. prison population grew by less than 1% in 2009, the slowest rate since 2000 (Glaze & Parks, 2012), but it still grew. Slowing the growth rate is good, but it cannot shrink the size of the Country Called Prison.

As if mass incarceration is not trouble enough, another crisis is heading our way. The event horizon—the point of no return—that makes this problem imperative to address is the aging of the baby boomers, those born between 1946 and 1964. Over the next 20 years, an average of 10,000 people per day will reach the age of retirement eligibility (Snyder, 2013). Who will pay into the Social Security system to fund the baby boomers' retirement? Since the correctional system is not really about correcting, and more about containment and control, the millions of offenders and ex-offenders (Solomon, 2012) are unlikely to be part of the employment pool. Eliminating millions of potential workers from the tax pool certainly does not help solve this problem.

When a problem is framed through an inaccurate paradigm, solutions, grounded in that paradigm, do not correct the problem. Rather than shifting the paradigm, however, those invested in the current system often just blame the offenders.

Although William Ryan (1971) in his famous book *Blaming the Victim* first described this rationale for justifying racism and social injustice against African Americans, the phenomenon of victim blaming is well established in human psychology. "She was asking for it" is said of a victim of domestic violence. For years, the "ex-con" has been blamed for returning to prison, for not trying hard enough, for just going back to his or her old ways—"once a crook, always a crook." Regardless of why a person returns to prison, the reality is that we are all worse off when it happens. It's bad for the public, bad for the taxpayers, and bad for the offender.

Our intention in writing this book is to share with you a new perspective of the mass incarceration epidemic and the latent effects that are threatening America's prosperity and potential. We use the word *epidemic* as a metaphor for the U.S. incarceration problem because public health uses it whenever there are significantly more people sick than would normally be expected from a specific disease in a given area during a specific time. We believe, as our earlier data demonstrated, that there are far too many people in prison than crime rates suggest there should be. We hope our perspective will shift the paradigm so that new solutions can be developed that address the foundation of the problem, not the structure.

We will not leave you scratching your heads as to what to do now that we have given you the bad news. Change will be hard. One of the most difficult obstacles to overcome is understanding that the United States currently locks up those they are not only afraid of, but also mad at. Most people don't realize that millions of citizens are being locked up for nonviolent crimes. The cost to taxpayers, as well as to the cost of human potential, is staggering. Until we fully understand the costs we as a society are incurring, change to the criminal justice system will likely never occur.

Another obstacle to change is the vast service and vendor industry that supports the criminal justice system. Imagine the money spent on toilet paper for one year for a 1,000-bed prison facility with about 500 employees. Now consider all the other necessities humans need to get through the day. A great deal of money is to be made from imprisoning others.

Last but not least, elected officials and government bureaucrats have built their careers on citizens' fear of crime. Frequently, the policies and procedures they put in place are difficult to defend. We realize that any suggestion we make will cause a ripple effect of policy and procedure changes. We hope that stakeholders in the status quo will be willing to take the long view and consider shrinking the size of the Country Called Prison.

When Mary was facing the daunting task of writing her dissertation for her PhD in clinical psychology, she mentioned to a friend that she didn't think she could do it. One room in her house was jam-packed with scientific articles and studies that she had been reviewing for her research. At times, she would walk into the room and not even know where to begin. Then she received a card in the mail depicting a beautiful Japanese watercolor painting of a mountain with a path meandering toward it. On the inside was written, "You can move a mountain, one stone at a time." A year later, she not only published her dissertation, but it also won an award for excellence in research.

We argue that there is a way to move the incarceration mountain one strategic proposal at a time. Most of the stones from the mountain will still be there, only in different places. Everyone can win. Allowing all life to flourish creates abundance. Stifling life only creates decay and stagnation.

By the end of this book, we hope you will come to understand the reason that affirmative and bountiful change must take place. Regardless of why someone has done what he or she has done, we still must figure out what to do with that person. We hope, in reading this book, you will experience just a little of the wretched-ness and desolation so many offenders and their families experience. We hope, then, that you will be inspired to do something, one little thing that could start whittling down the mountain. Throughout the book, we will suggest both small and large projects that address the issues discussed. These suggestions are also compiled in an appendix at the end of the book, with advice on ways to begin their implementation.

If nothing else, we hope that when you are finished with this book you will be more informed about the state of the prison system in the United States and see that we have built a very costly region within our nation, the Country Called Prison.

CHAPTER 2

What Makes Prisons a Country?

Facts do not cease to exist because they are ignored.

Aldous Huxley

James was a young man from a troubled home, not that much different from millions of other troubled youth in America. His father was a high school dropout, frequently absent, occasionally abusive, always addicted. His mother, who was in a codependent relationship with James's father, prided herself on keeping a job. Each night she worked stocking shelves at a local Walmart, leaving James home alone with his drunken father.

Along with absent parents, James was abandoned by his sister and brother as well. His older sister left the house when she was 16, and his brother was killed at 18 in a gang shootout. Thus, James, the youngest, spent a great deal of time by himself. He ventured out of his home to enter a dilapidated neighborhood where his friends all had similar backgrounds. As he aged, James joined the family business—addiction. By the time he was 14, he was using and selling marijuana and methamphetamine to his friends. Frequent run-ins with the law led him to juvenile court and repeated trips to a variety of programs, all poorly funded and all optimistically promising to provide hope to the hopeless.

At 17, James was caught in a drug sting; his prior juvenile record and age landed him in adult court. He pled guilty and accepted a three-year sentence for selling drugs on school property to avoid the ten-year sentence for trafficking.

James had been in prison for about a month when John met with him to provide crisis counseling. The morning John met him, James had been found in the shower, bleeding from his anus, after having been repeatedly raped by an undetermined number of prison inmates. While John attended to his mental health needs, a nurse provided emergency care. Later he was transported to a hospital, where he had surgery to correct the physical damage from the rapes. When he was released from the hospital, James was sent to a different prison, where for his own protection he was kept in seclusion for the remainder of his sentence. James wisely never revealed who had raped him. In prison, ratting out your fellow inmates could be grounds for murder.

James's story is similar to those of thousands of men and women who have been sent to America's prisons. A young man or woman with a troubled background commits a relatively minor crime. She or he is incarcerated in an unsafe situation for a long period of time. For many, that first incarceration puts them on the road to a lifetime of trouble. The options for life outside of prison for someone like James are quite limited. When he returned home, he reentered a community similar to prison because it, too, had few jobs. In addition the neighborhood had limited social resources such as educational opportunities, mass transit, and social welfare agencies designed to help former inmates reenter society. Add to this the fact that when the Jameses of the world return "home," they often reintegrate with the same unreliable, addicted, and criminal social networks they had left and you can see why this community, and many more like it across the United States, are merely provinces of the Country Called Prison.

Prison changes a person, and it certainly changed James. In our careers we have met many people like him. They come from dysfunctional families and are sent to prison for minor drug offenses. Then they are released from prison after a few years, only to return a few months or a few years later. This is the cycle of their lives. Men and women, just like James, made us realize that when a person enters prison in the United States they, in effect, cease to be American citizens. Instead, they become citizens of the Country Called Prison.

They enter a country with its own culture, language, rules, and regulations that they learn. Once released from prison, they rarely are welcomed in their original homeland. In fact, they could be compared to the millions of undocumented immigrants who enter the United States each year, people who live in plain sight but are not a viable part of American society.

James and those like him are members of a foreign country, living not on foreign land but within the borders of the United States. Of course, they are different from the thousands who cross U.S. borders illegally each year because they were born here. Now they are citizens of another country but live in America as *legal aliens*. In this chapter, we discuss the elements that make a group of people *a country* (or nation) and why the U.S. prison system fits those characteristics.

WHAT MAKES A COUNTRY A NATION?

According to the Oxford Dictionaries online (http://www.oxforddictionaries.com), a *nation* is a "large body of people united by a common descent, history, culture and language, inhabiting a particular state or territory." While on the surface this description doesn't seem to apply to inmates and prisons, we believe that each of these characteristics is present in the current prison system of the United States. Residents of the Country Called Prison form a national identity and develop a social personality that stems from shared experiences, which suggest that they have a shared culture. Therefore, to understand what makes prison a country, we must first understand the concept of *culture*.

Animals are born with instincts to survive. While humans are born with a basic survival instinct, we have something better than instinct to help ensure our survival. We have culture, and cultures can evolve just like animal species. The 1981 film *Escape from New York* depicts a culture that evolved from a prison environment (Carpenter, 1981). The movie depicts a future where the United States has turned New York City into one large maximum security prison. All access to the city is controlled by a large wall that surrounds it, essentially creating a fortified prison. The worst of the worst antisocial citizens are sent there for life and allowed to run the city as they see fit.

In the movie, the president of the United States ejects from a damaged *Air Force One* and lands in the middle of New York City. Through a series of plot twists, Snake Plissken (Kurt Russell), a prisoner held in a "regular" U.S. prison, is offered freedom if he can rescue the president from New York City. Of course, the prison lord of the city, known as the Duke of New York (Isaac Hayes), runs the city with his own gang of thugs who control every aspect of life there. This group, left to its own devices, created a culture with political, economic, and social norms. The film shows that in the absence of prescribed rules and roles humans will band together to survive. Out of this process a culture is created.

Culture is composed of material culture and nonmaterial culture. The material aspects of culture involve the physical stuff you can taste, touch, and feel. When you visit a prison, you experience an unfamiliar material culture. You enter through a "sally port," which is a secure sliding door. In prison, you become accustomed to locking doors, small windows, and bars. Razor-wire fencing becomes something through which you view the outside world. All shirts worn by inmates have "inmate" or "corrections" stenciled on the back. All of these aspects make up the material culture of the Country Called Prison. The nonmaterial aspects of culture include the shared knowledge of the customs and way that things are done in that culture. We will discuss nonmaterial culture further in later chapters.

Without culture, we cannot survive physically or psychologically. Culture serves some important functions. It teaches us values and beliefs. It gives us a language. It organizes our lives and helps us make sense of the world around us. Most of the time we take culture for granted, giving it little thought.

When John teaches about culture he asks his students to name the core components of U.S. culture. The class makes lists of values, beliefs, and expected norms or behaviors that are unique to America. It usually takes some time to compile the list. Once it is completed, and the students agree that the list accurately represents U.S. culture, the class has something to bind it together. Culture does much more than tell us what to believe, how to talk, and how we should behave. It binds us to other people from the same culture. In short, it creates a blueprint for social solidarity.

Culture, in any society, is not static. It is adaptive, meaning that it changes with the times. Since culture provides us with social norms and notions of acceptable behavior, it must be fluid. Social situations are always changing.

Culture teaches us the acceptable and unacceptable ways to behave in certain situations. For example, if you are at a football game, it is normal to yell. If you are at a funeral, it is not acceptable. The setting determines the appropriate behavior. As an intake psychologist, Mary meets men and women as they are entering into prison. First timers are always frightened and unsure of what they are supposed to do. Some hide their fear, acting calmer than anyone should upon entering prison. Others show their distress with an angry tone and derogatory statements. Occasionally someone breaks down and cries in Mary's office. She always tries to help new inmates deal with their feelings, but she also teaches them that crying and showing fear and excessive anger will likely cause them trouble in prison.

A culture is like a stream that meanders around rocks and erodes soft riverbanks. The stream never flows the same way year after year. Culture works in the same way. Think about how Americans have changed the way they socially interact with each other since the invention of the computer and mobile phones compared to 30 years ago. At one time we called people to see how they were. Today if we use a phone, we normally text. More frequently we use social media to catch up on old friends. All cultures change. What is the point of this discussion? Prison is a culture, and culture changes over time. Therefore, prisons have changed a great deal in the past 30 years, yet many are still operating with 30-year-old standards.

Culture is not innate in human beings; we are not born with an instinct for a specific culture. We learn culture through interactions with others and from adults, especially parents and teachers. Infants begin learning language and facial expressions the minute they are born. By age two, children have learned the language, gestures, voice tones, and symbolic meanings of their world and readily understand if mom is mad about the crayon marks on the wall. By middle school, preteens have learned the subtleties of flirting and the hurt of a sarcastic snubbing. If we were to move to another country, we would need to adapt to that culture in order to survive socially and psychologically, and sometimes even physically. As we move forward, let's review the characteristics of the Country Called Prison.

Land, in and of itself, does not a country make. If it did, Antarctica would be a country. People create a country. Even people living as a group do not always make a country. If they did, many U.S. universities with 20,000 students or more might be considered small countries. So why are we claiming that criminals and prisoners, as a group, are a country?

First, let us look at the demographic characteristics of those in prison in the United States (Carson & Golinelli, 2013). Table 2.1 shows the ages of male and female prison inmates in the United States. These data show that males enter prison at higher percentages at younger ages. The largest percentage for both groups remains in the 25 to 29 age group. The percentage of inmates 40 years and older begins to drop. In fact, slightly more than 69% of all inmates in American prisons are under the age of 40. Therefore, the population of the Country Called Prison is generally young. Demographically speaking, young adults contribute more to the welfare of society than do older adults. The lost potential of this group is difficult to measure but important to note.

As discussed in Chapter One, Blacks are overrepresented in the prison population. Generally speaking, White men are the oldest group in prison, and Hispanic women are the youngest. The data from the Bureau of Justice Statistics show minimal variability between age

Table 2.1. PERCENTAGE OF MEN AND WOMEN
IN PRISON BY AGE

Age Group	Total	Males	Females
18–19	3.5	3.8	2.4
20–24	17.7	18.1	15.3
25–29	19.3	19.1	18.0
30–34	16.7	16.5	16.3
35–39	12.4	12.2	12.5
40–44	10.9	10.7	12.2
45–49	9.0	8.8	10.4
50–54	5.8	5.8	7.0
55–59	2.6	2.6	3.3
60–64	1.1	1.1	1.5

Source: Carson & Golinelli, 2013.

group and the race of offenders (Carson & Golinelli, 2013). Thus, regardless of racial category, rate of incarceration generally follows the same percentages for the total age groups shown in Table 2.1.

Table 2.2 provides racial data on admission to prisons by the three largest racial/ethnic groups. Violent crime admissions to prison are higher for Blacks and Hispanics than for Whites. It is important to note that for all racial groups, assault is the most common violent crime and by percentage more common than murder or rape. In relation to property crimes, Whites have the highest percentage of new admissions to prisons, with burglary being the largest category. Finally, for all groups, drug crimes make up a large percentage of the reason people are incarcerated and the variability between these three racial/ethnic groups is about the same.

The data in Tables 2.1 and 2.2 provide a picture of people who were admitted to prison in 2011. We can see that depending on the group, drug

Table 2.2. PERCENTAGE OF ADMISSIONS BY CRIME AND ETHNIC/RACIAL GROUP

Crime 2011	White	Black	Hispanic
All Violent	25.3	34.4	35.7
Murder	1.4	2.8	3.2
Negligent manslaughter	0.9	0.6	0.7
Rape/sexual assault	6.7	3.7	7.0
Robbery	4.5	12.5	8.1
Assault	9.2	12.2	13.5
Other violent	2.6	2.5	3.2
All Property	33.5	24.6	21.2
Burglary	13.9	12.3	10.5
Larceny	7.4	5.2	4.0
Motor vehicle theft	1.9	1.0	2.3
Fraud	5.2	3.6	2.0
Other property	5.1	2.5	2.3
All Drug	23.1	24.3	25.5
Possession	8.2	7.4	9.5
Other drug	15.0	16.9	16.0
Public order	18.0	16.7	17.6
Other	1.1	0.7	0.4
Number of new court commitments	146,054	156,661	69,728

Source: Carson & Golinelli, 2013.

and property crime accounts for almost half of those going to prison. The crimes that we fear most—murder, rape, and robbery—in total account for less than 20% of those who went to prison in 2011, regardless of the racial category. These data support the main thesis of this book. Regardless of race, the majority of those who enter the Country Called Prison are generally not the people we fear. We may be angry because they stole our car, but we are not fearful that they will kill us.

The reason that one fears or does not fear criminals remains a contentious topic for many. If your home was broken into, you probably would not agree that you do not need to fear certain criminals. Victims of such crimes often wonder what would have happened had they been home.

Could our fear vary by the gender of the criminal? Men have always had higher rates of crime than their female counterparts. Table 2.3 provides data on new prison commitments in 2011 but breaks those

Table 2.3. PERCENTAGE OF NEW PRISON
COMMITMENTS BY GENDER

Offense	Male	Female
Total Violent	**31.5**	**18.4**
Murder	2.4	1.7
Negligent manslaughter	0.8	1.1
Rape/sexual assault	6.3	1.0
Robbery	8.3	4.9
Assault	11.2	6.9
Other violent	2.4	2.8
Total Property	**26.4**	**36.0**
Burglary	12.6	8.0
Larceny	5.3	10.6
Motor vehicle theft	1.7	1.5
Fraud	3.1	11.7
Other property	3.7	4.1
Total Drug	**23.9**	**32.5**
Possession	7.2	11.7
Other drug	16.7	0.8
Public Order	17.4	12.0
Other	0.7	1.1
Number of new court commitments	351,326	47,383

Source: Carson & Golinelli, 2013.

data down by offense and gender. You will quickly notice some key differences between men and women and how they end up in prison.

The reasons women and men go to prison differ by the type of offense they commit. For example, women are more likely to commit a property offense, with fraud (usually writing a bad check) and larceny (usually shoplifting) leading the way. Furthermore, women who enter prison do so at a higher rate than men for drug possession. Roughly a third of new female commitments to prison were for drug offenses, compared to 21% for their male counterparts. For comparison purposes, 68.5% of males enter prison for a nonviolent offense, while 81.6% of women incarcerated in 2011 were nonviolent offenders.

Again, these data support the notion that most of those we send to prison are nonviolent offenders. It is also important to look at the bottom row of the table. The number of new female commitments is about 7 times lower than the number for males. Generally speaking, we know women are convicted of fewer crimes then men. Regardless of gender, when we consider the different incarceration rates of both men and women, we note again that those entering prison are mostly nonviolent offenders. They make up the lion's share of the citizens of the Country Called Prison.

These data tell the tale of who is in prison. Many have addiction problems. Table 2.4 provides a different perspective. It provides trend data on offenders in the years 1991, 2001, and 2011, taken from statistics gathered by the Bureau of Justice Statistics. It breaks these data into two groups, first for new commitments that year, and second for those who violated parole and returned to prison.

The parole violator data are categorized by the offense that initially sent the criminals to prison, not by the offense that returned them to prison. Therefore, one should not conclude that the same type of crime returned the offender to prison. These data do not provide that level of accuracy. But the data do show that over this 20-year period the percentage of violent offenses remained relatively stable.

The last row shows the number of admissions for each category. You can see that, generally speaking, the group returning to prison via parole violation is roughly half the size of the group entering prison for the first time. Therefore, in general terms, about a third of those who went to prison in the years listed were parole violators. Across the

Table 2.4. TRENDS IN FIRST COMMITMENT AND PAROLE VIOLATIONS

Offense	1991		2001		2011	
	First Commit	Parole Violation	First Commit	Parole Violation	First Commit	Parole Violation
All Violent	**28.7**	**23.7**	**29.4**	**23.9**	**30.0**	**27.4**
Murder	3.0	1.7	2.5	1.3	2.4	1.2
Negligent manslaughter	1.3	0.5	1.0	0.4	0.8	0.3
Rape/sexual assault	5.6	3.6	6.3	3.4	5.7	4.8
Robbery	9.9	11.6	8.1	9.2	7.9	8.4
Assault	7.5	5.5	9.2	7.9	10.7	10.5
Other violent	1.4	0.7	2.3	1.8	2.5	2.2
All Property	**31.4**	**42.4**	**27.4**	**32.5**	**27.5**	**32.4**
Burglary	13.5	20.8	10.4	12.9	12.1	13.1
Larceny	8.1	11.7	6.6	8.8	5.9	6.6
Motor vehicle theft	2.4	4.1	2.0	3.9	1.7	4.9
Fraud	3.8	4.1	4.7	3.3	4.1	3.4
Other property	3.6	1.8	3.7	3.5	3.8	4.4
All Drug	**29.9**	**25.5**	**30.5**	**35.1**	**24.9**	**26.2**
Possession	6.9	7.0	8.7	9.1	7.8	8.7
Other drug	23.0	18.5	21.8	26.0	17.2	17.5
Public Order	8.9	6.1	12.1	8.0	16.8	13.2
Other	1.1	2.3	0.6	0.5	0.8	0.8
Number of admissions	317,237	142,100	365,229	215,344	398,709	200,481

Source: Carson & Golinelli, 2013.

board, the ratio of violent criminals to property criminals varies. In some years first-time offenders are more likely to be property criminals instead of violent offenders and in others it is just the opposite. The point is that generally these rates have not changed a great deal. The percentages of who goes to prison and for what they are going remains relatively stable over time.

While data on parole violations do not show us why the individual returned to prison, they do illustrate the prison population further. Many of those currently in prison had been released after serving their time but now have returned for some reason. We will discuss technical violations of parole in subsequent chapters. It is important to note that violating parole may or may not mean that another crime has been committed. Missing a meeting with the parole officer is enough to send a person back to prison under the right circumstances.

We have talked a bit about who lives or has lived in prison. But how many are in prison? This question should be easy to answer. After all, inmates are counted every night. However, the answer is more complex than you might think.

In an effort to curb crime, the United States began experimenting with large-scale incarceration. In the late 1970s the total prison population (state and federal) was approximately 300,000. Now, the number has soared to well over 1.5 million prison inmates (Glaze & Parks, 2012). However, if all individuals who are currently under some form of government supervision—via parole, probation, prison, and local jails—are included, that number explodes to more than 6.9 million. We suggest that everyone who is under supervision by the criminal justice system is a citizen of the Country Called Prison. Table 2.5 provides some comparisons for you to consider related to countries and their relative size to 6.9 million.

When one compares the number of people under supervision by the criminal justice system to the population estimates of countries around the world, relative to country size, the U.S. correctional system ranks 101st out of 239 countries in population size. It is larger than many countries, including New Zealand (which is 125th), Norway (119th), and Denmark (113th), to name a few (Central Intelligence Agency, 2013). The facts are that 1 out of every 33 people, or about 3% of the U.S. population, is under some form of supervision for criminal activity at any given time (Glaze & Parks, 2012).

Despite recent small declines in prison populations, the total number of individuals who inhabit the Country Called Prison is larger than the populations of half of the countries in the world. And this

Table 2.5. U.S. PRISON POPULATION COMPARED TO THAT OF SELECTED COUNTRIES

Population Rank	Country	Population
101	Bulgaria	6,924,716
	A Country Called Prison	**6,900,000**
102	Laos	6,803,699

Source: Central Intelligence Agency, 2013.

number does not include the millions who have been arrested and convicted of a felony but have not gone to prison. We suggest that once you are arrested and convicted of a crime, regardless of whether you go to prison or not, you become a legal alien in the United States as you cross the border into the Country Called Prison.

Estimates suggest that 65 million Americans have criminal records by the time they are 23 years of age. Having a criminal record can lead to employment problems and a host of other social ills (Glaze & Parks, 2012). At the same time, only 14% of the arrests are for violent or simple assault crimes (Solomon, 2012). Review the data in Table 2.6. It shows that those 65 million with an arrest record by the age of 23 make up a country with a slightly lower population than France but higher than Great Britain, making it the 22nd largest country on the planet (Central Intelligence Agency, 2013).

This does not tell the whole story, though. What about those who have been released from prison? In 2001, 4.3 million of the 5.6 million adults who had been incarcerated previously were no longer in prison. In other words, a vast majority of those we had previously sent to prison had been released. However, that does not mean they re-assimilate to U.S. culture. In fact, former prisoners account for 77% of all adult residents who had ever been confined in prison (Bonczar, 2003).

In 1997, research completed by the Bureau of Justice Statistics estimated that 5.1% percent of all Americans will go to prison in their lifetime (Bonczar & Beck, 1997). So, using current population numbers, we can estimate the current population who have been or will be in prison. As of March 2014, the Census Bureau estimates that the

Table 2.6. CRIMINAL RECORDS AND COUNTRY POPULATIONS

Population Size Rank	Country	Population
21	France	66,259,012
	Criminal Record by Age 23 (United States)	**65,000,000**
22	United Kingdom	63,742,977
23	Italy	61,680,122

Source: Central Intelligence Agency, 2013.

U.S. population was 317,712,320. If we take 5.1% of that number, we get 16,203,328 (U.S. Census [popclock], n.d.).

This number—16,203,328—represents the 67th most populated country in the world, as shown in Table 2.7. This country is only slightly smaller than Mali and the Netherlands. It is larger than Cuba and Ecuador, and its population is twice the size of Israel (Central Intelligence Agency, 2013). These data certainly support the notion that the U.S. prison population is sufficiently large enough to be considered a nation.

But let's consider one more comparison for the prison population. Table 2.8 provides the largest 10 states by population in the United States, according to the U.S. Census. The lifetime estimated prison population—16,203,328—would make the Country Called Prison the fifth largest state in the United States, just behind Florida (18 million) and larger than Illinois (12 million) (U.S. Census, 2012).

Florida sends 27 men and women to the U.S. House of Representatives and Illinois sends 18 (Directory of Representatives, n.d.). Prison could, therefore, be a "swing state" in any presidential election, if all current and former inmates were allowed to vote. But of course they are not. They are, as we hypothesize, legally here but essentially aliens in their own land.

We present these numbers to give you a perspective on the size of the Country Called Prison. They paint a picture of a large population

Table 2.7. COUNTRY RANKING OF ESTIMATED TO GO TO PRISON (UNITED STATES)

Country Ranking	Country	Population
65	Netherlands	16,877,351
66	Mali	16,455,903
	Estimated to go to prison (United States)	**16,203,328**
67	Ecuador	15,654,411
77	Cuba	11,047,251
79	Portugal	10,813,834
83	Belgium	10,449,361
90	Sweden	9,723,809
97	Israel	7,821,850

Source: Central Intelligence Agency, 2013.

Table 2.8. STATE RANKING OF ESTIMATED TO GO
TO PRISON (UNITED STATES)

State	Population	Ranking
California	36,961,664	1
Texas	24,782,302	2
New York	19,541,453	3
Florida	18,537,969	4
Estimated to go to prison (United States)	**16,203,328**	
Illinois	12,910,409	5
Pennsylvania	12,604,767	6
Ohio	11,542,645	7
Michigan	9,969,727	8
Georgia	9,829,211	9
North Carolina	9,380,884	10

Source: U.S. Census, 2012.

of people who share similar cultural experiences. Their crimes are generally nonviolent, and they are disproportionately people of color.

So how many citizens make up the Country Called Prison? Conservatively, we believe 16 million, since that is a statistical estimate built on firm research. However, since one does not actually have to go to prison to be a citizen of the Country Called Prison (they need only be convicted of a felony), we believe the population is much larger.

Recall that approximately 65 million people are convicted of a felony by the time they are 23 years old. The number of those convicted later in their lives would, therefore, raise our population estimate even more.

Being convicted of a felony changes lives permanently. Jobs, housing, and many career paths are limited for most felons. If someone is convicted of a drug felony, certain college funding sources become unavailable. Furthermore, once convicted of a felony, not only you but your entire family are more likely to suffer. For example, children whose fathers go to prison are at increased risk of incarceration themselves (Wakefield & Wildeman, 2014). When you consider all these facts, 65 million may be a more accurate estimate of the population of the Country Called Prison

However, even at the more conservative number of 16 million, which is based on empirical data, we are talking about a population that is greater than that of the fourth largest state in the nation and a country bigger than many of our allies. For this reason, we believe that the U.S. prison system can be considered a country with its own culture that exists within the borders of American society.

Regardless of its exact size, the population of the Country Called Prison is considerable. As we demonstrated earlier, about half of those who go to prison do so for nonviolent offenses, offenses that don't scare us but only make us mad. This raises many questions about social policies and the use of tax dollars. However, at this point, let us look further into why we consider the prison system to have its own culture, which makes it a country and not just a large group of people.

COMMON HISTORY

People from a country share a common history, which usually means, at least from a nation-state point of view, that they share experiences and historical connections to similar events. Americans all share a common history when we celebrate the Fourth of July or Thanksgiving. Clearly people in the Country Called Prison share these common historical events with all Americans. The question is, "Do they share other aspects of a common history that non-criminals do not share?"

Although most people in prison do not know each other prior to entering, many share a common history—that of poverty, abuse, and alienation from U.S. culture. Research has clearly demonstrated that prisons in the United States are disproportionately filled with people from lower-income homes (Reiman, 1998; Western & Pettit, 2010). Poverty, as we will discuss later in this section, is common to the lives of many who end up in prison.

As we mentioned in chapter one, in 1940 Donald Clemmer published the first research to suggest that prisons have a common culture. Working in a penitentiary in Illinois, Clemmer suggested that inmates create a culture and society with different values and norms. He termed the process by which prisoners learn these norms and values *prisonization*. With so many returning year in and year out, prison becomes a part of the common history all felons and inmates share. Many prison inmates are parents, and their children will likely also adopt this prison culture as normative. In many respects, the normalization of prison is a travesty of the modern age. Normalizing children's visits to see their incarcerated parents seems particularly problematic if our goal is to decrease criminality and incarceration.

Following the work of Clemmer, Gresham Sykes (1958) suggested that prison culture originates from the deprivation that the offender experiences in prison. Sykes identified five types of deprivation: loss of liberty, loss of goods and services that one is used to in the free world, loss of autonomy, loss of heterosexual relationships, and loss of safety. Since material goods are culturally important to Americans, the inability of inmates to acquire material possessions in prison is quite damaging to their self-worth and self-esteem. Based on our observation, deprivation of material goods is one of the main reasons that the predatory milieu and contraband exists in most prisons.

Another question to ask is, "Are the individuals who go to prison generally surprised by deprivation?" Jeffrey Reiman's book *The Rich Get Richer and the Poor Get Prison* (1998) provides ample evidence to support the claim that the poor are disproportionately represented in the prison population. While the poor may or may not be more criminal, they certainly are more likely to go to prison. Since social class differences permeate the prison system, perhaps many who enter prison are already set up for the deprivation that Sykes describes.

In 1995, Ruby Payne published her transformational book, *A Framework for Understanding Poverty*. In it, she identifies the differences between those who grow up poor and those who grow up in the middle and upper classes. Her description of individuals growing up in poverty mirrors Sykes's deprivation model in many ways. People who are poor struggle to obtain needed goods. They frequently must live in substandard housing in dangerous neighborhoods. Therefore, they suffer the deprivation of safety just as they would in prison. In addition, many suffer a loss of personal autonomy, primarily due to the poverty in which they live. Without expendable cash, individuals struggle to be independent and have limited choices.

When we add Payne's ideas to the work of others, we find it hard to deny that many in prison, particularly those who come from poverty, enter with an ingrained perspective of deprivation. As many have pointed out, when one lives in poverty, goods, freedom, and autonomy are difficult to obtain, which resembles the prison experience

(Brooks-Gunn, Duncan, Klebanove, & Sealand, 1993; Edin & Lein, 1997; Wilson, 1987).

A common history is the way a group of people thinks, perceives themselves, and believes about themselves in relation to other groups. While all people in the United States are free to choose, the choices are not always as plentiful as people might think. Choices are made in the context in which one lives. If, for example, you ask yourself why you married the particular person you did, you may find that a social context was involved. Most people marry someone who is geographically close to them. If you grow up in Montana, you are likely to marry someone from Montana. If geography is strongly linked to marriage, is your choice of a marriage partner really "free"?

Many life choices work that way. Instead of making choices using an objective thought process, people choose as a result of a complex series of social accidents. Put another way, the way we make choices is often influenced by the way we see the world, something that is often unconsciously and culturally learned (Edin & Kefalas, 2005).

For example, the university where we teach has a rival university in another part of the state. Students say they "hate" our rival. We ask our students, "If you happened to have been raised in the town of that rival university, and if you happened to have had a parent who worked there, might you feel differently about that institution? Would you hate it as vehemently?" The honest answer for most is, "Probably not." So why did they choose our university? For most of them, the university is geographically close to their home or they received a scholarship. Like the decision to select a life partner, selecting a school is hardly a free, unrestricted choice.

The poor in America make choices that many in the middle and upper classes may not understand. In the book *The Promises I Can Keep*, Edin and Kefalas (2005) suggest that many poor women make the decision to become mothers in a social context that is often difficult for those who are not poor to understand. For some women, the decision to become a mother is made because it is an event that they believe they can control. In a world where they have so little power, poor women believe that parenting is a promise they can keep. Therefore, many young, single women growing up in poverty choose to get pregnant, which does not always make sense to the middle and upper classes.

Most of our decisions occur in a context that is beyond others' experience. We both have taught at the community-college level and have known poor students who often miss class because they have child-care responsibilities. Others miss because their cars break down or their ride to school doesn't show up. Their childhoods were not filled with Little League baseball and summer camps. Their choices occur in a context that many "traditional" college students can barely understand. If you are a poor mother and your child is sick, you are going to miss an exam, even if it means you fail the course.

Conversely, the complications of choice are not all that influences the lives of those who may become citizens of the Country Called Prison. As previously mentioned, poor neighborhoods in America also tend to experience more violence. If you are poor and you live in a dangerous neighborhood, you do not have the financial resources to move. You are trapped. And sometimes protecting yourself means you end up committing a crime that lands you in prison.

Children growing up in such neighborhoods share similar disadvantages. When you are surrounded by drug abuse, violence, and underperforming schools, you are disadvantaged in U.S. society. When you know nothing else, you are truly disadvantaged. The limited availability of role models to teach children another way of life places limits on their potential, as well as their freedom and autonomy. Since inmates are more likely to be from poor backgrounds, many share this common history of disadvantage (Wilson, 1987).

Not only are poor people deprived of autonomy by their economic situation, but they also lack autonomy because of their limited opportunities. Nowhere is this more pronounced than in education. Numerous studies show that educationally the poor are underserved. The schools they attend are often poorly funded and the quality of public education they receive is not equivalent to that of their middle and upper class counterparts (Kozol, 1991; Roscigno, Tomaskovic-Devey, & Crowley, 2006)

The same holds true for higher education. The poorer a person is, the more difficulty she or he has completing a college degree (Alexander, Holupka, & Pallas, 1987; Dynarski, 2003; Haveman & Smeeding, 2007). Inmate populations reflect these educational differences. For example, slightly more than 41% of inmates have only attended some high school or less, compared to 18% of the general population.

Approximately 48% of the general population has some postsecondary education. Compare this to the incarcerated, among whom fewer than 13% have had educational experiences past high school (Harlow, 2003). If education is the key to success, then it is easy to see that those who enter the Country Called Prison are likely to be some of the least educated people in America and, therefore, the least successful.

Economic deprivation greatly complicates people's lives. American culture is dominated by materialism and equates wealth with success, thus making the poor the least valued. We often link self-esteem and definitions of success to wealth in the United States. In fact, economic success dominates the American scene. Some have argued that the disadvantages of the poor, coupled with the dominant cultural value of wealth and success, may be the reason some turn to criminal behavior (Messner & Rosenfeld, 2008). While this may or may not be true, one thing is certain: The Country Called Prison is filled with residents who come from disadvantaged backgrounds.

Having worked in corrections, psychiatric centers, and hospitals for years, we have witnessed a striking reality. Many people have never really been taught how to act properly in society. This is especially true of offenders. Many were never actually socialized into U.S. culture before they came to prison. Since many come from deprived backgrounds, it is not surprising that the rules they learned growing up hinder their success. Recall that James followed in his family's footsteps and embraced the addict lifestyle.

Rather than receive *re*habilitation in prison, many of the people with whom we have worked need *habilitation*. Why would we say this? Because many offenders were never educated in American social norms and citizenship standards of the United States in the first place. Not only do offenders find themselves excluded from U.S. culture while they are in prison, once they are released, opting back into society is extremely difficult for most.

NATIONAL IDENTITY

As both Clemmer and Sykes showed in their research, inmates maintain a separate identity from American society. Accepting a national identity is part of being a citizen of a country. Respecting the flag and watching fireworks on the Fourth of July are part of U.S. national identity. Most citizens of a country take pride in their national identity and believe their nation is number one.

For citizens of the Country Called Prison, national identity is a little different. First, inmates know they hold an identity that few want. In fact, most people, including those who go to prison, want to avoid this identity. However, there is no avoiding the distinctiveness that is associated with the Country Called Prison. Inmates have their own body language, slang, and dress. Just like America is known for cowboys, jeans, McDonald's, and Disney, prisons are known for shanks, cellies, contraband, canteen, and pulling chain. We will address prison jargon and cultural symbols in subsequent chapters. However, it is important to discuss these social elements now, since they clearly demonstrate that the Country Called Prison has its own unique national identity. Anyone who has ever worked in prison will agree that it is another land and that there is nothing like it elsewhere.

It is important to note that a person immediately gains a new identity when he or she enters prison. Those who move to another country often retain their citizenship from their birth country and never change their national identity; they merely adapt to the new nation's customs. People who enter prison accept their new national identity quickly because they are immediately given a DOC (Department of Corrections) number. This small and seemingly insignificant act immediately strips them of their American name and immediately brands them as citizens of the Country Called Prison. A new prisoner's given name is no longer relevant to anyone. Inmates are told to memorize their DOC number because they may be asked for it at any time. In addition, they must always have their DOC identification card clipped to their shirt.

Furthermore, new inmates experience "welcome" rituals when they enter prison, such as having their heads shaved, being strip-searched, or donning an orange jumpsuit. Gone are their old clothes and looks. New identities result from these rituals, which are meant to inform new arrivals that they are no longer a person but an inmate (Garfinkel, 1956). As they cross this border into the Country Called Prison, they are also no longer an American citizen. They have been cast out of their country of origin and forced to accept the customs, language, and roles of their new nation.

National identity can often be subtle. When Mary's daughters were preteens, the family moved from a metropolitan northern city to a rural area of Oklahoma. As a child, Mary frequently had visited her grandparents, who lived in a small rural town in western Kansas. So she was aware that the customary dress was different in rural areas. Before her daughters attended their first day of school, she bought them clothes that she thought would be appropriate—jeans, t-shirts, and cowgirl boots. However, they were upset when they came home after school because Mary had bought them Levi jeans instead of Wranglers. As a result, their peers made fun of them all day. The same is true for the Country Called Prison, where national identity shows up in subtle ways, such as prison tattoos, one long fingernail on one hand, or starching and ironing prison-issued, elastic, pull-on pants

From the outside, one might suspect that no one would be proud to have an identity of "incarcerated felon." We believe that this is mostly true, but we think it is a more complex issue than observation would suggest. We have observed that when a new inmate enters a prison yard, another inmate might yell out a welcome such as, "Hey, Big Mike, whatcha doin' back? How's Becka? Meet ya at the place later!" as if they just saw each other at a football game or the mall. Inmates have specific tattoos that designate the number of times they have been to prison and in which prisons they have lived. Prison gang tattoos designate leadership levels and special honors. We have often observed a group of offenders visiting with each other while waiting in medical for their appointments; they share stories of the various experiences they have had, the different prisons they have been to, and their opinions regarding different officers and staff and boast about the various crimes they have pulled off without getting caught.

At least at times, a country's citizens see each other as something more than a group of individuals who happen to live in the same area. When the United States was attacked on 9/11, Democrat and Republican, rich and poor, northerners and southerners, all rallied together to support their country. Students left college to enlist in the military to defend the homeland. External attacks—or the threat of them—tend to unite people.

This is true in prison as well. Behind bars, threats are both internal and external. Inside prison, security and staff have almost unlimited power over inmates, who as a result see them as threats. Prisoners know that these people can search them at any time, ask them to do things they don't want to do, take away their few belongings, lock them in solitary confinement, or disallow visitors. Internal threats from peers are numerous in prison. Prison gangs maintain a great deal of power in regard to prison activities, including who is accepted and who might be targeted for violence. In addition, some extremely violent prisoners prey on the weak because their sentences are so long that they have nothing to lose if they get in trouble. Some are severely mentally ill and can attack based on delusions that other prisoners are devils or monsters. Prisoners often find themselves in a catch-22 situation, since one way to protect themselves is to get in good with the prison staff and security. Of course, if one gets too chummy with prison staff, other inmates are likely to view this with hostility.

In prison, privacy and private property do not exist. Security personnel can search a prisoner's cell at any time and confiscate anything they want. They can stop a prisoner at any time to perform a strip search. Prisoners con each other out of items and steal from each other almost every hour of the day. The national identity that pervades the Country Called Prison is built on fear and mistrust. Americans proudly speak of their country as "the land of the free and the home of the brave." In prison, inmates derisively say, "Get what you can and don't get caught."

When someone, such as a missionary, has been living in another country for many years and returns to the United States, they are usually welcomed with open arms by family and friends with whom they have stayed in contact. While it may take them a few months to get reacquainted with the society they left behind many years ago, they usually adapt with little stress or difficulty. Not so for inmates leaving prison and returning to American society. They often seem to experience the same trouble re-assimilating as veterans who are returning from years of wartime deployment. Just putting a person back in a familiar environment doesn't necessarily mean they can blend back into what they left behind.

Once inmates leave prison, their identity is connected to having been "inside." Former inmates have a shared experience. In overhearing inmate conversations throughout the years, we have found that inmates and former inmates see themselves as alike in many ways and not like Americans who have not been "inside." The threats from within prison itself strengthen this sense of group identity much the same way that military war veterans are bonded for life due to the shared dangerous experience they survived.

Upon release, threats come from outside. These threats may be from the general public, which doesn't want former prisoners living in their neighborhoods, or from law enforcement, who keep track of their movements. Some police officers believe that they have probable cause to pull over a car driven by a former inmate. Threats may come from family members and former friends who now see an ex-con who is undeserving of attention and acceptance. In addition, employers are often resistant to hire former prisoners. These threats unify citizens of the Country Called Prison, which in turn strengthens their national identity.

COMMON TERRITORY

A country is more than just people. There is a geography that separates one country from another. The Country Called Prison has millions of acres of land, with millions of miles of razor-wire fencing. These acres contain hundreds of millions of dollars of buildings. Its geography includes everything from maximum security prisons to halfway houses to parole offices.

In school, when children are studying geography, they learn about different places around the world and the conditions people live in. Often children have discussions about places where it would be "cool" to live or places where it would be "horrible" to live. When Mary was growing up, she thought that Calcutta, India, would be a terrible place to live. Interestingly, she has worked in prisons most of her adult life and found many of them to be rather wretched indeed. While they perhaps are not as wretched as the slums of Calcutta, nonetheless prisons are dismal places to be.

Yet, in the United States, thousands of citizens are sent to these wretched and dismal places every day by the courts. Prisoners live in small cells with people they do not choose as roommates. The prisons at which we have both worked are in southern states. The cells have small windows on their doors and no windows to the outside that can be opened and are not air conditioned. In the heat of the summer, with temperatures rising to well over 100 degrees for weeks, these cells quickly become like ovens. Locked in a sweatbox with someone who may be your enemy is most definitely not fun. In the winter, our prisons are frequently cold, cells heated only to a minimal temperature, but at least the stench of body odor declines. All of this is a part of the geography of the Country Called Prison.

Of course, the geography of prisons involves more than cells and bars. Millions of acres of land and new buildings continue to be added every year. From June 2000 to December 2005, state and federal correctional facilities increased in number by 9% (from 1,668 to 1,821) (Stephan, 2005). But this increase does not tell the whole story.

During these same years, private, for-profit prisons increased from 16% (264) to 23% (415) of the total prison bed space (Stephan, 2005). Private prisons accounted for the highest percentage growth in adult prisons, with the number almost doubling in a five-year period. These prisons were generally built knowing that they would be put to use. Two-thirds were under state contract before they were completely built. The remaining one-third were under federal contract.

Prison geography involves more than just the sheer number of prisons; it also includes the size of prisons. During this same time period, from 2000 to 2005, prisons housing fewer than 500 inmates increased by 86 prisons (Stephan, 2005). The number of moderately sized prisons housing between 500 and 999 inmates remained relatively unchanged. However, the number of large prisons, housing from 1,000 to 2,499 inmates, grew by 57. Megaprisons, those holding more than 2,500 inmates, increased by 11.

In other words, during a five-year period of time, the United States increased the number of prisons by more than 200. Of these, most were built at the minimum security level (a total of 155). Minimum security prisons are just as you would expect from their name, minimally secure. Usually these prisons do not even have a fence around them. Men and women sentenced to such places are believed to be low escape risks and so the level of security needed to keep them in prison is low. Oftentimes prisoners at minimum security facilities are nearing their discharge date and so would be unlikely to attempt to escape, which would earn them more time in prison. Yet, inmates at these prisons are deprived of American citizenship, the opportunity for work and post–high school education and training, and their families. Most important, these low-risk inmates are tax-users, not taxpayers.

During this same time frame, maximum security prisons increased by a count of 40, while medium security prisons actually decreased in number by 42. Many of these were converted to maximum security institutions. What does this mean? Maximum security prisons house inmates that are deemed to be the most dangerous. This is the prison you probably have seen on television and in the movies. Razor wire, guard towers, and lockdown units are all a part of a maximum security prison. These prisons often lock down offenders for 23 hours a day and allow them out only 1 hour a day for court-ordered recreation, which usually involves standing in a small cage alone with a basketball hoop, with or without a ball.

The decline of medium security prisons may be of concern. Frequently medium security prisons provide meaningful jobs and job training for inmates. These prisons are circled by razor wire and inmates' lives are highly restricted, but less so than would be the case in a maximum security environment. Therefore, these prisons can offer rehabilitation programs, educational opportunities, and other activities, all of which are usually not allowed behind the walls of a maximum security prison.

If the decline in medium security prisons is the result of more people being convicted of less serious crimes and being given shorter sentences, then this bodes well for decreasing the population of the Country Called Prison. If, on the other hand, this is a sign that more people are living in maximum security facilities, it may not be. The data available are not clear. Certainly we have more minimum security beds then we had in the past, but we also have increased maximum security bed space as well. It appears that the loss of medium security prisons is related to inmates being transferred to either more or less secure facilities, which is accompanied by a significant loss in rehabilitation programs (Stephan, 2005).

If you drive across America, you may see other communities that create citizens for the Country Called Prison. These are the communities where you see bars on store windows, broken-down houses and cars, and yards filled with weeds and debris. These are the communities of the poor and the working poor, which are ignored by most of society.

COMMON LANGUAGE

Language is a system of combining sounds, hand gestures, and/or symbols to communicate meaning. Language is not just for communication but also provides an internal organizational system for thinking. Languages all over the world share common characteristics: grammar (rules about word structure and use), syntax (grammatical correctness), morphemes (smallest unit of language meaning), phonemes (basic language sounds), and practical aspects such as tone, inflection, etiquette, slang, and so on (Chomsky, 1975).

The Country Called Prison has its own language. It includes terms like "shipping" and "the wire" that do not mean the same thing in American society. In America, shipping is when you send a package; in prison, it is when you send a person to another prison. Bars in American society are places where you meet friends to socialize. In prison, bars are on all the windows, reminding inmates that they are captives. In American society, if you are being shaken down, you are being swindled. In prison, it means correctional officers are tearing up your cell, looking for contraband.

As Clemmer suggested long ago, the language and gestures that are part of prison life create a separate culture. When individuals enter such a setting, they must learn new language and understand its importance. When they return to American society, they must leave that culture behind. This bouncing back and forth between cultures is part of the reason that many former prisoners find it difficult to reintegrate into American society.

SHARED VALUES, BELIEFS, AND SOCIAL BEHAVIOR

In the Country Called Prison, personal choices are limited and social rules and roles are predetermined. An "us-versus-them" mindset becomes dominant. Prison inmates know that no matter to what degree a therapist, officer, or warden may be friendly, there will never be a genuine relationship. These people have power and prisoners do not.

The few choices prisoners have are not the choices that Americans have. This lesson can be hard to learn and harder still to forget. Lengthy prison sentences can create inmates who become institutionalized and thus find it hard to live in American society. As one man on parole whom John knew put it, "Prison has become my home. I don't know how to make it on the outside."

Trust also has a different meaning in American society and in the Country Called Prison. In most neighborhoods in America, we generally trust our neighbors. Trust is not likely in the Country Called Prison. In prison, friendship is tenuous. There can never be trust when there is no freedom of choice. While offenders may play a friendly card game with others in their unit in the evening, they each know that sharing personal confidences during the game will likely set them up for a swindle later. Although offenders form groups, much like civic clubs on the outside, these are really gangs that offer protection rather than friendships. No one in prison wants to become a victim like James.

Another value is the ability to manipulate staff. In one prison in which John worked, an inmate who worked in the kitchen would tip off the support staff he liked when the lunch should be avoided. The directive to avoid lunch usually meant that glass, human waste, or some other nonfood substance had been mixed into that day's offerings. While on the surface this seemed liked a respectful act of kindness, he actually used this "friendship" as a means for obtaining favors. He gained the trust of staff this way and would occasionally get extra privileges that his fellow inmates did not. Of course, no one ever really checked the food when the worker warned the staff, so it may have all been a con. Either way, John learned quickly to bring his own lunch to work.

Once offenders receive their prison birth name in the form of their DOC identification number, clothes and social roles quickly follow. Offenders are not "guests" or "clients." They are not people. They are "convicts," "inmates," "the chomo" (child molester) whose lives are no longer their own. When James was transferred to another prison after his surgery, he was "shipped" as if he were a UPS package. James became little more than an object to the Country Called Prison.

COMMON POLITICAL SYSTEM

A great deal of the literature relating to the culture of prisons supports the idea that inmates connect to others for a variety of reasons, but chief among them are status and self-interest. In every prison, there are security personnel who are friendly to inmates and some who are hostile; each of these relationships affects an inmate's level of status as well as comfort. At the same time, leaders of gangs call the shots in the inmate world. In some cases, the gang leader helps to determine who gets the best work detail or who gets beat up.

When you work and live in prison, you quickly learn that the political environment is clearly different than in the free world. While on the surface, prison life seems very structured by pages and pages of policies and procedures, in reality there are no clear-cut rules. For example, child molesters are often assaulted in prison. However, child molesters with marketable skills may actually achieve high status. An attorney who commits a sex offense is more likely to be valued for his ability to bring lawsuits against the state than to be shunned for his decision to abuse children.

Although security staff appear to be in charge of prison operations, with an average 1 to 7 officer to inmate ratio (ASCA, 2010), a small subset of inmates is really in charge. In some prisons, inmate gang leaders possess a great deal of informal power, and inmates follow their rules or end up dead. We have observed officers meeting with prisoner-leaders to arrive at a solution to calm a facility down when too many fights start breaking out among rival gangs.

MATERIAL CULTURE AND ECONOMY

In every country, certain materials and property are valued more than others. The items that are important to citizens of one country are often different than that of another. When you travel outside the United States, you need to exchange your U.S. dollars to the currency of the country you have entered. You won't get very far in France with dollars, but a Euro can take you anywhere.

Prisons have currency as well. In the movie *The Shawshank Redemption* (1994), the inmates are shown trading cigarettes as currency. Increasingly, U.S. prisons are becoming nonsmoking facilities. So what is used instead? Drugs are an obvious item of value. However, services, both sexual and personal, can be traded for favors. Candy, gum, and aspirin, all of which can be legally purchased at the commissary, can serve as a means of barter. Illegal cell phones may have the most value in prisons today. Smuggled in or thrown over the fence, these phones open the world outside of prison to the inmate; therefore, their economic value is high.

The material items you see in prison are different from those in the outside world. We have both traveled outside the United States and continue to be fascinated by items in other countries that are not available in America, such as a different type of light switch or a toilet that you stand over instead of sit on. The material culture of the Country Called Prison includes bars, jumpsuits, cells, trays, razor wire, and so on. A billion-dollar prison industrial complex is dedicated to producing items made to be used only in prison. For example, prison televisions must be securely built so that the electrical wiring cannot be taken out and used to open security gates.

Almost nothing from the outside world is allowed in prison exactly as it would be found on the outside. Why? Security always comes first. Everything must pass the security test to avoid the likelihood that it could be taken apart and *weaponized*. We have seen "shanks" (homemade knives) in prison made from soap and rolled-up newspapers. Imagine what a prison inmate could do with the metal box that surrounds an old radio.

Just as there are illegal materials in America, there are illegal materials in prison. In prison, correctional staff regularly search housing units to uncover contraband and find everything from homemade beer to heroin. Cell phones are commonly discovered. Prison inmates have an amazing ability to find a way to get what they need. In one prison in which John worked, correctional staff discovered that a prison inmate was editing a pornographic magazine using a contraband word-processor. How that was smuggled in is anyone's guess. Inmates are also skilled at conning people into helping them get whatever they want—another unique aspect of prison culture. For many inmates, the "con game" is as entertaining as watching a sporting match.

There is no doubt in our minds that prison is another country. It has a large and growing population with its own geographic location. It has separate rules and roles for citizens. It has a unique set of values and language. Former and current inmates frequently feel a sense of camaraderie because they share a national identity. While it is certainly true that prison inmates frequently fight for control over material items and power in prison, at the end of the day they all realize one thing. Once they were convicted and sent to prison, they became members of a new nation that they will continue to belong to even after discharge.

Offenders who enter this country are left out of the free world while in prison and generally have difficulty reintegrating into American society after release because of the cultural and identity issues we have discussed. After a stint in the "joint," ex-cons assume the identity of *legal alien* when they return to America.

We have coined the word *legal alien* to describe convicted offenders who are legally members of American society because they were born in the United States. However, once they were convicted of a crime, they officially entered the Country Called Prison, where they assume a different social status and, we think, a new national identity. And they are now excluded from many of the privileges afforded to Americans. In most states, a convicted offender will lose his or her right to vote. Depending on the crime, they may lose access to their children. They obtain a negative social status that they will carry with them throughout their lives, even after they are discharged from prison and released from probation or parole.

For this reason, we consider the elimination of the Country Called Prison to be a challenge to more than just prisons. In this book, we will suggest ways in which a warden can change a prison and the way policy decision makers can change the entire criminal justice system. But first we believe a discussion of our approaches is merited.

The first thing to consider is the way a society views crime. Is crime a matter of social control or a matter of public health? The answer may depend on the type of crime committed.

As we discussed in the preface, the United States has the second-highest incarceration rate in the world. Furthermore, drug crime is one area in which we tend to incarcerate at much higher rates than our counterparts that are also wealthy, industrialized, and democratic nations. So what do these other countries do about the drug problem that the United States does not?

In short, most of America's peer countries view drug addiction not as a matter of social control but as a matter of public health. Social control problems can be punished away, whereas public health matters must be treated. We would never consider incarcerating someone who goes to the county health department for a measles, mumps, and rubella vaccine. Free inoculations are a matter of public health. If we keep disease at bay, then we will all be better off. Most of America's counterparts throughout the world, who have lower incarceration rates of drug offenders, do just that. They believe that addiction is a disease and should be treated as a public health matter.

Another way to reduce criminality is to divide up the types of interventions we are going to use. Social workers understand that in any social setting there are levels of intervention. If we truly want to eliminate a problem, we will need a combination of efforts. The levels of interventions we will address are primary, secondary, and tertiary.

Primary approaches address the hands-on actions that people can take to bring about change. Frequently these include the organizational practices of prison. It could also include the use of nongovernmental means to address some of the social ills that set people up to enter the Country Called Prison. If you live in a neighborhood of poor quality housing, then a primary approach might be to make residences more livable. In subsequent chapters, we will discuss ways that prisons could be made more efficient, less expensive, and more humane by addressing some policy and procedure changes.

Secondary approaches deal with sociological and psychological factors that influence the way people live. As we have already discussed, poverty is a problem for many who end up in prison. Programs that address poverty would be considered secondary, because although it is related to incarceration, it is not clearly linked to it. One program that seems to have had a great impact on reducing incarceration rates is the famous Perry Preschool project.

The Perry Preschool program began at Perry Elementary School in Ypsilanti, Michigan (1962–1967). It measured the efficacy of early childhood intervention on the long-term ability of children to escape poverty and many of the problems associated with it, such as criminality.

Each week children attended 12.5 hours of school, and they were visited at their homes once a week. During home visits, parents were taught parenting skills, which mostly involved telling them what was effective from a developmental point of view (something we will discuss later). The results from this research project support the notion that high-quality, early childhood education improves the chances of long-term positive outcomes (Weikart, 1985). Most of the children in the project were poor and from single-parent homes. In addressing many of these children's structural problems, the project had amazing results.

Schweinhart (2002) did a follow-up study with these children after they had reached 40 years of age. They had improved educational outcomes, income, and much lower rates of arrest than one might have expected. In comparing two groups, one in the program and the other not, Schweinhart's study shows the positive benefits of early intervention on not just income and education but also on crime. In short, these children outperformed their counterparts and are taxpayers in the United States, rather than people in the Country Called Prison, who drain taxes from the U.S. economy.

Tertiary approaches address large system problems associated with incarceration. All of Chapter Six is devoted to these issues. In particular, we will provide a road map that we think will assist in changing the mindset of most Americans who believe that high rates of incarceration are acceptable. These tertiary approaches are usually structural and will require legal action to implement them.

We believe that the metaphor of the Country Called Prison clearly fits the current situation in the United States. We spend billions of dollars each year to support this new nation growing in America and seemingly get very little in return. As we have noted, at least half of those we send to prison have not committed a violent offense and yet we treat them as if they had killed or raped someone. In so doing, we turn taxpayers into tax users and expand a nation within America's borders.

The last time John saw James he was headed back to prison. He had once again fallen off the proverbial wagon, and this time created mayhem with his car. Luckily no one died in the accident, but James's life was once again spent idling away in a correctional facility. Many think this place will correct his behavior, but instead it will merely integrate him even more into a country that is growing ever bigger within America's borders, a country we call Prison. In the next three chapters, we will discuss the social and psychological realities of the Country Called Prison in the hope that you will come to understand how this new nation within America was formed.

CHAPTER 3

Who Are the People of the Country Called Prison?

In matters of truth and justice, there is no difference between large and small problems, for issues concerning the treatment of people are all the same.

Albert Einstein

Over the years, whenever we told someone that we worked in a prison, we invariably received one of two reactions. One had to do with the perception that prison is a dangerous environment, which then led the person to wonder about the way we managed our fears and protected ourselves. The other reaction was curiosity regarding the "evil" and "mentally deranged" inmates who live there. As we responded to people's reactions, we discovered that most really didn't want to hear about our jobs. They didn't want to contend with the reality of who actually lives in prison. Television is filled with crime dramas that nearly always result in the "good guys" capturing the "bad guys." Therefore, society has been trained to believe that the good guys win and the bad guys go to prison. However, in reality, the line in prison between who is "good" and who is "bad" is not always clear.

We have met some extremely dangerous people while working in prison. The majority of inmates, however, are not frightening. They are the people we discuss throughout the rest of the book: men and women incarcerated for nonviolent crimes. Although these men and women are not scary, they are psychologically and socially impaired. This perception of the criminal mind did not come about suddenly for

Mary. Early in her career, an event occurred when she was working at a medium security men's prison that caused her to question her own thinking about criminals. Until then, she had believed that most criminals were terrible people who deliberately broke the law and should be feared.

At this prison, the men were allowed to move about the compound unrestricted throughout the day but had to be in their dormitories right after dinner. Many of the men worked during the day and in the evening watched television, played card or board games, read books, or worked on art projects. One particular late afternoon, she was in the case manager's office in the dormitory, informing a prisoner that his mother had died. Afterward, as she tried to leave, she discovered that the front door was locked. The unit officer was in another part of the building doing her required population count. So here she was, a young woman, in a room with a bunch of male criminals. Her heart quickened a bit and she found herself momentarily afraid. Interestingly, though, when she turned around to make a joke to the men about her predicament, they were all staring at her, tense and afraid as well. They certainly were not afraid of Mary. But they did seem afraid of this out-of-the-ordinary situation. They obviously did not know how to react and froze in whatever activity they had been doing. An unlikely hero came to everyone's rescue. Jim was a middle-aged inmate in prison for growing marijuana in his backyard. He was playing dominoes with three peers and called out, "Hey, Doc, you're just in time to sit in for me. I've got to use the facilities. Me and my partner here have the highest score and I don't want to leave him hangin'. I figure an educated lady such as yourself surely can keep us in the lead. You feel up to helpin' us out till the officer gets back?" Just as a clear, blue sky appears after a storm passes, the tension in the room abated as Mary sat down to "save" the team.

These men were not that much different than Mary. They were not the "bad men" she expected. Everyone makes mistakes in life. While she had not violated the law, she nonetheless had hurt others and felt remorse for her actions. In her years of working with prison residents, she discovered that many also felt remorse for their criminal behavior. Yet, her regret for having hurt someone in the past prompted her to not make the same hurtful mistake twice, whereas many in prison seem to be unable to learn from their mistakes.

What is different about those who live in the Country Called Prison and those who do not?

On the surface, many of the prison residents we have met seem to have had fairly ordinary lives. They had jobs before they were arrested and lived with a spouse (or significant other) and their children in a home or apartment. Based on their own belief system, they tried to be good spouses and parents. They had active lives with friends and family. Beneath the surface, however, they frequently were addicted to drugs and/or alcohol. They had difficulty maintaining employment. Their relationships with their spouses and children were tenuous at best. They had poor grooming habits, their command of the English language was poor, and they generally used profanity as adjectives. They lived in the moment, with little thought regarding their future. They rarely had plans for ways their lives could be different. Most of them didn't even understand that their lives *could* be different.

Although generally prosocial people commit crimes, such as lying on tax returns or using their company laptop for personal business, they are rarely caught in the act. Some may feel guilty, but many excuse their behaviors with claims like "the government takes too much already" or "I don't get paid enough at work." Even if they get caught committing these types of crimes, society often excuses them. People often rationalize that "everyone does it once in a while." Considering the fact that nearly everyone does a wrong deed in their lifetime, one is left with a question. Why do some people cross the line of criminality and move past the socially acceptable crimes to those that can land them in prison?

Over the years, criminologists have proposed different theories regarding the ways people develop prosocial or criminal behavior patterns. Differential Association Theory, developed by Edwin Sutherland (1947), suggests that we learn to deviate from society's norms from the intimate relationships we build with others. This is particularly true as we reach our teenage years, when we quite literally adapt the behaviors of the different groups with which we associate. For Sutherland, deviant peers almost always lead to deviance. We learn different rules and norms depending upon the group with which we interact, which suggests that values and attitudes learned by members of street gangs and church groups are different. This difference leads to deviance for some and conformity for others.

In his Containment Theory, Walter Reckless (1970) suggested that all human behavior is contained by both internal and external forces. In childhood we develop internalized control mechanisms, such as a sense of morality or conscience, a fear of getting caught, guilt, self-esteem, and a host of others. These mechanisms lead to our *internal control* later in life. Strong internal control corresponds with low levels of criminality. We are also surrounded by external controls, such as the presence of the police, a teacher, or a parent. These external influences may control behavior immediately, but they cannot control us all the time. Why? Because the police cannot be everywhere at all times. Our internal desire to get our own way is only contained by our internal controls.

Travis Hirschi's Social Bond Theory (1969) postulates that children develop internal control because of the bonds they make. He agrees with Reckless that internal control is the key variable in predicting criminality. Internal controls are directed by the social bonds we formulate. Four key bonds—attachment, commitment, involvement, and belief—work against our self-centered desires to get our own way. According to Social Bond Theory, weak bonds lead to criminality, while strong bonds lead to conformity and pro-social behavior.

Attachment refers to the valued people in our life who are conformists. In short, if you bond with conformists, you are unlikely to become deviant. *Commitment* refers to the goals and aspirations that you may have related to living a prosocial life. If you're committed to becoming a doctor, you are unlikely to skip school. *Involvement* suggests that if we are active in prosocial events, like student government, we are unlikely to have the time and/or inclination to join a gang. Finally, if we *believe* that the rules of society are fair and applied fairly, then we are unlikely to break them. Our belief will direct our behavior. For Hirschi, the strength of these bonds determines who will and who will not commit crime.

Michael Gottfredson later with Hirschi developed a General Theory of Crime (1990). They hypothesized that lack of self-control—the ability to delay gratification—is a key element in criminal behavior in that it affects the bonds we create. People with a lot of self-control gravitate to others like them. Conversely, those who cannot put off short-term rewards in the hope of a better long-term consequence find others who are spur-of-the-moment types as well. People with high levels of self-control are unlikely to commit crimes because they consider the long-term consequences of their actions before they act. When individuals repeatedly commit crime and don't seem to learn from their behavior, they do so because they lack self-control. The General Theory of Crime hypothesizes that self-control, learned early in life, is resistant to any significant change throughout a lifetime. Here is where we disagree. We have seen many people make significant changes later in their lives.

The common element in all of these theories is *childhood*. How do we grow up? With whom do we grow up? The way adults model behavior and teach children directly affect children's perceptions of right and wrong. Psychologist Albert Bandura developed his theory on Social Learning (1963), which integrated behavioral and cognitive theories into a comprehensive model of ways we learn information and behavior. His concepts of vicarious reinforcement, modeling, and reciprocal determinism show that children learn in a social context through observation, imitation, and reinforcement as well as direct instruction.

As shown in Table 3.1, Bandura identified four ways that we learn while interacting with others. We learn by watching other people's behaviors and learning from their consequences. As an example, a younger child might see her older sibling being prevented from watching television because a chore was not completed; the younger child

Table 3.1. SOCIAL LEARNING THEORY

Element	How Learning Takes Place
Vicarious Reinforcement	Observe consequences of others' behavior.
Modeling	Observing and extracting information from observation and deciding to use it or not; learning something does not mean change occurs.
Reciprocal Determinism	Own thoughts, the environment, and own/others' behavior influence each other.
Reinforcement	Assists in learning but is not always effective.

Source: Bandura, 1963.

learns to complete her chores so she isn't punished. When the younger child obeys her parents because she has witnessed her sibling being punished, this is *vicarious reinforcement*. When the older child is prevented from watching television, this is *reinforcement* that misbehavior is not accepted. However, if reinforcement (either negative or positive) is too little, too harsh, or not immediate, reinforcement does not usually work.

A similar learning strategy is *reciprocal determinism*, which takes place through interactions with others and the environment. Here each person involved in the interaction learns from the other, as well as the environment. Following the previous example, if, when a parent confronts the older sibling about not completing the chore, the older sibling lies and tells the parent that she was helping her younger sibling with homework, she may receive a compliment instead of a punishment. The negative behavior is reinforced and is produced by the child herself. By lying she manipulates her mother and receives a reward for antisocial behavior. Such behavior sows the seeds of criminal thinking.

Today, many children spend more awake hours interacting with electronic media, much of it violent and sexual, than they do with adults. On average, children, ages 2 to 5, spend 32 hours a week watching television or videos and playing electronic games; 6- to 11-year-olds watch about 28 hours of television (McDonough, 2009). Research promoted by the Kaiser Family Foundation (Rideout, Foehr, & Roberts, 2010) identified that 71% of children ages 8 to 18 have a television in their room, 54% have a DVD or VCR player, and 37% have cable or satellite television. The Kaiser study identified that, on average, this age group devotes more than 7 hours a day to video games. In about two-thirds of households surveyed, the television was usually on during meals, and 51% reported that the television was on "most of the time." In the same study, 53% of families reported that there were no rules for teenagers about television watching.

In the past 20 years, there has also been an increasing number of latchkey children—children at home before and after school without adult supervision. According to research by New York University's Child Study Center, 15% of children, ages 5 to 13, are home alone before school, 76% are alone after school, and about 9% are left alone in the evening because the parent or parents work the night shift (Alston, 2010). The same study showed that 51% of latchkey children do poorly in school. After-school hours are the peak time for juvenile crime, with a 48% rise in juvenile crime between 1999 and 2010 during late afternoon and evening hours. Latchkey children are more prone to smoke cigarettes, use marijuana and alcohol, and suffer from depression.

The wealth of information obtained from social science research regarding the way children learn appropriate social and interpersonal behavior from adults is inconsequential if there are no prosocial adults interacting with children, according to William Golding's classic novel *The Lord of the Flies* (1954). In the story, preadolescent boys are stranded on an island. At first the boys are excited about the adventure and the lack of adult supervision. But the fun soon wears off, and savagery begins to take over. The story ends with one of the boys being murdered just before they are all rescued, and the boys realize the horror of their actions. The story is a timeless metaphor of the conflict between our need for group survival through a cooperative, civilized society and our desire to satisfy our selfish needs through power.

As what you have just read suggests and research has proven (Marquis, 1992), delinquent teenagers and antisocial adults likely come from chaotic, neglectful, and abusive families. Why? What happens in early childhood that is so important in the development of prosocial behavior? All animals need attention at birth; however, in comparison to most animals, humans come into the world and remain fragile for an extended period of time. Most animals are walking rather quickly after birth, while humans take around a year. Humans need a great deal of care in the first years of their lives. Therefore, parental caregiving is paramount if a child is going to reach adulthood with positive characteristics, attitudes, and social morality. (We will continue to use the word *parent* for ease of discussion. However, we are aware that many adults in prison had different types of primary caregivers.) Most people don't think of parenting as a job with goals and an outcome that can be measured.

But from a species-survival point of view, parenting is a job, a very important job, one that produces the next generation of adults who will further the human race. Recent research by Looman (2010) identifies three tasks (competencies) of effective parenting: nurturance, regulation, and attachment. These are summarized in Table 3.2. *Nurturance* is the

Table 3.2. TASKS OF EFFECTIVE PARENTING

Nurturance
- Warmth and unconditional acceptance
- Support and encouragement

Regulation
- Protecting child from harm as she or he explores and learns
- Socializing child to act appropriately

Attachment
- Bonding with child through consistent caregiving

Source: Looman, 2010.

ability to provide children unconditional love, demonstrated by acceptance, support, and encouragement. *Regulation* is the ability to protect children from harm as they learn and explore their environment, as well as help them learn important social skills so that they fit into the culture in which they were born. *Attachment* is the ability to form an endearing bond with a child that demonstrates that the child is wanted and valued.

Research by Christopher Mruk (2006), a leading expert in self-esteem development, suggests a way that we can identify the goals of parenting. As summarized in Table 3.3, Mruk's research indicates that competent parents help infants grow into adulthood with the ability to sustain their own lives; be autonomous yet connected to others; control their responses to environmental stimuli; accept responsibility for their actions; have a sense of purpose; and contribute toward humankind in some meaningful way. We believe that most of the teenagers and adults in homeless shelters, juvenile detention centers, jails, prisons, crisis centers, and inpatient mental health facilities have not developed these skills. This might be why offenders have higher suicide rates and lower levels of educational attainment than the general

Table 3.3. CHARACTERISTICS
OF WELL-FUNCTIONING ADULTS

Ability to sustain life in socially appropriate ways
Ability to be autonomous yet connected to others
Ability to appropriately manage responses to stimuli
Ability to accept responsibility for own actions
Ability to have purpose and contribute to society in a meaningful way

Source: Mruk, 2006.

public. The rate for offender suicide is 33% (Noonan, 2012), while the rate for the general population is about 12% (Centers for Disease Control, 2014). While 18% of the general public did not receive a high school diploma, 48% of offenders reported not completing high school (Harlow, 2003). As you will read later, offenders have poor relationships skills, tend to blame others for their problems, and have developed impaired thinking strategies, referred to as "criminal thinking." Frequently this appears to stem from poor modeling of appropriate behavior.

Just as studies have identified different management styles and their influence on organizational outcomes, research by Diana Baumrind identified different parenting styles that significantly affect childhood development (Baumrind, 1967, 1991). According to Baumrind's research, summarized in Table 3.4, authoritative parents are able to establish rules as guidelines but take a more egalitarian approach to enforcing them. When their children make mistakes, these parents tend to be more nurturing and guiding rather than strictly punishing. Other types of parents tend to either harshly enforce rules, disregard rules altogether, or are psychologically absent in the child's life. The thousands of prison residents we have met over the years were not usually raised by authoritative parents.

To become well-functioning adults, children must progress through a variety of developmental stages under the guidance of their parents and teachers. According to Eric Erikson's Life-Span Model of Psycho-Social Development (1959) and Stanley Greenspan's Emotional Development Model (1997), the first seven years of life lay the foundation for healthy adult functioning. Table 3.5 provides a description of these stages.

Table 3.4. PARENTING STYLES AND CHILDHOOD DEVELOPMENT

Style	Rule Orientation	Effect on Child Development
Authoritarian	Rules must be followed	Obedient but lack social competence
Authoritative	Rules, responsive to child	Obedient and socially competent
Permissive	Very few rules	Antisocial and do poorly in school
Uninvolved	Few rules, low responsiveness	Poor self-control, socially incompetent

Source: Baumrind, 1991.

Table 3.5. STAGES OF EARLY CHILDHOOD DEVELOPMENT

Age	Psychosocial	Emotional	Outcome
0–1	Trust versus mistrust	Making sense of sensations; relating to others	Hope
1–4	Autonomy versus shame	Intentionality	Will
2–5	Initiative versus guilt	Purposeful interaction; symbolic meaning, language	Purpose
5+	Industry versus inferiority	Emotional reasoning	Confidence

Sources: Erikson, 1959; Greenspan, 1997.

Within the first month of life an infant must be able to decipher sensations, organize stimuli, and maintain a minimum level of calm in order to survive (feeding, sleeping, and so on). Infants must learn to trust that the world is safe and that caregivers will provide for their needs. Within the first 3 months of life, an infant must bond with a primary human and be able to understand the caregiver's voice tone, expressions, and basic actions, then correlate sensation and emotions to decide intentional actions (for example, a smile response). With a sense of safety in place, infants can explore their environment and attend to important patterning, such as speech and emotional cueing. Within a year, infants begin to crawl, then walk, and learn that they are separate from their caregivers. By age 2, toddlers begin to separate from caregivers, becoming more autonomous and independent, thus developing a sense of self-identity. Competent parents provide a safe environment from which children can independently explore their social world. Parents can also instruct children in appropriate behavior, interact and play with them, as well as talk with them so that sounds become words with meanings.

As young children begin to interact with peers in play, they develop skills for planning, organizing, and initiating their own goals. By age 4, children develop a sense of purpose and understand, through play, that one thing can represent another. They learn moral reasoning when they break something or cause a peer to cry. Competent parents are actively involved with their children, listening to their stories, validating their feelings, answering their questions, and helping them solve problems.

By age 7, children begin to take pride in their ability to finish homework assignments, participate in sports, draw a picture, or play a musical instrument. They learn about the joy of working with others to accomplish a goal and sharing their accomplishments with others. Children are generally able to identify their strengths and weaknesses, share in peer group identity, recognize adults whom they like and admire, and take pride in obeying rules and participating in group and solo activities. They now have the foundation for their self-ego, which will continue to grow and carry them through life. Children raised by competent parents can form bridges between their own thoughts and feelings and those of others and begin to construct a cohesive internal reality that will develop into their sense of purpose in the world.

How does all this apply to those who go to prison? In our experiences, most criminals do not grow up with proper nurturance, regulation, and attachment. They report that their parents were either excessively strict or overly indulgent. In addition, they report that their parents were uninvolved in their lives and unresponsive to their psychosocial needs and that there was no routine or consistency in their daily lives. In short, they never knew what was going to happen next. Offenders report that they never could trust their parents because their parents would say one thing and do another. They often made promises they never kept. When people grow up this way, they develop sensory distortions regarding reality, often misinterpreting emotional and interpersonal cues. They tend to be impulsive and believe that there are no predictable consequences for actions. They get mad when someone "does them wrong" but steal from others if they need something. They tend to be vindictive and malicious, as Tammy's story demonstrates.

Tammy had been in prison for about 17 years when Mary met her. Tammy began attending meetings of Mary's Lifers' Club. The women who came to the meetings made items such as quilts or sweaters for elderly people who lived in the nursing home near the prison. As attendees worked on projects, they talked about issues in their lives, supporting each other much the way sisters do. Tammy had been sexually abused by her father, her brothers, and two of her uncles. By age 13 she was addicted to cocaine and began selling her body to get money to buy drugs. As an adult, she became a stripper and a prostitute. She lived with a man she had met at the strip club. He was an unemployed addict who beat her often. By age 25, she had given birth to two children who were taken from her at birth because they tested positive for drugs. After her seventh trip to the emergency room for another broken arm, she went home and burned up the man who abused her while he slept in their bed.

Why didn't she go to a battered women's shelter? Why didn't she call a women's hotline? Why did she endure abuse year after year until that moment when she threw the burning cigarette lighter on the bed? Children who grow up abused come to think of abuse as a normal family function and are likely to repeat the cycle when they grow up because it is all they know (Keeshin, Cronholm, & Strawn, 2011). A person's view of the world begins in infancy. The reality of right and wrong, normal and abnormal, develops in childhood. All future decisions and a sense of reality stem from this foundation. The Country Called Prison begins here, not at the prison gate.

Children who grow surrounded by chaos, abuse, and neglect generally develop poor self-esteem and have difficulty managing emotions (Greenspan, 1997; Mruk, 2006). They also tend to have poor relationships with authority figures, so they have difficulty in school and often drop out. As adults, they often suffer from chronic depression or personality disorders and have addictive personalities. They usually have difficulty maintaining employment and relationships, focusing on their own needs without understanding that their behaviors affect others. In a chaotic or abusive environment, children learn to tell stories to fit the reality they want or think their parents want, which might not always fit the true reality of the situation. When adults do this, prosocial citizens call it "lying." Psychologists call it "living in denial or fantasy." In the Country Called Prison, citizens call it "the truth, honest to God." Ineffective parenting practices patterns some children to chronically break the law (Moffitt & Caspi, 2001).

When Steve entered prison, he was a young adult and single. He had been raised in a family where his parents were often absent. When they were home, there was usually a lot of yelling and drinking and occasionally some beatings, if either parent got drunk. By the time he arrived in prison, he had a 5-year-old child in foster care because the child's mother was in prison for prostitution and possession of cocaine. Child Protective services terminated the parental rights of both Steve and his girlfriend. Steve was in prison because he had gone out with friends to celebrate completing drug court, with which he had been involved for the past three years. After leaving the bar, he was arrested for driving under the influence, possession of drugs, and illegal possession of a firearm. For three years, Steve had followed the rules of drug court and remained substance free; yet the very day that he was released from supervision he returned to his previous lifestyle. Why did he not integrate the lessons he learned from drug court?

Steve was motivated to leave drug court as soon as possible so he could "get on with his life." He learned in childhood to tell his parents and teachers what they wanted to hear so that he would get what he wanted. So he put on the show of being "the recovered addict." However, as soon as he was released, he "got on with his life" of getting what he wanted regardless of the cost to others. Society calls this antisocial behavior; Steve calls it a normal life.

Sociologists Gresham Sykes and David Matza studied ways that people learn to rationalize their self-interested behavior in order to avoid following social norms (1957). Sykes and Matza suggested that rule breakers develop ways to rationalize behavior when they go against social norms. Criminals tend to use these neutralizing techniques to protect themselves from self-blame (guilt and remorse) and to deflect the condemnation of others. Thus they don't easily learn from their mistakes. Table 3.6 provides a list of the techniques most used by rule breakers.

Following Sykes and Matza's research, Stanton Samenow has studied criminal behavior for over three decades. He ardently argues that

---

Table 3.6. TECHNIQUES TO NEUTRALIZE
DISTRESS CAUSED BY ANTISOCIAL BEHAVIOR

Denial of responsibility
- "It wasn't my fault."

Denial of injury
- "It wasn't a big deal. They could afford the loss."

Denial of the victim
- "After what he did to my friend, he deserved it."

Condemnation of the condemners
- "Like you've never done anything wrong before."

Appeal to higher loyalties
- "My sister needed help with her rent. What else could I do?"

Source: Sykes & Matza, 1957.

abuse, poverty, and media violence does not cause criminality. Instead, he believes criminal thinking causes crime. In the second edition of his book *Inside the Criminal Mind*, Samenow identified at least 36 thinking errors that characterize the thought processes of criminals (2004). His research indicates that all criminals view people as objects that can be used to satisfy their needs. While at times they seem to have a conscience and behave in a prosocial manner, they have the ability to turn it off at will, which insulates them from guilt and remorse. For a quick review of his thesis related to these characteristics, see Table 3.7.

Most criminals view themselves as decent people and their lives as exciting. They often think people who obey social norms are boring and unfulfilled. It is easy to feel sorry for people who return to prison for a second or third time. When you listen to their life histories, it is easy to see why they are in prison. Samenow does not deny this reality but suggests that if we wish to stop criminality we need to change criminal thinking.

Competent parenting is only one aspect of child development. Genetics, the environment, and the child's own temperament are also important components. At birth, the human brain weighs only about 10 ounces and needs to add another 38 ounces by age 20 to fully develop (Dawson & Guare, 2010). From their first breath after delivery, infants begin to absorb and assimilate millions of stimuli from their environment. The brain builds neurons and synapses as learning takes place, yet periodically prunes them as skills and information are

Table 3.7. TWELVE COMMON CHARACTERISTICS
OF CRIMINAL THINKING

Extremely energetic yet lazy

Chronically fearful

Periods of absolute worthiness and hopelessness

Chronic state of anger; used to control others

Grandiose; better and more deserving than others

Absolute need to control others

Concrete; very black-and-white thinking

Personality is fragmented; rapid shifts in personality

Belief that person is unique; not like others

Habitual lying; don't know how to tell the truth

Victim stance; blames others

Lack of empathy for others

Source: Samenow, 2004.

consolidated into concepts. Consolidation stages occur at ages 5, 12, 20, and 40. At each stage, crucial pathways must be able to lock into place for the next neurological stage to occur properly.

A good metaphor for brain development is the construction of a roadway. Generally, the width of the roadway is prepared first, then the bridges go in and finally the roadway. Many years ago, Mary discovered a bridge that had been put in the wrong location. As she approached the correct bridge, she saw a sign by the wrong bridge that humorously stated, "The McDonald County Bridge to Nowhere." Some inmates seem to have a bridge to nowhere in their own minds.

Although the brain takes nearly 20 years to fully develop, the most crucial of all neurological abilities, executive functioning, develops by age 7. Executive functioning, which assists in healthy adult functioning, is described in full in Table 3.8. It is like the foundation of a building. Mary once commuted to work on a busy highway and frequently had to stop because of a car accident further up the road. The stoppage usually occurred at about the same place where a 16-story building was being constructed. Since there was a tall fence around the construction site, for about four months no building grew above the fence line. Mary mentioned this to an engineer at work who taught her about foundations. A foundation has to be strong enough to support the building as well as manage the structural stresses caused by the earth shifting. The taller and larger the building, the

---

Table 3.8. EXECUTIVE FUNCTIONING CHARACTERISTICS

Definition of executive functioning
- The ability to manage emotions and monitor thoughts to regulate behavior.

Skills of executive functioning that help achieve goals
- Planning
- Time management
- Organization
- Working memory
- Awareness of own thinking processes (metacognition)

Behavior of executive functioning that leads to achieving goals
- Inhibit responses (delayed gratification)
- Manage emotional responses
- Be able to adapt to changes in the environment
- Persistence (manage frustrations)

Source: Dawson & Guare, 2010.

---

deeper and more structurally reinforced the foundation has to be. It is the same with humans, who must cope with stresses throughout their lifetime.

After observing and visiting with hundreds of people who live in the Country Called Prison, we believe that many offenders have poor executive functioning skills because of ineffective parenting (Greenspan, 1997; Moffitt & Caspi, 2001) and/or impaired brain development due to childhood abuse and neglect (Tarullo, 2012) or parental drug and alcohol while expecting, as well as secondhand smoke from recreational drugs and cigarettes (Blackburn, Bonas, Spencer, et al., 2004; Frank, Augustyn, Knight, et al., 2001; Zukerman, Frank, Hingson, et al., 1989). We have observed that offenders do not know ways to think about the pros and cons of choices. They do not understand their emotions and why they are feeling them. They are not able to incorporate emotional reasoning into their problem-solving process and tend to be impulsive and have difficulty delaying gratification. They generally don't understand that their behaviors affect others. If they do, they tend to minimize their own responsibility by blaming their behavior on someone or something else. Since many dropped out, they failed to go through the American socialization process that naturally occurs in high school. Most are governed by a deep underlying shame and sense of unworthiness that they frequently numb with drugs and alcohol. They know at some psychological level that they are outcasts in U.S. society long before they come to prison.

Ted's story illustrates the way poor executive functioning tends to make someone reckless and imprudent. Ted is a tall, middle-aged man with a weathered face that made him appear much older than he was. He came into Mary's office to receive his new arrival assessment. After welcoming him, she mentioned that he looked familiar. He shook his head and turned his eyes toward the floor and stated, "Yeah, I was here last fall [about seven months ago]." Mary asked him what brought him back. He looked up with tears welling in his eyes. "Oh, I got out about two months ago and even had a job in construction; my brother helped me get it. But I needed gas to get to work and hadn't gotten my paycheck, so I broke into a vending machine to get some money. I was going to leave the guy a note that I would pay him back. But wouldn't you know, the cops were just coming out of the restaurant across the street and caught me." Since Ted was out on parole, his parole officer brought him back to prison the next day.

Ted was not able to plan ahead. He was not able to think about what he would need to maintain employment. He was not able to organize and execute plans to be prepared for the next day. He was not able to manage his impulsivity in solving problems. He was not able to identify resources available to him, including supportive people who could help him with issues and problems. He more than likely had not had breakfast and had not prepared a lunch; obviously he did not have money to go out for lunch. He most likely did not have water, and he was probably not dressed appropriately for construction work. Along with poor executive functioning skills, Ted also had a second problem. He had become *prisonized*. For the last three years, prison had given him everything he needed. Now, on his own, he was supposed to suddenly figure out what he needed, where to get it, how to get it, and when to get it.

Throughout this book we refer to the problems associated with mass incarceration as an *epidemic*. We think this is a good metaphor. Ted was infected with the "unsocialized virus," of which the prison system has not cured him. Like many others, he keeps getting reinfected. Like many viruses, Ted's unsocialized virus flares up now and again and he finds himself back in prison. He also infects other people, such as his children or friends he convinces to use drugs and commit petty crimes with him. In epidemiology, a disease or illness is identified as an epidemic when the number of people who become ill significantly exceeds an expected base rate. America's incarceration rate certainly meets this condition. Usually epidemics happen when the ecology of a given population changes or a new parasite enters the area and the population has no natural immunity. Although illegal drugs were in use prior to the 1970s and 1980s, the punishments for their use increased a great deal. Instead of treating illegal drug use and addiction as a public health issue, policy makers made it a criminal issue. Think of it this way: What if we treated the flu as a criminal issue and stopped providing yearly vaccines?

The main goals of federal and state public health departments are to: 1) prevent epidemics by monitoring the community, 2) investigate and identify health hazards, 3) inform, educate, and empower people about health issues, and 4) mobilize community partnerships to identify and solve health problems (Office of Disease Prevention and Health Promotion, www.health.gov, 2014). Many of the changes we propose in this book are patterned after these public health goals.

We have also met nonviolent offenders who are shunned and outcast like lepers in ancient times. In Medieval Europe, people infected were often confined against their will and had to wear a bell while in public to identify their presence (Rodrigues & Lockwood, 2011). When you consider the plight of the mentally ill whom we incarcerate, the analogy of modern-day lepers certainly holds true. Consider the data in Table 3.9. Notice the high percentage of prisoners with mental illnesses. Is incarceration really the best way to deal with them? Furthermore, these inmate characteristics indicate high rates of substance abuse, homelessness, and a history of abuse.

Although we have known for more than 50 years that mental illness is caused by chemical imbalances in the brain and have developed effective medications and therapeutic rehabilitation protocols, society continues to fear the mentally ill. Health insurance companies, both private and public, fail to reimburse for services as adequately as they do for treatment of physical conditions.

Table 3.9. PRISONERS WITH MENTAL HEALTH DISORDERS

	Percentage in State Prisons	Percentage in Local Jails
Mental health problems	56%	64%
• Recent history	24%	21%
• Major depression	23%	30%
• Mania (bipolar)	43%	55%
• Psychotic (schizophrenia)	15%	4%
Substance dependence	74%	76%
Violent crime history	61%	44%
Three or more incarcerations	25%	26%
Homeless within a year of arrest	13%	17%
Received public assistance	43%	43%
Physical/sexual abuse	27%	24%
Guardian abused alcohol/drugs	39%	37%
Family member incarcerated	52%	52%
Lived in foster care	19%	15%

Source: Jones & Glaze, 2006.

History shows us that when the United States had fewer jails and prisons, the mentally ill were admitted to psychiatric hospitals. As prison facilities began growing in number nearly 30 years ago with "get tough on crime" legislation, social control agents (legislators, police, district attorneys, and judges) began to impose criminal rather than psychiatric definitions on people's behavior, thus shifting the management of mental illness to the criminal justice system (Fisher, Silver, & Wolff, 2006). And as we have already mentioned, the buildup of prisons coincided perfectly with the deinstitutionalization movement.

For many years social constructionists have argued that criminalizing mental illness has created a social response that no longer views mental illness as a medical issue but as a public safety issue (Erickson & Erickson, 2008). According to social constructionists, by identifying mental illness as a crime, society no longer has to view mentally ill people as sick and in need of compassion. Society no longer has to *feel guilty* about failing to provide adequate treatment and care.

What is the cost, in lives and money, of our lack of empathy? Between 55% and 65% of people living in jails and state prisons in the United States have a mental illness, nearly 4 times the number for the general population (Jones & Glaze, 2006). A quarter of this group reported that they had been to prison three or more times. Over half of the inmates with mental illness reported that a family member had been incarcerated and 15% to 19% lived in foster care at some point in their childhood. Nearly 40% reported that their parents abused drugs and alcohol, and 27% had been physically and/or sexually abused prior to arrest. Approximately 15% had been homeless the year before they were arrested, and nearly half reported that they had previously received public assistance. These figures reinforce our earlier discussion of the chaotic lives lived by many of those who are in the Country Called Prison.

Sam's story demonstrates the heartlessness of criminalizing mental illness. Sam entered prison when he was 52 years old. His developmental age was about 7, and he had been living with his parents in a small rural community. His parents, now in their 80s, were having more and more difficulty caring for themselves, let alone their son. One afternoon, Sam found a pellet rifle and shot out the lights in an old abandoned warehouse. Arrested and charged with destruction of property, he was sentenced to five years in prison.

Culpability for criminal acts is touchy. People like Sam with cognitive deficits find their way to prison with regularity. Often, these individuals are well known to the police for committing petty crimes. Because of their cognitive deficits, they struggle with issues of cause and effect and have trouble learning from their experiences. They can become frustrated easily and sometimes turn to violence as a result. John's experience as a disability social worker taught him an important lesson. People with cognitive delays are frequently not necessarily physically impaired at all. If their delays lead to aggression and frustration, they may be bound for prison because few states provide residential treatment for those with intellectual but not physical disabilities. At one prison where Mary worked, 168 men (an entire unit) all tested below the normal range on their intelligence tests. This unit attempted to provide the care that a community residential treatment facility could have done more easily and less expensively. While somewhat successful in keeping these fragile inmates from being abused by others, the long-term effects of incarceration on those with intellectual disabilities leave them with the same stigma attached to anyone who goes to prison. Is prison really the place to treat these people?

Our second story is that of Shamika, who not only had a mental illness but was also poor and African American. She had trouble all through school and was finally suspended. Afterward, the school counselor referred her to the community mental health center. But her mother was unable to take time away from her job to drive Shamika to appointments. At age 19, Shamika was caught shoplifting from a convenience store. When the police came, she thought they were demons coming to kill her, so she fought them. She was charged and convicted of assault and battery of a police officer and was sentenced to seven years in prison.

During Shamika's intake, Mary diagnosed her with severe mental illness, referred her to the psychiatrist for appropriate medication, and recommended placement in the prison's mental health unit. There she learned about her illness and ways to manage her symptoms as well as a few life skills. By the time she was discharged from prison, she had already been approved for Social Security disability and Medicaid assistance. She left prison with a future appointment with the community mental health facility.

Fourteen months later Mary conducted yet another intake interview with her. Why did this happen? Mary had done all the right things to set her up for success after her release—or so she thought. Shamika had been through one of the best treatment programs that the prison had. She had been housed in a mental health unit, where she learned effective coping and living skills. She had funding for housing and food on the outside, and she had been referred for follow-up services in the community. Unfortunately, the community mental health center rescheduled her appointment for later, and she ran out of medication. She relapsed into self-medicating with drugs and alcohol. Based on our experience, we believe Shamika returned to prison because the services for the mentally ill in prison were better than those in the community. But this is a costly way to deal with the mentally ill.

In 2011, women made up approximately 7% of the total number of people incarcerated, with 54% convicted of nonviolent crimes (Carson & Sabol, 2012). Yet incarcerated women have significantly higher rates of mental illness than incarcerated men: 73% versus 55% (Jones & Glaze, 2006). Female inmates report that 8 out of 10 were physically or sexually abused before entering prison, and 69% reported that the abuse occurred before age 18. Over 40% of women in prison exhibit symptoms of post-traumatic stress disorder (PTSD), while about 36% suffer from major depressive disorder and nearly 65% have addiction disorders that likely stem from abuse (Lewis, 2006).

Many women in prison are victims of heinous violent crimes but are nonviolent criminals themselves. However, a greater impact to society is that many female prisoners suffer from a serious mental disorder that will, for many, go untreated in prison, setting them up for failure when they discharge. They also are likely to have children who are in foster care or living with relatives. They often regain custody of their children after release. These children have a 25% greater chance of ending up in prison than children whose parents have not been in prison (Wakefield & Wildeman, 2014), and these children often have mental illnesses requiring inpatient care. And so the generational cycle of the Country Called Prison continues.

Since mental illness is often treated like a crime in America, we now tell the story of the growing number of veterans who have found their way to prisons instead of treatment centers. Devon grew up poor in a family where many of his relatives had been to prison. His neighborhood was a battlefield for gangs. By the time he turned 17, he had witnessed the deaths of two of his friends. He managed to make it through high school because he was a good athlete, playing starter positions on both the football and basketball teams. Teachers encouraged him to join the Army when he graduated. Unfortunately, Devon ended up in a war zone during Operation Desert Storm, where he experienced many horrors. After four years, he was medically discharged due to PTSD. He began working for a construction company and married his high school sweetheart. It seemed that everything was falling into place. However, as nightmares and flashbacks of the war worsened, he began using drugs and alcohol to try to make them go away. Driving home from work one evening high on drugs, he ran a red light and hit another car, injuring three people. He was sent to prison for 10 years for DUI, drug possession, and assault with a dangerous weapon (his car).

According to Wolfe (2013), 1 in 10 prison inmates have served in the military. Many veterans are unable or unwilling to get treatment. They compound their problem by self-medicating with alcohol and drugs. In addition, many nonviolent offenders suffer from PTSD resulting from years spent with a violent family and in neighborhood "war zones," where they never knew when the "bombs" of gang violence were going to explode. Research suggests that 20% to 33% of prison inmates display symptoms of PTSD (Scott, 2010). Research has also linked PTSD with high rates of drug and alcohol abuse (Meisler, 1996). In our experience, many nonviolent inmates convicted of drug crimes exhibited symptoms characteristic of PTSD and were using drugs to self-medicate. They often sold drugs as well to pay for their drug habits. Prison will not help these people. Prison time will only increase the tax burden by making them permanent citizens of the Country Called Prison.

We acknowledge that Ted, Shamika, and Devon committed crimes. But do they need to be in prison? And if they do need to be in prison, what kind of prison should it be? If we, as a society, can help them change, all of us, the criminal and taxpayers, would be better off. Why? Society won't have to pay to send offenders to expensive prisons and offenders can get treatment and rehabilitation. To accomplish this, society must change the way it thinks about prisons and criminals.

One of the reasons social change agents have not addressed the problem of mass incarceration is that they do not realize (or acknowledge) the long-term consequences of the numbers they see in criminal justice reports. Although we have already provided some general numbers, we now want to focus on some rarely discussed statistics that highlight underlying issues, which, if not addressed, will continue to increase the population of the Country Called Prison.

According to the latest report on people in confinement in the United States, published by the Bureau of Justice Statistics, 2012 marked the third consecutive year that prisoner population declined (Carson & Golinelli, 2013). Although this decline demonstrates that the United States is heading in the right direction, it does not mean that the population of the Country Called Prison is disappearing.

Approximately 47% of new admissions to prisons were for nonviolent crimes, with 20% of those parole violations. Prisoners aged 44 and younger accounted for more than 80% of all new admissions, and it is likely that they will be released from prison in four to five years (Carson & Golinelli, 2013). With a felony record, few job skills, and no treatment, as many as 75% are predicted to return within five years (Durose, Cooper, & Snyder, 2014). Although overall prison populations might continue to decrease, this group of people will continue to grow the population of the Country Called Prison, as will a percentage of new admissions year after year if prison operations do not change. Additionally, 68% of all releases were conditional, meaning that this large group of people are still under the supervision of the Department of Corrections and, therefore, remain a tax burden.

As shown in Table 3.10, new female admissions for property and drug crimes have continued to exceed those for males by nearly 10%. The reasons for this difference are not necessarily clear from the data. It may be that female offenders use drugs more often to self-medicate since women show a higher incidence of mental illness. It may be that women are punished more harshly for such crimes based on some gender discrimination. It may be that law enforcement sees this issue differently, frequently incarcerating mothers who birth a child while intoxicated but ignoring the father. Since women are the main socialization agents for young children, treatment, rather than punishment, would be better for everyone.

At the end of 2012, Blacks continued to have the highest incarceration rate of all ethnicities, with 18- and 19-year-olds being jailed most often. Among this age group, Black males have a 9.5 times greater likelihood of going to prison than White males, and Black females are 3 times more likely to be incarcerated than their White counterparts (Carson & Golinelli, 2013). These figures sound the warning bell of possible generational effects, since children of those who have been in prison are more likely to end up there as well.

As the stories in this chapter demonstrate, many criminals are poorly educated, poorly socialized, often addicted, and frequently mentally ill. Many believe that fear of imprisonment prevents crime. However, for many criminals, prison is not that much different from life at home. Many think that if prison were more punitive, people would never want to return. For some, prison life is actually less harsh than their life in the homes and neighborhoods in which they grew up or the box under the bridge in which they lived before they were arrested.

One question we've considered for several years is, "What is the Department of Corrections correcting?" With an unchanged recidivism rate for 20 years, it is undeniable that the department is not correcting anything. So the next question needs to be, "Why not?"

When solutions are based on erroneous assumptions, problems not only don't get corrected but might get worse. Criminal behavior is not the main contributor to prison population growth; the problem is socialization. Inmates behave as they have been socialized to behave in *their* culture. Their behavior in prosocial cultures, however, is not appropriate. In England, driving on the left side of the road is appropriate, but it is not in America. Since the root of the problem for many is a debilitated childhood development process, we must address this issue in the solution if we hope to prevent future crimes. Extending punishment to people who are used to being punished does little. If we hope to transform the current culture of the Country Called Prison to a more prosocial one, we will need a plan that focuses on resocializing the offender.

Although children learn culture through conditioning, Albert Bandura's research in social learning suggests that adults learn new

Table 3.10. BUREAU OF JUSTICE STATISTICS PRISONER DATA

Total 2011 federal and state prison population: 1,599,000

Total 2011 state population: 1,341,797

2011 State-only Data	Percent	Total
Total prisoners with nonviolent crimes	47%	630,645
New court admissions	80%	504,516
Parole violation admissions	20%	126,129
Nonviolent new court admissions		
Male	86%	433,883
Female	14%	70,632
White	43%	216,941
Black	40%	201,806
Hispanic	17%	85,768
Property and drug crimes		
Male	25%	126,129
Female	35%	176,580
Nonviolent parole violation admissions		
Male	91%	114,777
Female	09%	11,351
White	39%	49,190
Black	43%	54,235
Hispanic	18%	22,703
Property and drug crimes		
Male	29%	36,578
Female	38%	47,929
Nonviolent sentences under 10 years (in prison less than 4 years on average)	88%	554,968
Total nonviolent conditional releases	68%	432,366
White	40%	172,946
Black	39%	168,622
Hispanic	21%	90.797

Source: Carson & Golinelli, 2013.

cultural behaviors through observation and instruction, retention of new information and skills, reproduction and reinforcement, and self-motivation to continue or internalization (Bandura, 1963). Increasing inmates' self-esteem is key, since self-esteem is foundational to healthy adult functioning.

Branden (1994), a leading expert on self-esteem, believed that adequate self-esteem is essential to our success in life because "it is a motivator. It inspires behavior" (p. 4). Another leading expert in self-esteem, Christopher Mruk (2006), suggests that self-efficacy—the belief that we can learn new things and accomplish tasks—goes hand in hand with self-esteem. In other words, the internal traits of healthy adult functioning are found in self-esteem and the outward signs are found in self-efficacy. By blending the research of Branden and Mruk, six measurable traits emerge that demonstrate healthy adult functioning. These "Alpha Behaviors of Self-Efficacy" are listed in Table 3.11 (Looman, 2012).

With measurable goals, we have outcomes that can drive the transformation process necessary to take down the incarceration mountain. Obviously the mountain was not built overnight, and simple changes will not remove it. Transformation will require long-term solutions that will significantly change society's social structures. However, some immediate, smaller changes will start us down the road.

In this chapter, as well as the next two, we propose some relatively simple, inexpensive changes that we hope will start a chain reaction in shifting the culture of the Country Called Prison to include qualities that create full inclusion, rather than marginalization, within the American culture. You can also find these proposals in an action plan in the book's appendix. Our proposals focus on nonviolent offenders, who make up the majority of inmates.

Table 3.11. ALPHA BEHAVIORS OF SELF-EFFICACY

Trait	Self-Efficacy Behavior
Awareness	Can identify own thoughts, emotions, and behaviors.
Acceptance	Can identify own strengths and flaws.
	Can engage in an affirming manner with others by accepting their attributes.
Accountability	Responsible for own emotions, actions, and achievements.
Assertive	Able to overcome obstacles to achieve goals.
Admirable	Able to transform dreams and thoughts into productive tasks and relationships.
Altruism	Adheres to universal values of goodness.
	Contributes to the wellness of society.

Source: Looman, 2012.

PROPOSAL 1: INCREASE EXECUTIVE FUNCTIONING SKILLS

As identified earlier, one of the most important outcomes of childhood development is executive functioning, which is a prerequisite for learning prosocial behavior. Therefore, improving executive functioning (planning, organization, time management, problem solving and emotional reasoning) is foundational in transforming prison culture. Peg Dawson and Richard Guare (2010) and Sharon Hansen (2013) have developed educational curricula that teach executive functioning skills. These materials could be used in prison training and diversion programs. They also could be used to develop training curriculum for criminal justice personnel, teaching them ways to interact with offenders on a daily basis that will help improve the offenders' executive functioning skills. Practicing these skills throughout the prison is vital to reinforcement and changing old habits.

Another practical way to help prisoners improve their executive functioning skills is through electronic gaming technology. Many nonviolent, noncombative computer games are currently available that teach executive functioning skills, unbeknownst to the gamer. By succeeding in the game, the gamer improves his or her skills in time management, strategizing (setting goals and steps to achieve goals), organizing resources, emotional management (which might prevent the gamer from throwing the computer across the room when he or she isn't winning), and prosocial problem solving. Computer games could be placed on tables and perhaps even played online with other inmates.

Some in the prison industry believe that allowing inmates computer access is dangerous. They fear inmates would use the Internet to hack into websites, buy contraband, circulate hard-core porn, and so on. However, with a little ingenuity, these types of games could be made available to nonviolent inmates without creating a security risk.

Prisons could create training rooms in lieu of weight rooms. Instead of muscling up (which also is a security risk), inmates could learn executive functioning skills. Games designed specifically for inmates could create new business opportunities for Silicon Valley. If a reward structure was tied to successful completion of game levels, prison residents might be motivated to play in their free time. These games could also be used in halfway houses and diversion programs to accomplish the same goals.

When people have adequate executive functioning skills, they are able to curb reckless and dangerous behaviors such as using illegal substances, obtaining contraband materials, or being disrespectful to staff. They are able to establish long-term goals and identify behaviors and activities that will help them achieve those goals. They can manage work assignments and life obligations (laundry, room cleanliness, hygiene, and so on) effectively and make adjustments without undue stress. They can make good use of leisure time and engage in self-fulfilling, growth-oriented activities. They can develop humane attitudes toward others and identify ways to be altruistic. In other words, if inmates improved their executive functioning skills, prisons would experience fewer security issues and lowered medical costs for injuries resulting from violence. For community diversion programs and probation/parole officers, there would be less need for supervision and monitoring and more time could be spent on assisting their clients in reassimilating to American culture.

PROPOSAL 2: INCREASE LITERACY AND GENERAL KNOWLEDGE AND FOSTER VALUES TO BUILD CHARACTER, IMPROVE PARENTING SKILLS, AND PARTICIPATE IN CIVIC RESPONSIBILITIES
Increase Literacy through Education

To change a culture one must consider changing the language, values, and norms of that culture. These generally cannot be easily changed because they have evolved over time. However, research has shown that education is one of the most powerful and easily implemented processes to shift a culture toward democracy and cooperative, prosocial behavior (Harrison, 2006). Although the importance of education has been recognized by leaders in the criminal justice system for many years, implementation has not been easy due to security issues and funding for educational staff, especially in prisons.

Here too we suggest the use of technology as a low-cost alternative. Today we have computer programs that can teach literacy and prepare students for GED tests, college entrance exams, and licensed certification exams. Other programs teach technical skills and assist in learning vocational trades. Through the Internet and television, one teacher can present to several classrooms in different locations at once and interact with students.

Imagine if every prison inmate obtained a GED, learned vocational skills, and/or even attended college prior to discharge. Again, security remains a concern. However, if China can restrict Internet access to its citizens, why can't prisons? Online education is more available than ever. Inmates with access to a computer lab could even use this technology to plan for their lives after release, such as finding employment and housing. With proper monitoring, we believe this plan is viable. In November 2007, the One Laptop Per Child (OLPC) nonprofit organization began shipping their first hand-crank laptops to children in third-world countries where little access to electricity is available, in an effort to educate and connect these cultures with the 21st century. Surely we can bring this same technology to nonviolent inmates safely and with little cost.

Foster Values to Build Character, Improve Parenting Skills, and Participate in Civic Responsibilities

Beyond increasing literacy and general knowledge, inmates need training and education in three specific areas: character, parenting, and civics. *Character education* is essential to the dignity and development of society (Lickona, 1992). Character includes respecting the norms of society, self-discipline, honor, loyalty, consideration of others, and a desire to be your best while accepting failure. Curricula and resources for initiating character education programs and discussion groups can be found at www.charactercounts.org.

Although *parenting education* has been around for many years, typical curricula focus on skills and behaviors. Because lifelong patterning is developed within the first seven years of life through parent-child interactions, mothers and fathers are the primary source to help children develop prosocial values and attitudes. Since many who live in the Country Called Prison did not experience effective parenting, they first must learn to self-parent. Every Child Protective Services office in the United States recommends a set of parenting classes to families. These programs teach proper discipline, boundaries, and rules for healthy families. These parenting classes could be taught to the incarcerated to help inmates better understand their own childhoods, while at the same time preparing them for life beyond prison. Self-help groups are often effective in this regard, and, with proper training, long-term prison residents could lead the groups for little or no cost.

Civic education involves imparting the knowledge, skills, attitudes, and experiences that allow someone to be an active participant in American life. The United States needs informed, active, and thoughtful citizens to remain democratic. Civic education encourages personal responsibility for community endeavors, growth, and safety. An excellent guideline for developing curriculum for civic education programs and discussion groups is *Making Civics Count: Citizenship Education for a New Generation* (Campbell, Levinson, & Hess, 2012).

Increase General Knowledge Through Book Clubs

Research by Kong and Fitch (2002) has shown that students who participate in book clubs and current events discussion groups benefit greatly. They better their scores on standardized tests, improve their speaking and listening skills, increase their prosocial behavior, expand their problem-solving skills, and build their general knowledge base. These clubs also promote a sense of community and fellowship, which opens minds to alternative perceptions and improves the ability to empathize with others.

One of the best resources for implementing a quality book club program is the Great Books Foundation (www.greatbooks.org), a nonprofit organization that was founded in 1947. The original purpose of the organization was to promote the reading and discussion of great literature by the general public. In 1962, it expanded its mission to include children with the introduction of Junior Great Books. Over the years, the foundation has helped hundreds of thousands of people throughout the United States start their own discussion groups in schools, libraries, and community centers. One of the reasons for the great success of book clubs developed with assistance from Great Books is the foundation's use of the *shared inquiry* discussion method.

Participants learn to read more keenly, ask introspective questions, listen open-mindedly, and respond to others effectively. Participants also practice leading discussions and reflect on the discussion process.

Implementing these clubs in prison would allow inmates to reflect on their lives and to think about the larger world. Of course, a reward system would need to be instituted to encourage inmates to join. In one prison in which John worked, inmates earned a gold card for good behavior. The gold card allowed them to go first in the dinner line and provided an earlier shopping time at the canteen. No-cost rewards could be put in place to help the incarcerated learn to make choices that benefit them.

Knowledge and understanding of the world is a good thing. So too is connecting to others in the community. For good or ill, prison is a community. Currently the only connections available to many in prison are gangs. While church services and Alcoholics Anonymous (AA) meetings are provided in many prisons, we believe that expanding prison inmates' social interactions would only help. Busy residents are easier to manage, and if inmates work on a degree or a GED or just learn to read, they may see a future for their lives. In short, all of these ideas could help prisoners develop executive functioning skills, which would be good for both prison safety as well as the American society to which inmates will return.

Of all the proposals outlined in this chapter, implementing book clubs in prisons is perhaps the easiest and least expensive. It also has the highest probability of success and will quickly lead to positive change. The first step would be to contact a local librarian, either at the local high school or community public library, and obtain his or her help. In addition, many community organizations—churches, civic groups, book clubs—want to help those in need. As this book was being written, a professional men's group that was interested in conducting a parenting program for male inmates in the prison contacted Mary. These organizations might want to volunteer to facilitate discussion groups, help purchase books, or train prison inmate facilitators.

The next step toward implementation would be to assign a champion, an employee who works at the prison who is excited about the idea and understands the value of such a program. The champion would focus on implementing the program. Then identify prison residents who could be the first facilitators; they will need to be trained in facilitator skills. The final step would be to identify a group with which to start, perhaps a small minimum security facility or a few units in a medium security prison that have mature offenders willing to start something new. Obviously, policies and procedures would need to be written so the program could be implemented in all prisons. Different rules for different types of facilities would likely need to be written, but everyone should be able to participate in some fashion.

PROPOSAL 3: MODIFY PRISON ENVIRONMENTS TO INTRINSICALLY HABILITATE DELAYED PSYCHOSOCIAL SKILLS

In most correctional systems, prison residents are just thrown together without much thought to their age and rehabilitation needs. This practice is one of the root causes of the predatory culture of prisons. A minority of the prison population is sociopathic. Yet the sociopaths often prey on the majority of nonviolent inmates who, with a little help, could be transformed into taxpayers. This situation must change if we are going to stop the growth of the Country Called Prison.

Separate Predators from Prey

First, we need to separate the predators from the prey. Zoos with natural habitats don't let lions roam loose in the same area as antelopes. Yet prison administrators irrationally do the same thing with offenders. Predators can be easily identified by using one or two psychological clinical assessments, such as the Hare Psychopathy Checklist–Revised (Hare, 2004), Minnesota Multiphasic Personality Inventory–2 (Butcher et al., 2001), Millon Clinical Multi-Axil Inventory–III (Millon et al., 2009), and the Personality Assessment Inventory (Morey, 2007). These assessments, which are specifically designed to determine psychopathy and predatory behavior, are inexpensive and easy to administer to groups and to score and analyze. In public health, identifying and isolating the virus is the first step in stopping an epidemic. These same practices could make prisons safer.

The assessments would also identify mental health symptoms and socialization issues for all inmates, not just the predators. In our experience, we find that many inmates have undiagnosed mental disorders and frequently have dual diagnosis issues related to mental health and addiction. Couple this with the trauma from childhood abuse, and one can see the reasons for the poor interpersonal relationship and problem-solving skills. Inmates with serious mental disorders (such as schizophrenia and bipolar), intellectual disability, and serious medical disorders could then be housed in specialty units that offered standard mental health and medical services. These inmates require expert services and specialized discharge planning.

Smaller Is Better

Criminology theories of social control propose that when a society's moral codes are internalized and individuals have a stake in their wider community, they will voluntarily limit their propensity to commit deviant acts. Recall our early discussion of social bonding theory developed by Travis Hirschi (1969). He suggests that strong internal controls, which are influenced by social bonds, prevent criminality. While individuals with prosocial characteristics developed these strong internal controls by bonding with prosocial adults in their families and schools, most offenders did not because they likely grew up in families where prosocial values were not practiced. To correct this, prison environments need to support the four key bonds that influence internal control. First is affiliation with those who follow the rules. Separating prisoners from prey would go a long way to supporting this bond. Second, commitment to or investment in conventional action is vital, and it will increase when prisoners obtain adequate educational and vocational programs. Third, involvement in prosocial activities improves our social bonds. Activities such as participating in book clubs, playing computer games, and learning new skills and facts would be supportive as well. Finally, belief in or agreement with society's value system would increase through participation in civic engagement and self-help groups.

All of these bonds would be easier to strengthen if prisons were smaller. It is easier to bond in smaller groups. Research on school size showed that schools with fewer students have more commitment and involvement and, therefore, fewer delinquency problems (Kennedy, 2014). The military divides up companies into smaller units or platoons because it realizes that soldiers fight best when they bond to a group. Smaller is better for general learning as well. How we learn and grow is often a reciprocal process, where we observe and learn from each other during day-to-day interactions. Research suggests that reciprocity takes place more frequently in small groups (Nowak & Sigmund, 1998). Smaller living units can be created by fencing off larger prison facilities into smaller sections or dividing large units into smaller units via wall partitions.

Use Discernment in Placement Considerations

Prison residents need to be assigned to housing units based on demographic factors. Age, for example, is an important characteristic to consider. Separating inmates by age aligns them with natural growth and development processes. A school system would never think of placing high school students in the same building as first-graders. Humans naturally associate with people who are going through the same life processes, since we learn and grow by sharing concerns and experiences. If prisons are to become places for correcting behavior, we should use the natural socialization process of age to assist.

Length of sentence is another consideration for housing placement. Inmates should be housed according to how long they're going to be in prison because the needs of inmates with different sentence lengths are very different. *Fast-track units* designated for inmates serving sentences that are fewer than five calendar years should be created. Optimally, these units would be divided by age and offense, as well as number of offenses. It is important that first-time, nonviolent offenders not be housed with repeat offenders.

Developmentally, all young adults are figuring out their self-identity and their own moral principles. They are discovering their purpose in life, choosing a career, and forming close relationships with friends with whom they will stay connected throughout their lives. These developmental challenges for young adults in prison could be better addressed if they were housed in units with inmates of a similar age characteristics.

Prison residents in their midyears (ages 30–50) have often been employed and have families and aging parents. Developmentally, they are realizing that life is not just about them, that others depend on them. For this group, guilt and shame for their addictions and criminal behaviors often trouble them deeply and actually make their poor decision making worse because of fatalism and depression.

If we have to mix age groups, we propose housing the over-50 group with the midyear group and not the young. An "older and wiser" inmate serving a life sentence might positively influence younger inmates, like housing a college senior on the freshmen dormitory floor. The older student likely has gained some understanding and wisdom, which can help the younger student. In short, a deliberate effort should be made to house people in groups that are most likely to help them restart their development process and learn healthy prosocial skills so they do not return to prison.

We envision that these units will have rehabilitative milieus focusing on the particular psychosocial needs of the age group. Prison residents could be given planners and workbooks, appropriate for the different age groups, to guide them in their recovery. In college, we often create *plans of study* for students so that they know their roadmap to graduation. In prison, inmates could create *life roadmaps* to be used during their time in confinement and after their release.

Again, reward systems need to be in place to help motivate prison residents to develop self-discipline and improve their executive functioning and interpersonal skills. Of course, all units will have case managers and security personnel; however, in most rehabilitative programs, the goal is to have each group govern itself, just as families and neighborhoods do in the United States.

There also needs to be special *reintegration units* for inmates who have been in prison for longer than five years and who are about to receive parole. Inmates who have been in prison for this amount of time tend to be institutionalized. Some long-term inmates develop PTSD due to the warlike conditions of some prisons and will need to be treated before they are released or they will likely self-medicate with drugs and alcohol after discharge. Since reintegration is a major and complex process for inmates leaving prison, we discuss it at length in a later chapter.

Prison residents who are likely to spend their lives (or most of their lives) in prison might do better if they are allowed to create pseudo-family units where they form lifelong friendships and a support system (again, separating the predators from the prey). Reformed "lifers" can serve as unit program and club facilitators or as teacher's aides after completing training courses. Such responsibilities could provide lifers with a valuable way to contribute to their community and allow them the human dignity of atonement. Program facilitators can lead various club meetings, AA sessions, and educational groups (such as life skills, GED preparation, parenting skills, or employment skills) and assist with online classroom programs.

For over a hundred years, social scientists have recognized and identified that human development is based on peer group processes and patterning that intertwine cognitive, emotional, psychosocial, sexual, and moral internal systems. To disrupt this natural process assures functional impairment. By grouping prison inmates in natural developmental peer groups, they can fill in the gaps left by their incomplete childhood development. As inmates resume normal developmental growth patterns, they will be better able to appropriately care for their own needs. If inmates are to leave the Country Called Prison, they will need to be independent, able to maintain healthy relationships with others, and possess the skills to manage their responses to challenges in appropriate ways. While they have been taught that they must accept responsibility for their actions, they must also learn to self-correct their behavior.

The citizens of the Country Called Prison are diverse. In many ways, they are a lot like all of us, merely trying to get through life. However, for most of them, their socialization has been sorely lacking, leading them to make choices that land them in prison. The question for the taxpayer is merely this: Since most inmates will eventually leave prison, what do we want them to be like when they get out?

Currently, we tend to release people from prison in the same or worse condition than when they came in. The educational, social, and even spiritual resources that were lacking in the community are not provided in the prison system either. Thus, the boundaries of the Country Called Prison extend far beyond the walls of a correctional facility to neighborhoods all across America.

SUMMARY

If we want to decrease the number of people in prison, we need to reintegrate them into the rest of society. To transform prisons so that they actually rehabilitate inmates does not require a lot of money or a lot of staff. Transformation requires a belief that it can be done and that the citizens of the Country Called Prison are worth assimilating into American society.

CHAPTER 4
Living in the Country Called Prison

The vilest deeds like poison weeds bloom well in prison air: It's only what is good in Man that wastes and withers there.

Oscar Wilde

When people live in the same place long enough, the day-to-day process of living together eventually becomes a way of life, a way of life that is distinct from other groups of people who have lived together long enough in another place. It is a way of life that continues on long after the first people living together in that space die or leave. *Culture* is the word that social scientists use to describe the symbolic system that represents a specific people's way of life.

To change a culture, one must first understand it. Anthropologists study cultures in several ways. Most people are familiar with archaeology, physical anthropology (the study of bones), and linguistics (the study of language). Fewer people are aware of *social-cultural anthropology*, a subfield of archeology that focuses on the social and psychological behavior of a group of people who live together. Two basic schools of thought exist as to how one should study this behavior. One group of researchers assumes that social institutions create the cultural domains of a society, while the other assumes that culture drives the development of social institutions (Delaney & Kaspin, 2011). In this chapter, we are going to discuss both perspectives.

When anthropologists conduct research, they immerse themselves into the culture they are studying by living with the group; this is called *fieldwork*. They take extensive notes on their experiences and observations (research clues) in order to understand the reason a particular group of people does what it does, what motivates it, and how its way of life constrains or develops the group. Their findings are usually published as an ethnography.

In the years we have worked in prisons and ancillary community social service agencies, we have asked why prisons are the way they are. We have looked to research by others to find answers to our questions. While the research has been valuable, it has mostly come from "outside" the culture. There have been very few anthropological studies of prison culture.

James Waldram, who has conducted such studies for over twenty years, notes that "few are willing to venture into the 'belly of the beast' for three basic reasons: (1) prison inmates are not embraceable research participants in a discipline strongly focused on the innocent, disempowered, and disenfranchised; (2) it is often assumed that inmates will be uncooperative and too difficult to work with; and (3) prisons are highly regulated environments that constrain more than they enable research" (2009, p. 4). It is for this reason that we include our experiences in this book. Although our stories have not been generated from the rigorous notes of fieldwork techniques, we have tried our best to make our anecdotes accurate.

Why is culture important to understand when it comes to the mass incarceration epidemic? It is important because culture is the way each of us think, feel, speak, and behave. We all believe that the way we see and experience the world is the same for everyone else. In actuality, however, our mind interprets our life as we experience it based on cultural patterning from our childhood. As we grow up, we learn behavior patterns, values, and beliefs that are considered normal within the family, community, and country in which we live. As we learn these patterns, the mind stores this information as concepts and schemes—the framework for understanding relationships between different information. By the time we are young adults, these patterns have developed into our own unique sense of reality—the way we each interpret and experience *normal*. This is why, when two people witness the same accident, they often tell the police officer a different story. This is also why we have difficulty communicating with each other at times and why we have conflicts over the simplest things, such as the way laundry should be done.

Recent research by Wakefield and Wildeman (2014) illustrates why we need to study and understand the culture of the Country Called Prison. Their work suggests that children who are raised in households where a parent, particularly a father, goes to prison suffer throughout their lives. The act of incarcerating a parent sets a child up for a host of problems, including long-term economic inequality, increased likelihood of incarceration, higher rates of mental health and behavioral problems, higher rates of infant mortality, and a host of other complicating factors. Their findings clearly support our thesis that prison does not only affect those who live in it, but also the future generations who are raised in it.

Within a culture, we learn our roles and how to play them. The experience of life within a culture is dependent on the role a person plays in it. In 1971, Philip Zimbardo, a professor at Stanford University, designed a two-week experiment to study the way systemic power differences in prison corrupt people (www.prisonexp.org). Zimbardo divided students into two groups: One group was prison guards and the other was prisoners. He guessed that these roles would affect outcomes, but no one could have predicted what actually occurred. He theorized that four factors would contribute to the corruption of the student-guards: 1) anonymity of place and person, which creates states of de-individuation, 2) dehumanization of victims, 3) permission to control others, and 4) an environment that sanctions malevolence through significant differences in control and power (Zimbardo, 2004). Although the student-participants were assessed to be healthy in every aspect prior to the experiment, within six days, student-guards began mistreating student-inmates. As student-inmates grew more and more resentful, Zimbardo feared that violence was about to erupt and terminated the experiment. Over the years, we have witnessed Zimbardo's corruption factors play out time and again in the Country Called Prison with similar results; only no one stops the real-life scenario. Table 4.1 summarizes Zimbardo's findings related to who is most likely to abuse his or her authority if given the opportunity.

Mary's career in criminal justice began about the same time as Zimbardo's experiment, and the study greatly influenced her perceptions and attitudes toward the behaviors and relationships of and between criminals and criminal justice professionals. To this day, she

Table 4.1. FACTORS THAT CONTRIBUTE TO
ABUSE OF POWER

1. Anonymity of place and person, which creates states of de-individuation
2. Dehumanization of victims
3. Permission to control others
4. An environment that sanctions malevolence through significant differences in control and power

Source: Zimbardo, 2004.

sees great differences in the roles of people who live or work in the Country Called Prison. The imbalance of power often leads some who work in the prison system to act in a callous and uncaring way. At the same time, residents abuse and rape one another to maintain their own power. In prison, power is key. Everyone wants it, but few have it.

Before we continue, however, we emphasize that, for the most part, the people we have met working in the criminal justice system are good and compassionate and want to help offenders turn their lives around. Most understand, at least on some level, that offenders have had difficult childhoods and are not inherently bad people. In other words, the criminal justice system is not an industry where budding despots come to work for the sole purpose of being mean to other people.

We believe that the abuse of power, the inhumane care of prisoners, and the callousness sometimes exhibited by employees stems from the overall objective of the system, which is to *contain* criminals, not correct their behavior. Therefore, we have observed that as soon as a person is charged with a crime and given a number-name that person becomes an object, no different than a piece of furniture that needs to be moved from here to there or stored in a warehouse. To work with this "number-name object" and ignore its humanity, criminal justice personnel must shut down, or at least turn down, their emotional reasoning. When humans detach from their emotional reasoning center, they become insensitive and potentially cruel.

Why haven't prison operations changed much since Zimbardo's enlightening research? Beyond isolating people we are afraid of, do prisons serve a psychological or sociological purpose? Philosopher Kenneth Burke (1954) coined the term *scapegoat mechanism*, which Rene Girard (1986) developed more broadly as a cultural phenomenon that occurs when a person is singled out to be expelled from society, or sacrificed, in order to psychologically reduce tension created by the human desire to have what someone else has. Although the initial conflict over an object likely started a long time ago, the antagonism between the two groups or individuals builds to the point that the desired object is forgotten and only the antagonism remains. Since growing antagonism ultimately threatens human survival, the antagonistic feelings are projected onto a designated scapegoat who can, then, be destroyed, thus restoring peace between the individuals or groups.

Although he was not speaking directly about criminals, Carl Jung, a Swiss psychiatrist, described the role scapegoats play in society when he stated, "There must be some people who behave in the wrong way; they act as scapegoats and objects of interest for the normal ones" (Jung & Campbell, 1976, p. 108). The killing of Native Americans in America's early history and the killing of Jewish people during World War II are examples of large-scale scapegoat events.

About the same time Girard and Jung were developing the scapegoat theory, American social scientist Lee Ross proposed a slightly different idea (1977). His Fundamental Attribution of Error Theory postulates that humans have a tendency to explain a person's behavior as a choice rather than as a result of situational context. For example, if I have no money and I steal medication to take care of my child, Ross's research suggests that people would judge me as "bad" because I was obviously a thief and ignore the extenuating circumstances of my poverty and my sick child.

In our experience, we believe that many people judge offenders the same way. Over the years, we have heard many people say, "Well, she's a criminal; she gets what she deserves"; "What did he expect; he should have thought about that before he stole the car"; or "All of 'em lie, don't believe a word they say." Yet, as we identified in previous chapters, statistics demonstrate year after year that the majority of people in prison are poor and undereducated and have poor problem-solving skills. Add to this that most are in prison for nonviolent offenses and the picture becomes cloudier. Most people from the Country Called Prison are not inherently *bad*; yet we treat them as if they are.

We wonder if society has made prisons, and the millions of nonviolent offenders that fill them, the scapegoat for society's frustrated desires. What is it that society believes it cannot have? What is society projecting on the millions of nonviolent offenders who have been expelled from the general public over the past thirty years? And did the use of this scapegoat reduce any tension?

Obviously, mass incarceration has not made our society any better. We contend that it is making things worse. So when solutions don't solve the problem, oftentimes it is because the wrong question was asked. Instead of asking, "What should we do with people we think are bad?," we might want to ask, "How can we help humans make cooperative choices rather than antagonistic ones?" or "How can we change the environment so that antagonistic choices don't have to be made?"

The concept of culture is complex and entails many dimensions and attributes. A major dimension of culture is the way a group of people view the concept of "self" (Storti & Bennhold-Samaan, 1997). In *individualistic cultures*, members identify primarily with themselves; independence and self-reliance are valued. Although members may join groups or clubs and attend family get togethers, they tend to distance themselves psychologically and emotionally from each other. In other words, a person's sense of identity and success is not tied to what others think but to his or her sense of accomplishment. The United States, Great Britain, Australia, and Canada are examples of individualistic cultures.

Within this typology two divisions identify the way individuals relate to one another. In *horizontal individualism*, each person views him- or herself as autonomous and relatively equal with others. In *vertical individualism*, each person views him- or herself as autonomous but unequal with each other; thus, competition is valued. This describes America's culture.

In a *collectivist culture*, one's sense of identity stems from one's membership and role in a group; the harmony of the group and the interdependence of group members are valued. Group members are relatively close emotionally and psychologically but distant toward members of other groups. Japan, Pakistan, and India are examples of collectivist cultures.

Within this typology are two divisions that specify the way group members interact with each other. *Horizontal collectivism* encourages collective decision making among equal individuals and is based on decentralization and egalitarianism. *Vertical collectivism* stresses hierarchical structures of power and conformity; it is based on centralization and hierarchy. Vertical collectivism generally describes the four major groups we have observed interacting with each other in jails and prisons: prison residents, security personnel, administrative staff, and licensed professionals (see Figure 4.1).

We believe each of these four major groups experience life in prison differently and have developed a subculture within the larger prison culture. Inside prison is the only place Mary has worked where the different employee groups do not seem to have a common purpose regarding prisoner care. For example, Mary worked at an inpatient treatment facility for teenagers where everyone focused on treatment objectives. At the facility, even the housekeepers, security officers, and kitchen personnel were trained to interact with each patient in a therapeutic and compassionate manner. This facility housed very difficult patients who were one step away from being sent to juvenile prison. Yet the treatment facility's success rate was high because everyone worked together to create an environment focused on a common goal. In this environment, where everyone holds the same values, belief system, and social expectations, the different role groups did not develop into subcultures. Prison is not like this.

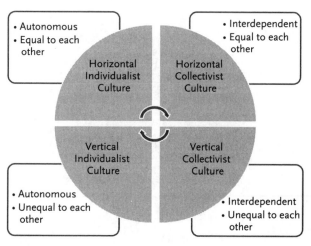

Figure 4.1: Individualist and Collectivist Culture Typology.
Source: Storti & Bennhold-Samaan, 1997.

Over time, role groups in prison develop into collectivist subcultures because the individual group goals are not linked to a common goal. In other words, each group within the prison focuses on its own goals, which frequently don't support inmates' behavior correction. Prison then sets up a culture similar to that found in the Middle East, where different subcultures exist together in a relatively small space but are often at odds with each other. Since each subculture has its own goals, peace is hard to achieve. So it is with prisons.

Figure 4.2 provides a visual image of the four groups—security, administration, licensed professionals, and prisoners—found within prison walls. Each has different goals to which their efforts are usually directed. For instance, the goal of the mental and physical health professionals who work in prisons is different from that of the "break-even, fill-the-beds" mentality of administration. Security always holds the trump card in a prison.

Later we will further discuss the characteristics of the different subcultures. First, we relate one of Mary's prison experiences that led her to the insight that the four subcultures within prison work against each other.

"Doc, it's Sgt. Lane on Unit 6. Jane's acting up again; I think she's probably going to start cutting herself again." "Can you send her up to my office?" "No, the yard's locked down and everyone has to stay put." "Is there an officer that can escort her?" "No, our roving officer

Figure 4.2: Goals of Four Main Role Groups in the Prison System.

had to make a medical run; someone got hurt in the kitchen." Mary knew better than to ask if she could come and get her. She had tried to escort an offender several months earlier and had received a scolding from the chief of security, who adamantly reviewed the security regulations with her. In another thirty days Jane would be out in the community without a police escort. Why couldn't security use some common sense? Resigned to the situation, Mary told the officer she'd be there soon.

Mary hung up the phone feeling frustrated. Jane had some very serious mental health problems and should never have been sent to prison in the first place. Mary had been expecting this acting out behavior, this cry for help, for the last few days. Now that Jane was going to be discharged soon, she didn't want to leave because no one in her family wanted her. Mary wasn't sure what good she could do visiting her in the corner of the dayroom surrounded by the other residents.

Mary first spoke to Jane's case manager to see how her discharge plan was coming along. The case manager explained, "Well, I've called a couple of shelters to see if they've got any beds open. To tell you the truth, though, I've had six discharges this week, and I really haven't had time to work on her plan. There's very little out there for anyone with her issues. I don't know what can be done. She's probably not going to make it anyway." Although Mary knew he was probably right, she was a little perturbed by his pessimism. She wondered if he was really trying to find her a good placement or just going through the motions.

As Mary walked into Jane's unit, about a third of the residents were in the dayroom. There weren't enough jobs for all the prisoners, so many residents spent the day trying to figure out ways to occupy their time without getting into trouble. Some of them were styling each other's hair, while others ironed or drew. They all smiled at Mary when she entered, obviously glad that help had arrived for Jane. They knew not to say anything though; the officer on duty was fussy about residents talking to staff without permission. This officer had once said, "Doc, you got to set better boundaries with them. They're going to take advantage of you. You gotta make sure they know their place."

Jane was sitting on a bench by a window off to one side of the dayroom. Two residents were doing their best to befriend her, although one of them had just about as many issues as Jane. The friends stood up to leave when Mary arrived, but Mary asked them to stay. Without divulging anything her friends didn't already know, Jane said she was distressed about her imminent discharge. However, she also made some statements that suggested that the real issue concerned a known gang member pressuring her to do things before her discharge. Mary validated her concerns and educated her friends on ways they could help her cope with the stress. After talking with her for about 30 minutes, Mary invited her to her office as soon as lock-down cleared so the two of them could talk more privately.

Mary feared that helping Jane would get her into more trouble, but she wanted to try. If you tell on someone in prison, you're setting yourself up for a savage beating if not death; but if you don't, your life can get pretty wretched. As a licensed professional, Mary was supposed to be caring and helpful, but as a Department of Corrections employee she is supposed to follow policy, which states that Jane should request separation from the gang member who is threatening her. Each day is a catch-22.

Mary then went to speak with the duty officer. Upon entering the control room, she surprised a couple of officers excitedly discussing the fight that had broken out in the kitchen that initiated the need for the medical run. A resident who owed money for drugs had been stabbed by the woman who sold her the drugs. The officers' language was coarse and filled with expletives. Mary told them of her plan and assured them that Jane was not suicidal. They complained, but only because they feared she'd create more problems for them if her mental health continued to deteriorate. Mary walked back to her office feeling tired and irritable, recognizing the absurdity of prison life. No one worked toward the same goals for Jane or anyone else. How could she ever hope to recover in such a setting?

As this story demonstrates, the subcultural group in prison that is viewed as essential is security and it therefore has the most intrinsic power. After all, there are dangerous people in prison, and it is security's job to keep them there. In addition to supervising prisoners and ensuring their safety, security is also responsible for keeping all staff safe as well. The security subculture tends to be based on a military-style system that includes a hierarchical structure of decision making. It tends to have exact rules of conduct and defined roles, ranks, and statuses.

Members tend to have a strong sense of tradition and adherence to values that often remains even if someone leaves the group. There is consistency across units and organizations (for instance, if you are a captain at one place, you know you will be a captain at another place). There is a clearly defined career path with expected promotions based on the passage of time as well as abilities. Bill's story illustrates the general beliefs and attitudes of this subculture.

Bill was convicted of possessing a relatively large amount of methamphetamine. It was his first time in prison. As he got off the transport bus and began walking toward the prison entrance, a security officer told him to get in line and walk straight. Bill had difficulty walking straight because of a limp. The officer, a kind-hearted family man outside of prison, pulled him from the line and berated him, screaming, "Hey Gimpy, walk where you are told!" Bill cowered in terror and tried to comply. Later this officer joked with the staff, saying, "It's good to find one and make him an example; it keeps the others in line." Everyone laughed and agreed. John knew this man well and knew he would never laugh or yell at a person limping at the mall or in his church. Yet in prison, he submitted to the dominant value of the security subculture, which is to maintain power over the residents. No one cared if Bill's feelings were hurt. That was not the point. After all, he was just an inmate.

Employees in the administrative subculture are responsible for the business end of criminal justice organizations. They are concerned with such activities as processing prisoners, filling beds, overseeing facility maintenance, providing for personnel supplies and needs, and managing the finances of the organization. This subculture tends to have a collaborative, matrix structure, with rules of conduct that are generally implied rather than specifically identified. The roles and statuses of members are more flexible and ambiguous, with both formal and informal decision-making practices. Considerable variation across units exists within this subculture, with leadership usually establishing the distinctiveness. Career paths are open and usually based on individual abilities and personal interest. The following story highlights the values of this subculture.

A prison at which Mary worked experienced an unusual flood of new residents. Over the course of three weeks, the prison received more residents than it would normally see in six months. Clothing ran short, food at the intake unit grew scarce, and hygiene products, such as toilet paper, disappeared. When security brought the situation to the administration's attention, the secretary in charge of ordering supplies stated in front of her manager, "What's the hurry? They're not going anywhere. If they're a bit dirty, it's no big deal. Eventually they'll get what they're supposed to get." The secretary was a grandmother who loved to tell stories about how she spoiled her grandchildren. Kindness in one arena, disdain in another.

Although the subculture of licensed professionals (mental and physical health care professionals and religious ministry) is similar to that of administration, there are some unique differences that are important to understand. Of all the subcultural groups, this group tends to be the most educated, and members are professionally licensed or certified, which can put them at odds with the criminal justice professionals because their allegiances are to an external professional code of ethics, not just the prison. This may be the reason that this group is sometimes seen by security or administration as "soft" on residents.

At a prison in which John worked, Dion, a 20-something resident incarcerated for drug offenses, received news that his mother, with whom he was close, was dying. He went through the proper channels in an effort to obtain permission to contact her, but because he had previously had some conduct issues his requests were denied. As a social worker, John knew that his code of ethics required him to advocate for the client. In this case, Dion was his client, not the prison. He began with security and worked his way up to the warden, asking, "Can Dion have a private phone call to speak with his terminally ill mother before she dies?" The reaction from the other two subcultures was telling. He was accused of "babying" the resident. The most fascinating part of this story was that most of the people who refused to allow a phone call were the same ones who gladly gave him permission to attend her funeral.

The fourth subculture is made up of the prison residents. Within the Country Called Prison, they are the largest subculture, but they have the least amount of inherent power. Of course this is with good reason; after all, they are convicted felons. Interestingly, residents outnumber security and staff in every prison. Yet most willingly submit to the authority of smaller subcultures. It certainly seems possible that at any given moment prison residents could easily overtake a prison, but prison riots are rare. Why?

As mentioned in an earlier chapter, Donald Clemmer (1940) believed that prisoners become institutionalized by the submissive position that they assume in prison to avoid harsh consequences. Several years later, Martin Seligman published his theory on learned helplessness (1975), which supports Clemmer's research. Learned helplessness occurs when someone endures adversity or a painful situation for a long time. Later, when the person has the chance to leave the situation, he or she doesn't leave, because he or she believes that he or she has no control. This can occur over time as residents must repeatedly play a submissive role.

Recent research by Terence Gorski (2014), a leading expert on the long-term effects of incarceration, suggests that the learned helplessness that occurs in prison should more aptly be called *institutionalized personality*. The institutionalized personality results from people living "in an oppressive environment that demands passive compliance to the demands of authority figures, passive acceptance of severely restricted acts of daily living, the repression of personal lifestyle preferences, the elimination of critical thinking and individual decision making, and internalized acceptance of severe restrictions on the honest self-expression of thoughts and feelings" (p. 1). Gorski's research demonstrates that prison residents can develop marked hopelessness, intense immobilizing fear, free-floating anger, and impulsive violence with minimal provocation, which can lead to a host of problems, particularly the use of addictive substances to self-medicate after discharge. Gorski believes, and we agree, that this learned helplessness from prison significantly increases the chance of failure after discharge.

We have personally seen this happen. Monique was given a three-year sentence for possession of methamphetamine. Upon admission, she was defiant and angry. It was her first round of incarceration, and she made it known to everyone. She frequently raised her voice with staff and complained about living conditions. Mary spent nearly twice the normal amount of time with her intake assessment in the hope that Monique would better understand the culture of prison. Mary introduced ways that would help Monique assimilate before she ended up in solitary confinement with a longer sentence. A year passed before Mary saw her again, walking alone across the prison yard, head bowed, eyes on the ground. Mary greeted her with a "Good morning," which Monique ignored. Mary asked what her plans were for her imminent discharge. She mumbled, "I don't know; I'll have to see where they send me." Her spirit was gone. She was an ideal inmate because she'd learned to be obedient and to depend on authority to make decisions for her. Most important, she was getting out on time because she hadn't caused any trouble. Unfortunately for society, she had not learned anything that would help her stay out of prison.

Although at first glance prison residents appear to be a homogenous group, with their similar nondescript attire, they are not. Residents make up the most complex subculture in prison, for there are several factions within it; prison gangs, in particular, are powerful groups that directly influence the overall milieu of jails and prisons. Although residents are adults, as we pointed out in an earlier chapter most are developmentally and psychosocially delayed in their early teen years. Additionally, while prison is home to residents, they are not in charge of their home; they are supervised much like teenagers are by their parents. Is it surprising that these "mental teens" would form gangs?

From our observations, prison residents have many of the cultural characteristics of an American middle school (CA-EDU, 1989). Residents display a wide range of individual intellectual development, as some are still in the concrete stages of adolescent reasoning while others have progressed into the abstract thinking of early adulthood. They tend to learn through active experiences and often argue merely to exhibit independency rather than knowledge.

Their behavior is inconsistent, at times conforming and cooperative, at other times anxious and needy or aggressive and devious. Typical of teenage behavior, residents tend to challenge authority, testing limits of acceptable behavior; yet at the same time they want frequent reassurance that they are accepted and cared about. They experience intense conflict regarding loyalty to their subculture in prison, while at the same time they want to get out of prison and stay out.

From our experience, much of the conflict in prison between staff and residents, as well as among residents themselves, stems from the fact that most residents are egocentric. They are easily offended and believe their personal problems, experiences, and feelings are unique. Residents are also idealistic and demand fairness from their own perspective. Conversely, they often lack the capacity to understand the unfairness they caused their families and victims through their wrongdoing, as the following story illustrates.

Jim was always a large kid and the anchor of his high school football defensive line. Throughout school he'd had issues related to fighting and learning. Although school never came easy for him, he was good enough to have a shot at playing college football. One night, after a big game, Jim, who had just turned 18, got drunk with some friends by the local river. He then tried to drive home. On the way, his car slammed into an elderly couple who were returning home after a movie, killing the wife. In a panic, Jim fled the scene but was quickly tracked down thanks to numerous eyewitness reports. The manslaughter charge stuck, and he was sent to prison. In John's intake interview with him, he asked Jim if he was sorry for his crime. He said, "Of course! I'm here, aren't I?" He did not mention the grandchildren who will never see their grandmother again nor the lost football scholarship or the shame brought to his family. The consequences of his actions were assessed only by how they affected him. So Jim was a good fit for prison. Everything was all about him.

We want to emphasize something that we believe directly affects how good people working in prison can be cruel. As we noted earlier, American culture is vertical individualist, where competition is valued; however, the three employee subculture groups—security, administration, and licensed professionals—are part of the vertical collectivist category. So employees of the criminal justice system pass between two very different cultural worlds every day.

Both American culture and prison culture have their own beliefs, expected behaviors, communication styles, and reward systems. They are fundamentally incongruous to each other, one individualist and the other collectivist. When people experience significant cultural differences for extended periods of time, they develop something known as "cultural stress" (Koteskey, 2014). They become anxious and disoriented as they lose all familiar cues, which leads to frustration, verbally (and sometimes physically) aggressive behavior, an irrational need for familiar and comforting things, and disproportionate anger at trivial restrictions and delays (Delaney & Kaspin, 2011).

It has been only recently that we have begun to understand this kind of behavior as cultural stress. In particular, we have noticed that employees get irritated if the security gate does not open quickly and they usually make a disparaging remark about the officer operating it. When Mary observes this behavior at work, she now humorously reminds the irritated person, "Just think. We get paid the same whether we are standing at the gate or not." The irritation seems to then subside.

This kind of humorous statement helps people relax because it reminds them that they are employees (a familiar cue) who can therefore go home at the end of the day (safety). We believe cultural stress accounts for many episodes of cruelty toward prisoners by otherwise healthy employees. We also wonder if cultural stress is the reason for the unexpected extreme violence that erupted during the Stanford study.

Stanley Milgram's (1965) famous obedience experiment also shows the powerful external control that prison environments have on good people. Recall that Milgram tested a subject's ability to reject the orders of a perceived superior. In the experiment, subjects are told that they are going to be a part of a study to test the effects of punishment on learning. The person being studied is called the *teacher*, and it is his or her job to give an electric shock to the *learner* when that person fails to answer the given question correctly. The teacher cannot see the learner, and the learner is not really getting shocked, but the teacher doesn't know this. With each error, the teacher was instructed to increase the voltage of the shock. Eventually the learners begin to cry in pain, and Milgram instructs the teacher to continue.

Milgram found that 65% of the teachers administered up to 450 volts, even when the learner stopped responding and the dial on the machine for this voltage read "danger." Some people quit the experiment before their session ended, but most continued to administer what they thought was a strong electric shock even after the learner had supposedly passed out. After observing thousands of participants, Milgram wrote, "With numbing regularity good people were seen to knuckle under the demands of authority and perform actions that were callous and severe. Men who are in everyday life responsible and decent were seduced by the trappings of authority, by the control of their perceptions, and by the uncritical acceptance of the experimenter's definition of the situation, into performing harsh acts" (p. 74).

The same seems true for prison employees. Frequently they seem callous and uncaring. But how can employees hope to correct a resident's behavior when many of their interactions are adversarial? Certainly strong boundaries are needed with the hardened criminals who occupy today's prisons. However, in the Country Called Prison, most are nonviolent drug offenders. Could the use of abrasive and demeaning authoritarian techniques be partly the reason for high recidivism rates? Why don't criminal justice professionals see this?

Groupthink is a term coined by social psychologist Irving Janis (1972). It is used to describe decisions that are made without objective reasoning. When in groupthink mode, people conform to what they believe is the consensus of their peers, which can lead them to make decisions they would not normally make. Groupthink frequently results in bad decisions that people later agree were a mistake.

The prison environment is prone to groupthink for the following reasons:

- **Cohesiveness:** Groups that are highly integrated are more likely to engage in groupthink. Prisons have subcultures, and workers see themselves as the status they occupy. Thus, security doesn't care if the toilet paper runs out, because that's administration's job. Add to this the hundreds of policies and procedures that specifically govern nearly every action needed to operate a prison, and these statuses and roles become thoroughly entrenched in the culture of a prison. This provides predictability in an environment where at any moment things can get out of hand and become dangerous.
- **Threats:** When groups encounter an external threat, solidarity increases because common enemies unify groups. In prison, all staff realize that they are outnumbered by the residents and their control of the institution hangs on a thin margin.
- **Strong leadership:** Since administrative and security personnel follow an almost military-like authority structure, directives from wardens and their assistants are rarely questioned.

Here is an example of the way groupthink plays out in prison. When a prison resident reported a rape, he was immediately placed in protective custody, which means he was locked down 23 hours a day in a private room. When the time came for the resident to testify to the investigator, policy required the resident to be handcuffed and escorted through the facility to the interview office. Now, we have a victim of a prison rape with the courage to report the crime being paraded through the prison facility in handcuffs. Imagine if we did this to a rape victim in a hospital emergency room setting.

When Mary asked if the interview could be conducted more privately, the shift captain said, "Sorry, Doc. It's policy. You'll have to talk to the warden." When Mary asked the warden, the warden seemed quite irritated that she asked and referred her to the state deputy director over prison operations. The director mindlessly told Mary that this was current policy. However, in a feeble attempt to be helpful, he said, "Well, the policy is up for review next year, and you should write a letter then and make your suggestions to the review committee." No one knew why rape investigations were handled this way and no one questioned it. Groupthink at its best!

The various subcultures of prison are all likely to be wrapped in groupthink. They each have different goals for their jobs, but they tend to have one thing in common: They carry out their roles without much thought. This is true for both the employees, who forget that their job includes inmate rehabilitation, and the offenders, who forget that they're supposed to learn from this punishment.

Now that we have a better idea of the factions and ideologies that make up prison culture, let's try to understand the life residents lead within the boundaries of prison. We could write a lengthy book if we told everything we knew about life behind the razor-wire fences. So we are only going to discuss the characteristics that we believe contribute to an unhealthy prison culture and that our proposals hope to change.

Daily life in prison is strange, to say the least. No babies are born, but people grow old and die. The people who live there just wait for the sentencing clock to run out so they can leave. While many count the minutes until they are released, feeling their life slipping away, others work at meaningless jobs in order to earn enough money to buy something special, like a chocolate bar, at the overpriced prison commissary. In prison, the natural human sex drive is often reduced to animal barbarianism, and materialism and status rest on a few pictures on a cell wall and a bag of goodies purchased at the commissary. Rules define what relationships can form, how they form, and for what purpose. Rules and security are the most important things, and human dignity is always the least.

For prison residents, cultural stress is even more problematic than it is for employees. While residents tend to be poorly socialized, they did grow up in a culture where autonomy and competition are valued, just like most employees in the criminal justice system. Offenders are incarcerated into a dual society where authority figures no longer view them as people but as objects with a number-name. Prison residents must also form allegiances with the collectivist subculture groups formed by residents with which they live while at the same time strive to be individualistic and autonomous in order to change and not return to prison. Since continuous stress is not healthy and can cause many physical and psychological problems, prison residents must let go of their familiar American cues and adapt to prison life.

Two processes can help people adapt to a different culture. One is assimilation, in which a person's language and culture comes to resemble those of the different culture. While the process is usually gradual, full assimilation occurs when the new member of the society is indistinguishable from current members of the culture. In prison, these residents are often referred to as "convicts" because they have become prisonized. Second is acculturation. Acculturation is the process by which the new person keeps some of his or her customs, which the other culture embraces. In prison, many of the orderlies and trustees starch and iron the clothes they wear to their jobs, which can be likened to people wearing suits rather than casual clothes to work. Rather than being a positive change agent, prison life often duplicates residents' lives in the community outside of prison. Many grew up without caring, loving parents. In prison, many staff would like to be more caring toward residents, but policy prohibits the behavior. Other staff treat residents as if they are a bother, just as their parents did when they were children. Rules and discipline in prison are as arbitrary as they were in their childhood, depending on the officer in charge at the moment, just like if mom or dad were drunk or sober.

Education was not often valued by parents of prison residents; prisons don't seem to value education either, since many residents leave prison without a GED even though they had time to earn one. Much like on the outside, many residents in prison do not have work assignments, and if they do the work assignments are usually meaningless. Many residents did not have jobs prior to their arrest, and those that did worked at jobs that just covered their basic human needs. Most did not have a career, and they likely will not receive training on the inside to begin one when they leave prison.

Another way life in prison is similar to the outside world is the living conditions. Prior to being incarcerated, many inmates did not have their own place to live and drifted from one friend's couch to another. In prison, some people are difficult to get along with, and officers move them from one cell to another. Friends come and go, as individual security levels change and residents are transferred to other prisons or other units. Just like on the outside, nothing is permanent and relationships are unpredictable. Relationships have very little continuity. How can you develop trust and respect for others when you aren't given enough time to bond? How can you develop social allegiance if the members of society continually shift and change?

The threat of danger is with all of us all the time. We never know if a car accident will take our lives or if someone will attack us. Most of us, however, are able to put these fears to rest when we get home, locking ourselves into the safety of our nest. But if you're a prison resident who has been placed in a cell with an inmate who wants to regularly dominate you, you have trouble. Tell staff, and you will be isolated, moved, and singled out as a snitch. Ignore it, and you're a punk, a sex toy for a domineering and violent inmate. Certainly not everyone is tormented in prison, but residents never know if their new cellmate might be that kind of a person. Few people in the outside community have this worry.

Of course, for many residents life might not be as absurd as we might think. After all, most come from fractured backgrounds, so perhaps their lives are not much different from when they lived outside. If they were homeless and poor, perhaps prison has improved their lives. At least once a week, an offender tells Mary that prison saved his life. Usually the resident notes that if he had remained in the community, he would have probably died from violence or drugs within the year. Nonetheless, even in these circumstances, prison culture makes little sense compared to the American way of life.

It is important to understand the dynamics that create a specific culture, especially if that culture needs to change. The main dynamics we will explore in this chapter are language, customs/etiquette, clothing, spatial relations, economics, and social relationships.

Just like other nations, the Country Called Prison has its own language and style of communication. Communication is not just words; it also includes body language, voice tone, eye contact, and the use of silence. All communication, sent and received, must pass through cultural filters. Therefore, one of the first things we learn as children is language. Language is important to the Country Called Prison as well.

A major dimension of communication is *context*—the amount of innate understanding a person can be expected to bring to a particular communication setting (Storti & Bennhold-Samaan, 1997). Language in the Country Called Prison varies a great deal depending on the subculture to which you belong. Security, administration, and licensed professional staff all use similar terms. For example, the number-name that is given to offenders and the process of stripping them of their birth name turns them into an object, a non-person. Since they are deemed objects, other words reinforce that perception.

An offender is *booked* at the police station when the district attorney decides the person will be charged with a crime and placed in jail. The judge asks the *defendant* to rise prior to the verdict being announced, instead of saying, "Mr. Smith, please rise." When a convicted felon is transferred from jail to prison, it is referred to as *pulling chain*, which originated as a term in the 1800s, when prisoners were chained together in a line and an officer pulled on the chain to lead them.

In prison, offenders are called *inmates*, implying that all criminals are the same, that they are all mates. Residents live in *cells* on *units* or *quads* with a *cellie*. When young adults go off to college, we say they live in student dorms. They are referred to as dorm residents, and they are assigned a room with a roommate. Offenders are often referred to by the crime they committed—thief, chomo, murderer, druggie—again, not their name.

Why are prisoners objectified? Recall that the Fundamental Attribution of Error Theory, developed by Lee Ross (1977), suggests that humans have a tendency to explain a person's behavior as a choice rather than as a result of situational context. Carmon has been housed in a medium security prison for two years and has earned the privilege to be transferred to a minimum security facility. The minimum security prison she will be sent to has cottage-like residences with two sets of bunk beds and a private bath area; everyone eats in a main cafeteria area. The prison has no fence, but residents can easily tell where the boundaries are because of the tree-line. No one leaves the prison because being caught trying to escape would land them back into medium security, along with an extended three-year, day-for-day sentence. Almost everyone at the minimum security prison is within two years of discharge. Carmon has to complete only nine more months of her sentence, and she will go home to her mother, who is caring for her 3-year old son.

Here's the power of objectification and the fundamental attribution error. Before Carmon can get on the bus to be transported to the minimum security prison where she will be free to walk off any time, she has to be strip-searched, then handcuffed to a belly chain with her ankles shackled. Although she has earned the right to be trusted at a prison without a fence, on the bus her ankle chains will be locked into the floor. From security's point of view, Carmon is an object that is being shipped. How does Carmon feel about herself as she is riding in the bus? Is there a difference between being shackled and unshackled? It seems that if she were unshackled she might see that she's being rewarded for her good behavior.

In prison, communication involves more than just words. Customs and etiquette are the observable signs of the cultural beliefs of a nation. These dynamics of culture dictate the way we greet people (handshake in the United States or a bow in Japan), appropriately eat a meal (belching at the end of a meal is expected in some countries), enter someone's house (in Japan, shoes are removed first), or respect someone's privacy (the tendency not to talk in an elevator full of strangers). The Country Called Prison has customs and etiquette as well. But in America, if someone does not follow a custom or display proper etiquette, that person will be looked at with disdain or merely laughed at. In prison, not following customs and etiquette rules can get you killed.

In talking to and observing residents, we have learned that *respect* is the number-one aspect of most of the customs in the Country Called Prison. Conflicts in prison usually involve the dayroom, which often has a television; the telephone area; and chow hall. These are common areas where behavior toward an inmate can show respect or disdain. There is a pecking order for inmates that determines who gets which seat, how closely you stand to someone while they're on the phone, and who gets to be first in line for meals. These are just some of the unwritten rules that substantiate residents as a collectivist culture. Remember that in nations in which people have limited space and know each other well, customs and etiquette develop to create psychological space and privacy for everyone.

Since prison residents spend a great deal of time in their units, it is important to learn quickly the proper way to act in the dayroom. Rules dictate the use of dayroom property, such as the television, microwave, coffeepot, and laundry equipment. Residents usually develop an unwritten schedule for use of dayroom property, which residents are expected to know. Telephones are usually tightly spaced on a wall in the dayroom. Residents expect each other to act as if they are in a telephone booth, being sure not to touch each other and to talk quietly so as not to disturb the person next to them.

Since food in prison is limited and the chow hall crowded, offenders are expected to stay in the space created by their chairs and to share any leftover food on their tray. However, the leftover food rule gets a little tricky, as sharing food with someone might be a lure to later use the recipient for something inappropriate, such as sex or a mule carrying drugs from one unit to another.

The most important etiquette rules to quickly grasp are those governing toilet use. Obviously, when the toilet is in the bedroom, which is shared with other people, residents must use the toilet in a way that reduces the smell. The rule is to flush quickly and often while using the toilet. Cellmates turn their backs when others use the toilet or step outside the cell if the door is unlocked. How might this daily prison etiquette affect you when you were released from prison? Generally these roles and rules don't translate very well to American culture.

Interestingly, cleanliness and good health are important in prison, no doubt because of cramped quarters. Obese people are perceived as weak and are preyed upon. Sickly people are also perceived as weak but also as a threat because of possible contagion. Residents are expected to practice good hygiene such as washing their hands after using the toilet and brushing their teeth. It is a sign of respect; it shows that a resident cares about his or her peers' health.

There are also very specific customs and etiquette rules regarding interactions between residents and employees. Residents must never whisper with staff or be seen talking with an employee alone or they might be suspected of snitching. Many prisons require residents to refrain from talking to employees unless employees first talk to them. Residents are mindful of their closeness to staff and maintain an adequate distance; this applies even to trustees and others who work in the offices with employees. When a security gate opens, all employees go first and then residents.

Culturally, clothing has meaning in terms of status, age, gender, occupation, and degree of formality (Delaney & Kaspin, 2011). Cultures identify the type of clothing one should wear to celebrations, to work, and for leisure activities. One would never consider wearing athletic wear to a formal wedding. Clothing for prison residents is as bland as their lives. They have no choice in what they wear, but of course that's part of the point. All "inmates" are the same. Choice of dress isn't really needed because not many activities require different styles of dress. Residents are also told how to wear their clothes as well, much like parents instruct their young children. As might be assumed, clothing for residents is designed to identify them as inmates; residents' shirts usually have "inmate" or "corrections" printed on the back.

Clothing provided by prisons is designed to be worn by many different sizes of people and is made with easy-to-launder material. Clothing usually consists of a T-shirt, a long-sleeved shirt with buttons, and an elastic-waist pull-on long pants. For men, the T-shirt and pants are not much different than T-shirts and sweat pants that they wore on the outside. For women, prison clothing is often demeaning because the clothing looks unfeminine. Many state systems just make one style of clothing, and do not differentiate between male and female styles. Thus women frequently wear unisex clothing, another subtle form of punishment. Is this because having one style of clothing is cheaper? Or is this a fundamental attribution error? Is genderless clothing provided because no one wants to acknowledge the increasing numbers of women in prison?

While space (geographic location, structures, landscapes, physical distance) is a universal concept, the meaning it holds is different for each culture. Mary worked in and visited many different prisons in several states. Prisons are like little towns and are often reminiscent of castles. They have razor-wire fences that serve as moats that separate those inside the castle from those on the outside. Once inside, it is difficult to get outside.

Most prisons have 2 rows of 20-foot high fencing with razor-wire in rolls along the top and bottom. Why are there two rows of fencing? Per foot, the fencing is very expensive. The probability of someone making it over the top of one razor-wire fence is very small. It could be a security precaution to prevent an outside person from throwing something over the fence and into the prison. Many of the prisons that we have been inside or have seen on state Department of Corrections websites look structurally like small college campuses from the outside. Yet once inside the buildings, the solid cement walls and clanging steel doors that echo throughout the building remind one of a cave. The echoing sound effects in units and hallways make it difficult to hear staff requests, so residents don't respond when they should. Staff also cannot hear inmates' responses. The diminished ability to hear each other often leads to conflicts between staff and residents. Prisons are loud places.

If the staff already think residents are "just a bunch of lazy criminals" and residents think staff are "mean and deliberately unfair," it's difficult to mediate disputes. For residents, this dynamic may be reminiscent of their childhood. They would come home from school, walk in the door, and get yelled at. They would ask for something to eat and get yelled at. Mom would tell them to do something, only she'd be drunk and not make much sense, so they would ask mom to repeat the instructions and get yelled at.

Most prisons are a contradiction in spatial elements. While the landscape is large, the space for residents is very small. While the entrance is often beautifully landscaped, the living conditions for residents are deplorable. Often employee work space is lacking as well. Although there is plenty of space for residents to do various things (for example, classrooms, craft shops, vocational training areas, leisure activity areas), residents sit in their units for long hours and are often confined to their tiny cells, with nothing to do except read or draw, usually in the name of security.

One of the annual training courses that Mary attends focuses on "games offenders play." Its goal is to educate staff about ways prison residents attempt to manipulate them. According to the training, residents are expert at getting staff to give them things they are not supposed to have. Year after year employees are reminded that "they don't have anything to do all day long but watch staff and think about ways to use staff weaknesses to their advantage." If prison leadership knows this to be true, then why haven't they done something to keep residents active in a productive manner? Groupthink?

Providing productive opportunities for residents would improve their lives and make the prison community safer and more egalitarian. If inmates learn and grow, then they will likely be successful in society when they are released. Recidivism would decrease and corrections departments would actually correct criminal behavior. And taxpayers might not be so angry about the billion-dollar corrections budget.

Prisons are supposedly designed to control the movement of prison residents. We use the word *supposedly* because, in our experience, the reason that we have stayed safe when we worked in prisons has nothing to do with security. We are safe because the prison residents choose to not hurt us. We have seen security gates left open, officers asleep in control rooms because they were working a double shift, too few officers managing too many offenders outside of their cells, and easily weaponizable items left accessible to prison residents. So if prison residents choose to "do no harm," then why all the security and its resulting costs?

Obviously, some prisons house violent offenders, and security is very important. At these prisons, though, residents are usually confined to their cells most of the day and only one to two residents are allowed out at any given time. But this is not the norm. Remember that we are talking about nonviolent offenders who are going to be in prison for only a few years. They just want to get back home. Shaming them with overzealous control mechanisms only makes them more prisonized, more helpless and angrier. If you treat adults like children, you are going to get childish behavior.

Mary was once on a unit with an officer who was controlling and mean. This officer had let about 20 residents out of their cells to get their lunch. The lunches lately had been of poor quality and small. So the men were already grouchy. One of the residents did not have a slice of bread on his tray, and so he politely asked the officer who had let him out of his cell for a slice. The officer snapped back, "Be quiet and go to your cell." Not a good call on the officer's part. The resident, of course, got angry and began arguing with the officer using profanity. The other residents became alarmed, with some backing away and others moving closer to fortify his stand, no doubt. Mary could tell that the situation was going to escalate quickly, so she intervened and was able to calm everyone. Although the officer and resident were still angry, they stopped yelling. Although most of the time residents will have their say and eventually back down and return to their cells, there are moments when an episode like this one could go the wrong way quickly. However, most nonviolent residents don't want to be tagged with a misconduct charge, which could result in more time being added to their sentences. The threat of a longer sentence keeps most nonviolent offenders in check.

All nations have their own economy and legitimate and illegitimate ways to obtain items to satisfy needs. So do prisons.

The money that prison residents have is referred to as "money on my books." If they have a job in prison, they receive a small "salary." Family and friends can also send money to be placed in residents' accounts. Residents are not supposed to flaunt their money by buying large amounts of commissary items or having lots of items in their cells to demonstrate wealth.

Residents can also earn money through *self-employment*. Some residents make greeting cards in exchange for something another resident can do for them. Some residents make money illegally the same way they did on the outside, selling drugs, sex, and cell phones. These kinds of trades are where most of the trouble between residents begins. If you owe a debt, you pay or you die; there are no bankruptcy laws in prison.

One of the most important dimensions of a culture is kinship. Social relationships are significant because humans need to be with others; we do not do well in isolation, as Abraham Maslow's research on human needs identified (Maslow, 1954). Relationships are important because they affect who we are and who we will become; they connect us to a family. Prison residents, for the most part, do not get to choose with whom they have a relationship in prison. They are assigned to a specific group of people day and night. They eat together, sleep together, play together, shower together, and get in trouble together (even if an individual in the group doesn't do anything wrong). Residents are forced to form familiar relationships with people they do not call a friend. Imagine going to a public restroom where there are no stalls. In prison, two people who may actually hate each other share a small room with bunk beds, a sink, and a toilet.

As in all cultures, hierarchies and politics are closely related in prison. All prison yards have their hierarchies, with one or two residents serving as the informal leaders—and they are usually gang leaders. Officers work with resident leaders to keep the prison manageable since residents outnumber security officers. Some inmates who are not gang leaders have a lot of influence in the prison, usually in terms of mediation and common sense. In some ways, all prisons have a dual leadership that mirrors a traditional family, with the father-figure (gang leader) as the protector and controller alongside the mother-figure (non-gang leader) who focuses on relationship and harmony.

Knowing the gangs, and the hierarchy within the gangs, is crucial to survival in prison. Gangs are often ethnically oriented, but residents can choose to stay out of gangs. Staying out of gangs is harder for younger residents, since gangs are eager to increase their numbers. Gang members threaten new residents by promising retribution if they don't join. Residents must be politically savvy to avoid a problem. Young residents often join out of fear, believing that ties to gangs will make prison easier for them. Later, if a person wants out of the gang, the resident sadly finds out that membership is not easily dropped.

Since friendships develop most often with people with whom we have frequent contact, healthy friendships do in fact form among prison residents and can be a source of comfort and nurturance. Unfortunately, security often sees any kind of close relationship as dangerous and will transfer a friend to another facility or unit "because they must be up to something." Residents and employees also spend a lot of time together, so friendships are bound to happen between these two groups as well. These kinds of relationships, of course, are prohibited by policy—thus, once again, criminalizing a natural and important human need.

As social scientists, we believe that human relationships are paramount to healthy living. After all, everything we have done, and will do, generally occurs within the framework of a relationship. In the world outside of prison, relationships might persist or they may come and go. Think of your best friend at work at your first job. Odds are that you were very close and now you have no idea where that person lives. In prison, relationships are no different. For some who can establish a relationship with a mentor, prison gives them an opportunity to develop their self-identity, complete their GED, learn a vocational trade, and develop the socialization skills needed to successfully emigrate from the Country Called Prison. Others connect to gangs and dominant residents who might make them even worse off, sealing their fate to live their entire life in the Country Called Prison.

In America, people form friendships based on race, ethnic heritage, age, gender, and religious beliefs. Prison residents also bond in the same way, although there are some differences. Some prison residents form relationships with each other based on interests or skills. However, other relationships are chosen for survival purposes. Men tend to be competitive and hierarchical and therefore where a man stands within the pecking order is important. Smaller men or men who are not accustomed to fighting might form relationships with larger men or men who know ways to fight. These relationships are often mutually beneficial. The protector might desire sexual favors or need help in learning a skill such as reading or writing. The protected can benefit from such a situation because of the protection he receives.

In American culture, women form friendships based on their family status. Women with children tend to make friends with other women with children, and so forth. In prison we've seen similar affiliations. In prison, women also tend to form more family-like relationships. An older woman might have "children" (younger offenders) that she looks after. A middle-aged female resident might care for an elderly resident, much like she would care for her mother outside of prison. Just like with male relationships, female relationships are seen by security as troublesome. Our experiences show that women in prison tend to place very high value on their relationships with others in the institution. This surrogate family is important to women and yet frequently discouraged by security. In prison, when a female breaks off a relationship with a friend, serious consequences can result. The first day Mary worked at a female prison, she had to counsel a resident whose ex-friend threw boiling syrup on her face because of the break-up; they had been friends for only three months.

Dating and marriage are universal concepts in all cultures, even in prison. Just because prisons house a single gender does not mean that sex doesn't take place. Sex in prison, much like in the outside world, takes place under three circumstances—consensual, prostitution, and rape. Some residents abstain from all forms of sexual activity while in prison. Some are not homosexual outside of prison but choose to be while incarcerated. When they are released, they return to a heterosexual lifestyle. Some homosexual residents choose a consensual partner, and some may actually form a monogamous partnership. Other residents willingly prostitute themselves as payment for protection, drugs, and other needs. And then there is rape, which is not about sex at all; it is about power and control.

Prison rape is perhaps the ultimate abuse of power and most symbolizes the corruptive nature of prison. In 2013, the Bureau of Justice Statistics collected data on the incidence of prison rape in the United States in all forms of secure confinements (Beck, Rantala, & Rexroat, 2013a, 2013b). When John addresses the issue of prison rape in class, students usually snicker. Some suggest that the "fun" of prison rape is just part of the cost of committing a crime. In short, our perception is that few people actually understand the data on prison rape and most don't care. However, the research is clear; there has been a steady increase in prison rapes over time. While not all reported rapes are substantiated, of those reported in 2011, only slightly more than half involved nonconsensual acts between residents. The rest involved staff-on-resident sexual violations. Resident-to-resident rape generally includes the use of force or threat of force. Most staff-resident rapes were reported as consensual; however, no state allows staff to have sexual relations with residents. Although sexual activity between staff and residents appears to be consensual, true consent can never be obtained due to the power differential. So these acts are classified as rape. The research indicated that female staff most often engaged in illegal sexual activity with prison residents, accounting for almost 60% of the crimes. Resident-on-resident sexual violence is most common in the victim's room, while staff victimization tends to occur in program service areas. For a complete look at this topic, one should consider Michael Singer's book, *Prison Rape: An American Institution* (2013).

Every weekend and on most holidays, families and friends visit residents in prison. Visiting a prisoner is not like visiting your son or daughter at college. Visitors must have passed a background check and can only bring with them an ID and some coins for the vending machine. Visitors must pass through a security checkpoint, much like at an airport. Visitation is public, with all the residents and visitors in one large room. Little to no touching is allowed, but that does not mean it doesn't happen. We have seen residents create disturbances to cover a conjugal visit of a friend right in the visiting room. Conversations are limited since everyone can hear everyone else. Some residents don't want their families to visit because the heartache after they leave is worse than not seeing them at all. Many just choose to keep in touch by phone.

Life in the Country Called Prison is different than life in America. We may have told you more about it than you really wanted to know. Many Americans believe that people in prison are locked away in dingy, dark cells or building roads on some chain gang. What most people don't realize is that prison is a place where criminals live out their lives in a town rather similar to any town in America. The biggest difference is that this prison town only teaches those who live there to become more disenfranchised from American society, to become more mentally ill, to become more angry, and to become more criminal.

So how can prisons change? Nowak and Highfield (2011), experts on evolution and game theory, have recently demonstrated that cooperation is as fundamental as DNA in terms of human progression. Their research indicates that altruism and cooperation are not just nice things we do but are essential to our struggle to survive. "Our ability to cooperate is one of the main reasons we have managed to survive in every ecosystem on Earth, from scorched, sunbaked deserts to frozen wastelands of Antarctica to the dark, crushing ocean depths" (p. xvi). In terms of genetic selection, far too many people are involved in the mass incarceration epidemic to ignore its effect on all of us.

Cooperation, as a survival mechanism, is not about being nice to one another. It is about competitors voluntarily helping an enemy. Every November we celebrate Thanksgiving, which reminds us that without the help of Native Americans we would not be the country we are today. Nowak points out that when individuals are forced into the same area, working together helps everyone do better. In his research he noticed that when you take out the concept of forgiveness you create a vendetta rather than the ability to move toward a better condition.

Nowak identified five mechanisms that lead toward evolutionary social change:

- Direct reciprocity: *I will if you will.*
- Indirect reciprocity: *I will help you because you are my sister's friend.*
- Spatial selection: *We live in the same unit. Let's work together.*
- Multilevel selection: *We all work for the same company. Let's help each other.*
- Kinship selection: *You're my cousin. Come live with me till you find your own place.*

In terms of helping offenders emigrate from the Country Called Prison, the most important part of Nowak's Cooperation Instinct Theory is that cooperation does not require an institution to direct altruistic behavior. Cooperation is an instinct, an innate part of who we are. Correctional departments merely need to let it flourish.

The computer-animated movie *Ice Age* (Wedge et al., 2002) provides the perfect metaphor for Nowak's theory, as well as the situation America finds herself in, with latent consequences of mass incarceration piling up. The story takes place during the end of the Ice Age, when animals had to migrate to survive. The story's main characters are three prehistoric animals—a sloth, a mammoth, and a saber-tooth tiger—who are natural enemies. At first the annoying and pathetic sloth joins with the depressed and irritable mammoth. The mammoth is sad because human hunters killed his wife and child. Upon the sloth's insistence, they rescue an infant human boy from a riverbank as the mother drowns. Soon the devious tiger joins the team; he's been ordered by his herd to lead the heroes into a trap so the baby can be killed and eaten.

Along the way, the three animals must cooperate with each other in order to survive. A friendship begins to emerge, and each of their personalities becomes more affable and gracious. The pathetic sloth assumes responsibility and develops courage. The mammoth overcomes his grief and self-centeredness in order to save the child, who may grow up to hunt mammoths. The tiger learns to think for himself, rather than taking orders from his leader; he becomes willing to give up his life to save his new herd. In the end, the baby is returned to the humans, and the three natural enemies create their own herd based on friendship and altruism.

Just as the great glaciers of Earth's Ice Age melted so that land could be formed and humans could eventually populate the Earth, the mass incarceration mountain has to melt away. We have to migrate away from a belief system that causes us to see enemies where there are none. We need to create prison environments that encourage cooperation and altruistic behavior, that help people self-actualize, to become what they are innately capable of. A human is a terrible thing to waste.

We recognize that prison culture has evolved over many years and will be difficult to change. However, if we want people to leave prison and never return, then we must try. Changing a culture requires not only new rules and regulations but new psychological and social acuities, which are hardest to acquire. Therefore, the proposals that follow are intended to only get the ball rolling. Our hope is that as small changes take place and life within prison becomes more psychologically healthy for everyone, people will be motivated to try more healthy ideas until we have a society that more closely resembles the egalitarian America we all want to live in. Once again, our proposals are focused on the nonviolent offender population. You can also find these listed in the action plan found in the appendix.

PROPOSAL 1: MODIFY PRISON ENVIRONMENTS TO PROMOTE COOPERATIVE BEHAVIOR AND PROSOCIAL AMERICAN VALUES

Promote Prosocial Behaviors, Cooperation, and Compassion

Procedures should be put in place whereby residents and staff are rewarded for being charitable to each other. In the outside world, people are often rewarded for compassion. In prison, compassion happens rarely; when it does it should be encouraged.

Perhaps some simple reward structure could be instituted so that when a resident does something nice for someone else, a note is placed in his or her file, which will be reviewed when that inmate comes up for parole. So too with staff. Currently, a staff member who loans a book to a resident or goes out of her way to assist a felon in contacting his or her children is often deemed to have "bad boundaries." While it is certainly true that residents try to "con" staff for favors, this is not universally true. Prisons should reward prison workers for going above and beyond their jobs. Much in the same way schools vote on "teacher of the year," perhaps prisons could have "staff of the month" awards based on who showed the most compassion. Policies and procedures, as well as reward systems, should be created to encourage both prison residents and employees to follow the five mechanisms of cooperation: direct reciprocity, indirect reciprocity, spatial selection, multilevel selection, and kinship selection.

Promote Personal Pride and Self-Respect in Prison Residents

In sociology, the symbolic interactionist paradigm suggests that how we talk about things creates the social world. We believe such a paradigm should be applied to prisons. It would cost almost nothing and could create great change in prison atmosphere.

We should remove objectifying language from policy and procedure by using words to describe tasks that are affirming of human dignity. Instead of "shipping" a resident to a new prison, we should talk about "transferring" people. Prisons could easily improve civility by insisting that all people use niceties (please, thank you, excuse me) and greetings that are respectful (such as Mr. Smith, Ms. Jones, rather than someone's last name only).

Only changing prison language will not change everything, any more than eliminating racial slurs has eliminated racism. However, no one questions that reducing racial slurs has been a good thing for race relations in the United States. If we were to eliminate terms that do not translate to life outside prison walls perhaps life would improve within them

Imagine if instead of "inmates," we had "residents." What if the "cell" was called a "room"? What might occur if we used the same terminology we use in the public arena to describe prison functions. Instead of going to "chow," prisoners would go to "dinner." If residents could purchase a candy bar from the "store" instead of the "canteen," the prison experience could be more normalized, thereby helping prepare residents for life outside the walls and reducing the effects of institutionalization.

Reduce Learned Helplessness and Institutionalization

We should promote opportunities for residents to make choices that reduce learned helplessness and increase their sense of competence. Research by McRaney (2013) shows that when people in prison were given responsibilities and choices, such as choosing their roommate or the movie to watch for group movie night, they were more cooperative, less argumentative, and less demanding. Making good choices is central to maturity and the development of proper executive functioning. While security must remain a primary concern, residents can make many choices, such as electing a resident leadership group to help make decisions on matters like meal menus, store hours, and even paint colors for common areas.

The point is that the more power people have over their own lives the more cooperative they become. Prison exists to protect the public and to eliminate harmful behaviors from society. If we hope for that to happen we need to teach proper social skills that will translate to the community.

Establish Multidisciplinary Unit Teams

Multidisciplinary health care teams have been in existence for over twenty years, and research has shown that they are highly effective (Fay, Borrill, Amird, et al., 2006) with complex cases. When unit teams consist of members from security, case management, and social work (health care and discharge planning), they are able to focus on individual cases. Much like individual departments in corporations, multidisciplinary unit teams should have the power to establish unit rules and procedures that provide structure and social development based on the unique needs of the unit as well as complement the larger organization. The team should teach and model civic responsibility through unit meetings and democratic processes with residents.

Increase Employees' Knowledge and Understanding of Social Science Principles

We need to encourage all employees to obtain at least an associate's degree in one of the social sciences (psychology, sociology, social work, and criminal justice) and encourage management personnel to have a bachelor's degree and senior management to have a master's degree. By expanding employee training programs to include information on childhood development, social psychology, mental illness, addictions, diplomacy, mentoring and coaching skills, and egalitarian principles we could radically change prisons. Research in progressive cultural change shows that education is crucial to successful transformation, along with structural changes in the environment and clearly identified behavioral outcomes (Harrison, 2006). Training curricula should cover a broad range of social science topics as well as pragmatic how-to skills for learning new behaviors. If processes were implemented within the context of a multidisciplinary team, prison could be transformed into an environment where all subcultures in prison—administration, security, professional staff, and prisoners—work together. If we reward staff and residents both intrinsically and extrinsically for practicing these new skills, life within prison walls could change. We transform the coercive culture that currently exists within prison toward one that is more cooperative and altruistic.

SUMMARY

When Mary was a child, she often visited her grandparents' farm in western Kansas. Their home did not have a bathroom; it had an outhouse about 50 feet from the house. Even though her father volunteered repeatedly to pay for and build a bathroom in their house, they did not see a need for it. They did not see how it would improve their lives.

We think people cannot envision a prison ever being a place where people will be nice to each other voluntarily. Yet, kindness and cooperation is the foundation of our culture, as evidenced by our celebration of Thanksgiving. We have seen the same kind of kindness and cooperation that we celebrate occur every day in prison.

Although these acts of kindness and cooperation only last a few minutes, random acts of kindness do happen, which means they can happen again. Once or twice a week, a resident will tell Mary that his cellmate is having a rough time and asks if she can help. An elderly resident was having trouble walking, and another resident broke the rules to assist him. The weather outside was extremely hot one day, making the cells feel like ovens. An officer went against policy and unlocked all the tray holes in the cell doors so air could circulate. My coworker's office wall is filled with beautiful pictures drawn by residents as thanks for her help with their problems. A gentler, kinder prison environment will allow both employees and residents a greater opportunity to grow and is fiscally prudent as well.

CHAPTER 5

Visiting America from the Country Called Prison

Compassion, in which all ethics must take root, can only attain its full breadth and depth if it embraces all living creatures.

Albert Schweitzer

In 2010, 700,000 people were released from U.S. prisons. From this group, about 59% will return within three years (Guerino, 2011). For the past 30 years, the recidivism rate for corrections has changed little (Cooper, Durose, & Snyder, 2014). However, the number of people that rate accounts for has grown. Roughly 30 years ago, that statistic meant approximately 130,000 people a year, while today the number is about 413,000. That is a lot of people burdening the economy. Imagine what might happen to the national debt if these people paid taxes instead of using them.

Why do so many return to prison? After living in the dreadful conditions of prison, why would anyone ever do anything to risk going back? Some simply say "prison must be too easy." But with all the violence and isolation in prison, we can't imagine that prison could be any harder.

As we've shown, for some prison conditions are quite similar to the environment in which they were raised. For others, return to prison might occur because they've become prisonized, a tragic end to a wasted life. For others it may not be a clear decision, but the result of years of flawed thinking. One thing is certain: For most people adequate support is unavailable to them to help them change, so when they leave prison they often repeat the same mistakes.

What do we not understand? All over the world, people successfully transition from one country to another, from one culture to another. How does this happen? Can we duplicate this successful immigration with prison residents returning to their communities? What can we do differently that will make their homecoming permanent and beneficial?

Over the years, Mary helped three people during their first year out of prison to reassimilate to American culture. Her experiences with these three were part of the reason we wrote this book. The main focus of this chapter is Avalon's story, which is a good representation of Mary's experience with the people she helped. We have also met many former prisoners who shared their experiences with us and have read books by former prisoners that relate their experiences, such as *Beyond Bars: Rejoining Society After Prison* (Ross & Richards, 2009). While the anecdote about Avalon is a compilation of several experiences, it is an accurate portrayal of the challenges and difficulties newly discharged prisoners face.

Mary met Avalon while working as a psychologist at a women's prison. Avalon related that she was going to leave prison in a couple of years and wanted to "get better and not come back." She met with Mary for psychotherapy twice a week for several months until Mary left the facility for another job. Mary learned through these sessions that Avalon's childhood was filled with psychological trauma from severe abuse and neglect at home that was offset by nurturance from caring teachers and a female neighbor she thought of as her aunt. Avalon had gotten pregnant at age 15, left school, and began living with her boyfriend. By their mid-20s, they both had been convicted of drug crimes and child neglect and Avalon had also been convicted of prostitution. A year after their arrest, they lost their parental rights, and their two children were placed in an adoptive home. Avalon and her boyfriend both ended up in prison.

In 1996, the late Stanley Greenspan, then clinical professor of psychiatry and pediatrics at George Washington University Medical School and chair of the Interdisciplinary Council on Developmental and Learning Disorders, invited leading researchers and clinicians on

Table 5.1. UNIVERSAL NEEDS OF CHILDREN

- Safe and secure environment
- At least one stable, nurturing, and protective adult
- Consistent, nurturing relationship with same caregivers
- Rich, ongoing interactions with caregivers
- Child allowed to progress in own style and timeline
- Opportunities to experiment, take risks, and find solutions
- Structure and clear boundaries
- Stable neighborhood and community

Source: Greenspan, 1997.

childhood development to form a study group to determine the universal needs of children. Although he thought the group would need several weeks to create the list, they finished within a few days. The list can be found in Table 5.1.

Without stability and nurturing guardianship, children develop learned helplessness and exhibit many of the symptoms of Terrence Gorski's institutionalized personality (2014): passive acceptance of deprivation, impaired critical thinking and emotional reasoning abilities, and a deep-seated rage that is often drowned out by drugs and alcohol use. By the time Avalon became a teenage mother and a drug addict, she had already been socialized as a member of the Country Called Prison. In many ways, she was destined to become a felon as children who grow up with abuse and neglect are significantly more likely to develop addictions and commit nonviolent crimes (Dube, Felitti, Dong, et al., 2003; Wakefield & Wildeman, 2014).

About two years after Mary had left the prison where Avalon was housed, her case manager asked Mary if she was still interested in helping her. Their journey together began about a month later.

On the day Mary met Avalon on the "prison border," she was wearing the clothes Mary had mailed her two weeks earlier and was carrying a small bag containing two weeks' worth of medication she took for a psychological disorder, a form confirming that she had been released from the facility, and a piece of paper on which was written her parole officer's name and address. As the metal gate clanged behind her, Avalon said with a slight smile and a bit of a quivery voice, "Hi. I didn't know if you were really going to come."

Mary's maternal instincts kicked in, but she resisted the desire to hug her. Instead, with the most nonchalant voice she could muster, she said, "Of course I came. I said I would." Avalon stared at Mary, her eyes betraying no hint of her emotions. They walked to Mary's car without a word. Avalon got in, and they drove toward America.

Mary assumed Avalon would need time to adjust to her knew freedom, so she waited for her to initiate a conversation. When she did, she asked about Mary's job and other trivial things. Mary responded with brief answers, but let her know that she didn't have to talk. Mary told her, "I know you must be having all kinds of emotions and thoughts running through your head. Take care of yourself. If you want to talk, we can, or if you want to be quiet that is good too." Avalon responded, her voice uncertain, "I don't know what to do. I don't even know what to think. It's been so long since I've even let myself have feelings that I don't know what I am feeling. In the facility, kindness is used for no good and to hurt people. Even though I know your kindness is a good thing, I don't know what to do or what to say to you." Mary said, "Avalon, I cannot imagine what you are going through right now. . . . Whatever you need to help yourself adjust to your new surroundings, just tell me."

As they rode on in silence, the music from the car radio offering some relief from their uncomfortable feelings, Mary thought about Avalon's comment about kindness and her disbelief that she would really honor her commitment to her. Even though Mary had heard the statement "kindness is weakness" many times in prisons, she thought of it colloquially, much like Americans saying "How's your day going?" yet not expecting an honest response.

As Mary reflected on the hundreds of residents of the Country Called Prison she had met over the years, she had an aha moment. Their stories followed similar themes—abuse, neglect (either physical or emotional), and poverty. She realized these themes were the observable patterns, not the foundational issue. The real issue was that children who grow up the way Avalon did were not usually socialized for human attachment.

Attachment is the emotional bond that forms between an infant and a primary caregiver. Attachment is crucial to the social and emotional development of the infant, and it needs to form within the first eight months of life. Table 5.2 identifies four types of

Table 5.2. HUMAN ATTACHMENT: PARENTAL INVOLVEMENT AND OUTCOME

Secure	Predicable caregiving Child secure
Ambivalent	Unpredictable caregiving Child passive and very independent
Avoidant	Abusive caregiving Child insecure and anxious
Disorganized	Inconsistent caregiving Child very impaired

Sources: Ainsworth & Bell, 1970; Bowlby, 1960.

parenting styles and the resultant outcome regarding child development (Ainsworth & Bell, 1970; Bowlby, 1960). During this time, the child must master two-way, intentional communication, which can only be achieved by routine interactions with a nurturing caregiver. Without this skill, further cognitive, psychological, emotional, and social patterns develop in an idiosyncratic, piecemeal, and disorganized manner (Greenspan, 1997). Attachment creates the trusses that allow the brain to interconnect cognitive and emotional reasoning centers so the mind can operate with intentionality and purpose, grasping ever more complex concepts, meaning, and empathy that make relationships possible. Poor attachment in children is highly correlated with having a caregiver who consistently avoids the infant's needs or who is coldly rejecting, indifferent, inconsistent, or abusive.

Poor attachment results in long-term problems with emotional control, interpersonal relationships, learning, organizational and planning skills, self-identity and self-esteem, task completion, and perseverance. For many offenders like Avalon, the early years are filled with violence and deprivation, which means that they are not able to organize their experiences and information into a logical order from which they can develop solutions and consider consequences. Their emotions are not able to corroborate their experiences so that their needs can be satisfied through relationships with others. Therefore, they are often overwhelmed by situations, and their reactions to events can be irrational and, at times, counterproductive.

Mary and Avalon had driven about 30 minutes when they arrived in a town. Mary asked her, "Avalon, did the facility give you a cashier's check before you left?" When Avalon replied that it had, Mary asked her if she wanted to cash it at a bank. When they arrived at the bank, Mary, as a matter of habit, started going through the checklist of items needed for banking. Suddenly she realized that Avalon did not have a driver's license. When, upon questioning, Avalon said she did not have a state ID card either, her face shifted to an "oh-no" look as she realized she had no way to prove her identity. She would not be able to cash her check.

Even though for the last four years Avalon had to carry her prison ID card with her at all times, she left prison without an ID card of any kind. The moment the gate closed behind her, she became a "legal alien"— an American without any legal status. In disbelief, Mary wondered if this was some kind of cruel joke that correctional employees played on the inmate. Was this the last "gotcha," the last little reminder that felons, even those who have completed their punishment, are not wanted in America? Surely this was just an oversight. Many Americans do not realize that a state ID card or a driver's license signifies American citizenship. Although an oversight by correctional personnel, for Avalon it was a huge stumbling block toward successful reassimilation into American culture. Not only was she not going to be able to cash her check, but she also would not be able to get a job, rent an apartment, or go to a doctor's appointment.

As soon as the shock of this oversight passed, Mary came up with a plan. Avalon would sign the check over to Mary, who could deposit it, then withdraw the cash and give it to Avalon. Mary could tell Avalon had been crying when she returned from the bank. Mary laid the cash on her lap and confidently said, "Well, we solved that problem. No doubt we will have more ahead of us. I'm frustrated, but I'm not going to give up and you aren't either." Looking out the window, Avalon tearfully mumbled, "Thanks." It was at this point that Mary realized that helping Avalon would require a lot of patience.

When they arrived at Avalon's father's house about two hours later, the welcome that was not given said everything. Her father did not come outside. When the two women walked in the door, he grumbled,

"Hello." No hug, no smile, no thanks for bringing his daughter home. One didn't need to be a forensic expert to understand the body language of father and daughter—neither of them wanted to be with each other. "You can have your old room," her father again grumbled.

Mary and Avalon then carried the bags of clothing and personal hygiene products that Mary had bought her back to her room. Even after spending nearly $400, Mary realized that the summer clothes she'd purchased would only be suitable for another couple of months, as winter was coming. There was no way Avalon would have her own income by then. Since the signs of poverty were everywhere in the house, it was clear that her father would not be able to provide much for her. Mary made a mental note to locate a church in town that offered clothes for indigent people.

Mary had wanted Avalon to return home to a deserved celebration. In an attempt to salvage the moment, Mary suggested that Avalon might enjoy going through her new clothes. Although her heart wasn't in it, she obliged by pulling the outfits from the bags and making favorable comments about them before hanging them in her closet. Although she seemed happy with her new clothes, her body language portrayed only rejection, shame, and unworthiness. How could Avalon's father have been so insensitive and impassive? Mary grew up in prosocial, middle-class America. Maybe there was something about Avalon's culture that was being missed.

Most people view family as necessary for obtaining food, clothing, shelter, and, most important, nurturance. According to Collier (1982), "Nurturance is a certain kind of relationship that entails affection and love, that is based on cooperation as opposed to competition, that is enduring rather than temporary, that is non-contingent rather than contingent upon performance, and that is governed by feeling and morality instead of law and contract" (p. 77). However, this idealized concept of family prevented Mary from understanding Avalon's choice to live with her father, someone who had beat her as a child and terrified her with his drunken rages. To Avalon, however, this was normal. This was her family.

As we grow and experience life, we form attitudes—positive or negative viewpoints about ideas, relationships, people, objects, or situations. Attitudes develop as a result of our experiences, either through direct behaviors or through observation. Social roles and norms, especially in childhood, have a strong effect on attitude development. Attitudes involve our thoughts about something and emotions, the way something makes us feel. We can be consciously (explicit) or unconsciously (implicit) aware of our attitudes. Nonetheless, our attitudes influence our beliefs and behaviors.

Not only do we form attitudes about other people, situations, places, and so on, we form them about ourselves. Our attitudes about ourselves are referred to as "ego-identity." Although grounded in childhood development processes, ego-identity is constantly in flux and influenced by one's experiences all through life, especially the way people react to your decisions and behaviors.

The attitudes that children growing up in abusive and neglectful homes form are the ingredients for intergenerational criminality and learned helplessness. These children believe that they cannot have what others have. They believe that they are incapable of doing things "right." They believe that they are worthless and a burden. Drugs, alcohol, and sex temporarily numb their despair and sense of hopelessness.

From Avalon's point of view, she had basically three choices of where to live when she left prison—with her father, with her mother, or at a homeless shelter. Although some offenders choose homeless shelters, for Avalon, the homeless shelter was definitely out; it would bring back too many horrible memories that would likely return her to a life of drugs and prostitution. Avalon did not want to live with her mother because she felt betrayed by her for not protecting her from her father's abuse. Avalon rationalized that her father beat her occasionally, but only when he had been drinking. And now he was sober. As a child, when he was not drinking, her father would often take her places and was nurturing and fun. He worked, and the family had food and clothing. She believed that she would be safe with him and that he would provide for her needs.

Unfortunately, Avalon was blinded by a false image of her father's ability to provide the love and nurturance she needed because of her idealized concept of family. She viewed her father's house as a place where she would be accepted, supported, and encouraged. However, according to Ruby Payne's research (2005), living in poverty can lead to expectations on men to be lovers and fighters and women to be martyrs and rescuers. In such a setting, frequently the mother is all-powerful if she is viewed as nurturing and attentive while men are seen as largely irrelevant to the family structure. Avalon did not view her mother as such. After all, her mother turned a blind eye to the abuse she had suffered as a child.

Avalon's childhood memories of her father caring for and loving her occurred when he fulfilled his nurturing ("lover") role as a father toward his little girl. But she was no longer a little girl, and he obviously was unable to nurture her in that way. Therefore, he no longer had a culturally prescribed relationship with her; Avalon was now merely someone living in his house.

Later Mary discovered that Avalon also chose to live with her father in order to care for him since he was ill. She had unconsciously assumed the "rescuer role" and would later take on the role of "martyr," since she gave up her needs to care for him. These gender roles may have worked out well for both father and daughter if her father had had the financial resources to provide for her and they had lived in a community where she would have access to resources to meet her social and psychological needs.

Because Mary didn't share Avalon's idealized concept of family, she was unable to understand Avalon's choice to live with her formerly abusive and absent father. However to Avalon, her father was her family. Avalon had related during sessions in prison that she was going to live with her father because he had worked and provided for the family when she was a child. She rationalized that his abuse and ambivalence only happened when he was drinking and he no longer drank. She believed that since she was now an adult, she would be safe with him and that he would provide for her needs.

When you grow up in one culture or value system and change to another, a distressful mental state called *cognitive dissonance* can occur. In this mental state, you experience a myriad of emotions, such as frustration, anxiety, guilt, dread, embarrassment ,and anger, as you attempt to shift from one value system to another. For this reason, humans resist change. They want their expectations to meet reality and to avoid situations or information sources that may cause them to feel uneasy. When we encounter the uneasiness or dissonance caused by change, we attempt to reduce our tension in one of three ways:

1. Lowering the importance of one of the factors that makes us uneasy.
   a. "I know cigarettes are supposedly bad for me, but no one in my family ever got cancer."
2. Adding elements that help us feel better.
   a. "I know cigarettes are supposedly bad for me, but I don't have the smoker's cough so I should be okay."
3. Changing one of the factors that make us uneasy.
   a. "I know cigarettes are supposedly bad for me, but I eat healthy and exercise a few times a week. So I think I'll be alright."

People who are unaware of the unconscious influence cognitive dissonance has on decision making have difficulty managing their frustration and tend to make quick decisions without fully evaluating consequences. While Avalon was in prison, she did not want to think about not having a home to go to when she discharged. She did not want to face the reality that she had been abandoned by her parents, not only as a child, but also as an adult. Therefore, she rationalized the fact that her father was abusive by saying that he only was abusive when he was drunk. She also changed one of the factors by believing that since she was an adult, he would not abuse her anymore. Therefore, she could justify her decision to live with her father after discharge.

Mary realized that she had been naive and that she would need to be involved in Avalon's life longer than she anticipated after she witnessed Avalon's father's behavior. She told her, "Avalon, I have just realized that the plans we made for getting you back on your feet again are going to need a little adjusting. I can see that your father is not going to help you and you are very uncomfortable being here." Avalon stared at Mary with sad eyes while she made fists with her hands, driving her nails into her palms, hoping that the pain would stop her from crying. Mary had seen this behavior in prison when residents did not want to show their fear, anger, or sadness.

Mary said, "Avalon, I will come back in the morning, and we will go into town and see what we can get accomplished. Do you think your father will hurt you?" Avalon stoically stated, "No, he'll just ignore me and watch TV. I'll be okay. Don't worry about me. I've been living in a cell the size of this room for four years with a cellmate. At least tonight I can be by myself." Avalon's mind was already busy figuring out ways to survive, to make do, to escape if she had to. Although Mary wasn't experienced in this kind of problem solving, clearly Avalon had had a whole childhood of training.

Mary already knew from her sessions with Avalon that she was an intelligent young woman. But why was she not able to solve problems effectively? Why was she not able to think about her options, make plans, or come up with different solutions? Why did she choose to live with her father who lived in the country? How could she not realize that she would have fewer resources available to her and she would need transportation? Why did she seem to set herself up to fail?

In prosocial cultures, young children learn fundamental ways of processing information from their parents and other caring adults. These people guide them through problems by identifying the situation, telling them the meaning or importance of it, and helping them solve the problem. As an example, Aaron bites Lilly because Lilly took a toy from Aaron. The adult stops the action. The adult asks the children to explain the situation and helps them identify the details. Then the adult explains the prosocial way to handle the situation, by teaching rules about sharing or providing ways to appropriately manage anger. Over time, children develop cognitive and emotional neurological pathways for processing complex information, which is critical for problem solving, interpersonal relationships, and developing prosocial attitudes and behaviors (Feuerstein, 1980).

Many children in the Country Called Prison do not have these kinds of adult-child interactions. They generally have to figure things out on their own, which might work for some but not for others. The problems in childhood are relatively minor, so the methods children develop on their own are rarely effective in adulthood. Many people in prison continue to use problem-solving methods from childhood. If someone disrespects them, they try to get even. If someone has something they want, they take it. If they get in trouble, they complain that it's not their fault. As a child, when they complained, their parents either scolded them harshly or rescued them. A whipping or a candy bar were the natural outcomes of complaints. These outcomes can be duplicated in prison, where complaints rarely are rewarded but might result in a transfer (punishment) to another unit or prison.

The next morning Mary retrieved Avalon from her father's house. Mary had realized that the first thing Avalon needed was a copy of her birth certificate—the one document that would prove she was an American citizen. Avalon did not know the process for obtaining a copy of her birth certificate or replacing her Social Security card. How would Avalon have been able to get these critical citizenship documents if Mary did not assist?

By mid-afternoon, the task had been completed, but it was more difficult than expected. They had to stand in line for nearly an hour, with crying babies and mothers scolding misbehaving children all around. The crowded room was making Avalon anxious. The clerk asked Avalon for her driver's license, which she did not have. All she had was the paper showing that she had been discharged from prison. As the clerk read the paper, his body language slowly began to display aversion instead of boredom. His eyes were filled with disgust and in a terse voice said, "I'll have to check with my supervisor." Avalon's eyes began to fill with tears. Finally, the clerk returned and processed the paperwork necessary for Avalon to get her birth certificate.

After they got in the car, Avalon reminded Mary that she had to see her parole officer the next day. After Mary told her that she would drive her to the meeting, Avalon began to sob. Mary felt powerless and inept. The government agency they had spent the day dealing with, with their policies and procedures, was just like the fence that surrounded the prison Avalon had just come from. She was still in prison, only now at a community province. She had finally acquired a passport but still knew little about America's culture, norms, and hidden social rules. Culturally, Mary realized that she had always been a "legal alien." Mary realized at that time, based on her experience, that many illegal aliens understood the American culture better than Avalon did.

More than 11,000,000 undocumented immigrants are in America on any given day, and about 8,000,000 work to support their families (www.numbersusa.org). While they might be breaking immigration laws, illegal immigrants are generally prosocial and abide by and appreciate the customs and laws in the United States. Unlike legal aliens like Avalon, who have poor coping strategies and planning skills, the undocumented immigrants had to plan and save money for several years to cross the border in search of a better life. Most of these immigrants had support from employers, family, and churches. Not so for the Avalons of the world.

Legal aliens rarely have a support structure, either emotionally or physically. If they do, it is usually ineffective in meeting the numerous needs formerly incarcerated people have. For the most part, children who grow up in the Country Called Prison do not learn prosocial coping strategies as children. They do not develop goal-directed attitudes. No one teaches them the self-talk that helps us persevere through difficult times. Rarely are lessons taught about positive, nonviolent ways to solve conflicts that promote satisfying interpersonal relationships. While some may believe that illegal immigrants are a financial threat to the United States, we suggest that legal aliens like Avalon create a greater burden on taxpayers and will likely continue to do so.

When Avalon visited her parole officer the next day, she was told that she had to pay a monthly parole fee as well as $1,750 for court fees that were incurred prior to her imprisonment. Mary was stunned when she told her this news. How was she supposed to pay for these expenses? Avalon's prison sentence was her punishment and that was over now. How was she going to find a job with her felony record so she could pay these fees? After all, nearly every employment application asks if you have been convicted of a crime. And, if Mary hadn't assisted, she would not have been able to get a job anyway since she left prison without two forms of legal identification. No wonder so many former prisoners turn to drugs and crime.

In a longitudinal study conducted from 2001 to 2006, sponsored by the Urban Institute, 740 ethically/racially diverse male offenders, who had been in prison at least 1 year, were monitored for their post-release income and employment sources. Table 5.3 identifies some of the key findings. After eight months, nearly half of the men did not have employment. Although 65% of the men had employment training in prison, it did not seem to help many obtain a job in the community. Former prisoners must overcome prejudice and the stigma of incarceration regardless of their job skills. Sadly, nearly half of the men did not know where to get help in the community for learning or improving their job skills. Why were they not given this information prior to their release?

The Urban Institute study showed that nearly half of the men had been financially supported by their family and friends both before prison and after prison. Research by Petersilia (2005) suggests that about 40% of prisoners have neither a high school degree nor a GED and about 30% have physical impairments or mental conditions that often prevent adequate employment. The similar percentages regarding the lack of education and need to be cared for by others are not surprising.

As we have discussed throughout this book, once someone has been sent to prison, their lives are forever changed and re-entry to America is hard. Note in Table 5.3 that 61% of the men had been working prior to prison, yet 8 months after release, only 41% were working at a traditional job. Although an additional 47% were working at informal jobs, these jobs usually do not produce adequate or steady income. While the study indicated that illegal income dropped significantly from pre- to post-prison, we are not sure that percentage would hold the longer the person was out of work.

Without a job, how can you live? Although research by Petersilia (2011) has shown time and again that employment for former prisoners is crucial in reducing recidivism, parole officers often are unable to provide much assistance. The barriers for obtaining employment

Table 5.3. EMPLOYMENT AND INCOME FOR FORMER PRISONERS

Key Findings			
Percent employed in prison			53%
Percent received employment training in prison			65%
Percent employed 8 months past release			45%
Percent who had no knowledge of how to obtain training			48%
Sources of Income	Pre-Prison	Time Past Release	
		2 Months	8 Months
Family/Friends	43%	66%	48%
Formal Employment	61%	30%	41%
Informal Employment	—	28%	47%
Government Program	10%	25%	24%
Illegal	35%	02%	06%

Source: Visher, Debus, & Yahner, 2008.

are huge. Even with the federal government's Work Opportunity Tax Credit program, which gives tax breaks to employers for hiring former prisoners, many employers are reluctant. But even if all the barriers to employment were removed, it is difficult to look for work without a car and money for fuel. Money is needed for a haircut and clothes so you look presentable for interviews. You need a phone so that employers can request you come for an interview. How does all this happen without money?

Since Avalon's father clearly was not going to drive her to work, she was going to need a driver's license. As for a car, maybe her father would at least let her borrow his truck.

Much like getting a copy of her birth certificate, obtaining a driver's license took much longer than expected. At the driver's license agency, Avalon was told that she had to pay an extra $150 dollars because the court had fined her for an old traffic violation that she did not even remember. Although Mary offered to pay, Avalon became so upset that she was not able to take her written test.

Avalon had acted like this every time she interacted with a clerk at a government office or a volunteer at a social service agency, such as the church that provided her winter clothes. She became extremely anxious and frustrated, and Mary had to translate most of the communication from the workers at these places. In response, Avalon talked about trivial information or related stories about other government workers she had encountered in the past, which had nothing to do with the present day. Mary sometimes wondered if she had an auditory learning disability. She needed a significant amount of encouragement to stay with the processes that had to be gone through in order to obtain documents, appointments, and possessions. Mary found that on the days that she worked with Avalon she would end up mentally exhausted, with little energy for her own chores.

Mary's struggles with Avalon reminded her of the foreign exchange student she befriended in high school. While the student could speak and understand English, Mary often had to help translate, especially when formal processes were involved. Avalon grew up speaking English. Why did Mary have to translate for her?

Language in any culture is spoken in five registers (Joos, 1967). Differing situations determine which register is appropriate depending on the audience (who), the topic (what), the purpose (why), and the location (where). These are summarized in Table 5.4. Static register is rarely used; prayer or the Pledge of Allegiance are examples. Formal register is usually one-way and used to give instructions or make announcements. Consultative register is commonly used and is a two-way dialogue based on social dialogue etiquette. Casual register is informative and used by peers and friends in a group setting. Intimate register is used for private conversations and generally contains endearments.

For those growing up in the Country Called Prison, frozen and casual register are most often used, whereas school, work, and professional settings use formal and consultative register. During conversation, formal register information is organized, and the goal is to get to the point quickly and precisely, conveying information, meaning, and importance; there is little body language. In casual register, "The pattern is to go around and around and finally get to the point" (Payne, 2005, p. 28). This accounts for the frustration Mary felt when Avalon produced meandering responses when Mary tried to explain things to her. Research by Montano-Harmon (1991) identified that to function in a prosocial culture, one must be able to move back and forth from formal to casual register, much like someone who is bilingual and can move easily between English and French.

For Avalon to acquire the skill of easily changing language registers, she would need to immerse herself in the formal language register through a relationship with someone who speaks formal and consultative register regularly, just as one might live in a foreign country to learn

---

Table 5.4. LANGUAGE REGISTERS

Frozen: always the same, such as "time to get to bed"

Formal: complete sentences with specific word choice

Consultative: formal register in conversation where information is exchanged

Casual: language between family members and friends; word choice is general and not specific; body language and voice inflection are significant elements

Intimate: language between lovers or very close friends

Source: Joos, 1967.

a language. In short, she would need to be taught this register, much as students are taught a foreign language in school. Unfortunately, in prison, personnel are not supposed to have consultative conversations with residents; they are only supposed to talk with them when they ask them to complete tasks or paperwork, which requires frozen register. Therefore, while residents live day after day immersed in an environment where they could learn important skills for success in America, they cannot because of the us-versus-them mentality of prison.

The more Mary worked with Avalon, the more she reminded her of her daughters when they were teenagers. Although teenagers can often make good decisions, they can also make some big mistakes. Since Mary was Avalon's teacher and mentor, and not her mother, she had to be careful in the way she talked with Avalon about these issues.

As we discussed in Chapter Three, most people from the Country Called Prison are psychosocially delayed. They generally stopped developing in their early teens, which is usually when they also began using drugs. In order to help Avalon, Mary needed to review the psychosocial goals for adolescent development. Adolescence is the most complex of all the developmental stages. It involves five areas: physical, cognitive, emotional, social, and behavioral.

Table 5.5 identifies the four major psychosocial goals that need to be met during adolescence. First, teens must achieve a new level of closeness with and trust of their peers. Mary needed to help Avalon try out more adult ways to interact with others. Mary would need to model the behavior as well as give Avalon feedback regarding her attempts. Second, teens must gain independence from parents and develop a new status within their family. Rather than just telling Avalon the rules for their relationship while mentoring her, Mary would need to involve her in the decision-making process. Third, and most important, teens must develop a sense of their own personal identity that distinguishes their abilities, skills, and unique personality. Mary would need to engage Avalon in discussions about her preferences and her thoughts about different ethical and moral problems and give her feedback regarding her decisions. Finally, teens must move toward autonomy. Mary would need to help Avalon take on more responsibility without overwhelming her with too much, too soon. She would also need to

Table 5.5. ADOLESCENT DEVELOPMENT GOALS

Goal	Task
Achieve new level of trust with peers	Practice different ways to interact
Gain independence from parents	Collaborative rule-setting with guardians
Develop new status with family	Evaluate and consider different options
Develop own sense of identity	Increase responsibility
Become more autonomous	Increase activities in the community

Source: Pruitt & AACP, 1999.

get her involved in work, social activities, and planning future goals, such as an education.

During the months that Mary worked with Avalon, she would get frustrated and impatient with her. She kept expecting her to act like an adult, but then would remind herself that, developmentally, she was working with a teenager. A few times Mary needed to be stern with her, since she made a few serious mistakes that could have led her back to prison. But, just like a typical teenager, she was testing limits. Slowly, though, she began to move along the developmental pathway, assuming the qualities of a young adult, although she was already in her 30s. With luck, she would continue to grow and catch up with her peer group.

Three weeks after Avalon's release, she applied for food stamps and Medicaid. Although she was able to get food stamps right away, she was unable to get Medicaid immediately. She was able to go to a community mental health clinic without medical insurance, but she had no money to pay for medications. Although her father was not abusive, he remained emotionally distant and resistant to offer financial support. Avalon grew more and more discouraged and depressed.

Nearly six weeks passed before Avalon was emotionally ready to look for a job. Before she went to prison, she had worked at a fast-food restaurant and at a daycare. She did not believe she could handle being around a lot of people, so she did not want to work in either of those jobs again. After some discussion, she agreed to apply at a temporary services employment agency.

Thanks to the local church, Avalon was able to find a couple of outfits that were suitable to wear when applying for work. Without telling

Avalon, Mary had already checked with her parole office and discovered that this particular agency was willing to hire former prisoners and worked with several companies willing to accept them. Avalon was able to get through the application process relatively calmly, and within a few days she was offered a job by a small company that needed someone to mail brochures. Although the job was only going to last a month, Avalon was happy and proud to have it.

Mary kept in touch with her over the next month. Although she needed a lot of coaching on employment skills and relationship situations, she steadily improved.

Mary's biggest worry was that she would fall in with a bad crowd and get back into drugs. Mary discussed Avalon's situation with a friend who sponsored adults in AA, learning some valuable mentoring skills. Even in the absence of addiction problems, former prison residents would probably do better if they had a sponsor as well as a support group to help them stay on the right path.

Avalon had been out of prison for about five months when she called Mary wheezing and coughing. After seeing her in person, Mary realized she was very ill and took her to the nearest emergency room. Her breathing was labored and the beds of her nails were blue, indicating that she was getting little oxygen. Diagnosed with severe pneumonia, Avalon was admitted to the hospital, where she stayed for about two weeks. The nurse told Mary that she would have died within a week had she not gotten medical attention.

Mary visited Avalon in the hospital the day after she was admitted. Avalon told her that she'd been sick for days but had thought her father would recognize it and get her help. By the time she figured out that he was not going to help, she was gravely ill. She told Mary, "I thought I was dying. I knew if I died that you'd be mad about all you did for me and that I let myself die. So I called you." While her logic was a little off, Mary noted her learned helplessness. She was still struggling with being a victim. But one positive result was that she finally realized that Mary was trying to help her because she genuinely cared about her.

A few weeks earlier, Avalon had told Mary that she did not think she was "going to make it." She thought she should just go back to prison. She said, "If I don't go see my parole officer next week and I don't pay my fines, then the officer will just revoke my parole, and I can go back to prison. At least I'd have a place to live and I have friends still there." Remembering that conversation, Mary wondered if Avalon's reason for not calling her sooner about her illness had been a form of suicidal thinking. Mary remembered the character in *The Shawshank Redemption* (Darabont, 1994) who hung himself a few weeks after being released from prison.

Individuals raised in the Country Called Prison tend to think in black-and-white terms, much like children. They tend to have little self-awareness and make decisions to neutralize their internal anxiety as quickly as possible. If the decision turns out to have bad consequences, then they quickly rationalize their situation by explaining it away, blaming others or convincing themselves that there is no problem. They often use anger to intimidate others so that they can feel in control of the difficult situation they created by their impulsive decision. They have developed numerous thinking errors that help them defend against their fear of change. The severe anxiety that comes with change is extremely difficult for many former prisoners as they shift from the culture of prison to the culture of prosocial America. We believe this is why so many return to the familiar rules and expectations of the prison culture.

As Avalon began to recover from her illness, Mary approached her with the idea of finding another place to live. Mary offered one idea after another that Avalon always found a reason to dismiss, even though she acknowledged that living at her father's house was not working out. She again would talk about "just going back to prison," which caused Mary's frustration to grow. What was causing this impasse?

As children grow up in a structured and nurturing home, they progress through three levels of prosocial maturity, as shown in Table 5.6. In his book *The 7 Habits of Highly Effective People*, Covey (1989) points out that, at first, children need a great deal of help from their parents but

Table 5.6. LEVELS OF MATURITY

Dependence	"You take care of me."
Independence	"I take care of myself."
Interdependence	"We can cooperate and do things together better."

Source: Covey, 1989.

gradually learn to do more and more things on their own. Parents often view teenagers as difficult to parent because one minute the teen is able to function independently, sometimes too independently, and then suddenly he or she becomes clingy and needy again. By age 25 or so most young adults realize that achieving goals requires working with others.

Children growing up in the Country Called Prison do not encounter situations or form parental relationships that help them move through these levels. Although humans have an innate drive to seek positive reinforcement and avoid punishment, the chaotic environment of most homes in the Country Called Prison prevents children from learning patterns by which to predict outcomes. Therefore, they do not develop self-efficacy—the confidence in one's ability to succeed at a task or in a given situation. Self-efficacy is critical in developing independence. Without a sense that one can control the outcome through choices and relevant behavior, one falls into the pattern of learned helplessness, depression, and criminal behavior to meet needs (Peterson, 1995).

For adults in the Country Called Prison, antisocial dependent maturity is demonstrated in a pattern of manipulation, anger, threats, and violence as the person expects to be cared for and the mentality of "when you don't come through for me, I will blame you for the results" arises. This is one of the main reasons for the predatory milieu in prisons and the hundreds of grievances filed by residents against prison employees. Prison residents demonstrate antisocial independent maturity also by seeking to get their way through criminal behavior (lying, stealing, breaking rules, and so on).

Although prison is an environment that could provide prisoners with positive role-modeling and reciprocal interactions through which they could learn appropriate expectancy patterns, corrections personnel often believe that prisoners will manipulate them to obtain illegal items or special privileges. Therefore, personnel limit their interactions with prisoners as much as possible. Once again, the us-versus-them mentality prevents residents from interacting with role models and mentors who could help them develop the skills necessary for success in America.

Once Mary realized the reason that Avalon was being so resistant to change, she tried a new approach: talking with her about her mother.

Avalon proudly said that her mother had divorced her father after Avalon left home, then went on to earn a medical office management certificate at the local technology school and had been steadily working at a medical clinic ever since. After hearing Avalon talk about her mother, Mary realized that Avalon's mother was in a better position to care for her than her father.

After leaving the hospital, Mary took Avalon to her mother's house. Although her mother also offered no hugs of welcome, she was polite and appeared to care. In addition, Avalon's mother lived in the city where Avalon grew up and Avalon hoped to reunite with some of her school friends who could offer her emotional support as well as drive her to job interviews. Avalon also had more access to social services and would be able to continue her counseling.

Once Avalon moved in with her mother, her life began to slowly improve, although Mary still periodically received a frantic phone call and a request for help. Mary spoke with Avalon for the last time a little over a year after Avalon was released from prison. She was still living in her mother's home but was on the waiting list for housing through the U.S. Department of Housing and Urban Development. She had found a job at a florist's shop and was being encouraged by two friends to attend the community college where they had gotten associate degrees. She was seeing a therapist and was taking her mental health medication.

In that last call, Avalon told Mary, "I'm never doing drugs again or hanging out with anyone who does. I'm never doing anything that will get me sent back to prison." Avalon had learned to love herself enough to keep the gift of freedom. She had fallen off the human development pathway when she got pregnant and dropped out of school as a teenager. Now she was back on track, developing her authentic adult self.

Avalon's story ended without her going back to prison. While Mary had the training, knowledge, and maturity to manage the frustrations they experienced and the problem-solving skills to overcome challenges and barriers, Avalon certainly did not. In trying to help her help herself and not treating her like a child, Mary had to develop new ways of thinking about solving typical life challenges and a whole new level of patience and compassion.

What did Mary learn from her experiences helping former prisoners emigrate from the Country Called Prison? First, while paying for a host of social services for former prisoners may seem expensive, it is actually cheaper for taxpayers than incarceration. If we're going to make a choice based on fiscal responsibility, then dollars spent for community support and programs will beat dollars to incarcerate hands down.

Second, many former prison residents are socialized in a culture with which they have little experience. They unconsciously see the world as rejecting them and themselves as unworthy. Psychologically, they are immature, helpless, and chronically fearful of people. Cognitively, they have poor problem-solving and social communication skills. They have no understanding of the Internet, word processing systems, or other technology that could help them find and keep a job. They have impaired adaptive skills and little understanding of ways to achieve their goals and are frightened of authority figures or people "in the government." A team of people is needed to help released offenders; Mary found herself emotionally drained any time she tried to help someone by herself.

The former prisoners Mary helped entered the criminal justice system with poor social skills, few problem-solving abilities, and no idea about how to improve their lives. While at the correctional facility, nothing about this framework was corrected. These offenders were merely contained like toddlers in time-out. While in time-out, they learned more about isolation and abuse. They were degraded as human beings and viewed by the prison system as a package to be shipped to the next facility. They witnessed peers being stabbed and raped. They had to be strip-searched every time they had a visitor. They did not receive occupational training so they could support themselves when they returned to America. When they were released from prison, they left without proof of citizenship. How were people with few problem-solving skills and no self-esteem or self-confidence supposed to crawl out of that deep hole?

Hierarchy of Needs, the humanistic psychology theory developed by Abraham Maslow (1954), provides a foundation for ways to help Avalon and those like her (see Figure 5.1). The theory suggests that human motivation is based on a series of needs that must be met for human development to occur. The first two needs are physiological and safety.

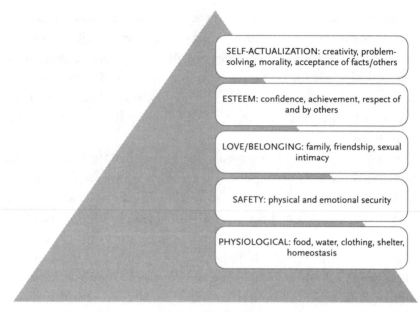

Figure 5.1: Abraham Maslow's Hierarchy of Needs Model.
Source: Maslow, 1954.

You might think of these as survival needs that include food, clothing, shelter, and a safe environment. Next comes needs related to love and belonging. In other words, we need social relationships. The fourth need—self-esteem—comes after meeting physiological, safety, and belonging needs. One way to build self-esteem is to succeed cognitively in areas we thought were weaknesses. Finally, we cannot feel comfortable in our own skin and reach self-actualization, where creativity and resourcefulness develop, until all these lower-level needs are met.

Since Maslow's theory was published, hundreds of social science and business research endeavors have used it as a basis for their studies. His theory is taught in high schools, colleges, and universities all over the world, not only in social sciences courses but also those in business, marketing, management, leadership, and law. Why? His model provides structure and intuitive clarity from which to create effective strategies for transformation involving human growth and development. To ensure that prisoners will leave prison and never come back, we must help them satisfy these needs through prosocial cultural norms and standards. Remember, these are innate human needs, and they will be satisfied one way or another.

PROPOSAL 1: PROVIDE PRISON RESIDENTS WHO ARE DISCHARGING WITH THE IMMEDIATE AND ESSENTIAL NEEDS TO REENTER SOCIETY SUCCESSFULLY AND WITH DIGNITY

Most case managers who supervise prison residents have a list of things to do prior to a resident's release date. But the focus is on discharge needs—getting them out the door—rather than helping them flourish when they leave so they don't come back. In doing research for this book, we found a workbook designed by the Peace Corps (Storti & Bennhold-Samaan, 1997) that helps to prepare people for life in a foreign country. Containing more than 250 pages, it includes information and self-directed study assignments. It covers all the important things one would need to know about assimilating and adapting to another country's culture.

We also searched the Internet for the topics "checklist for going to college" and "checklist for going on a trip." We found numerous websites with fairly comprehensive lists, some containing as many as 60 items, of things to do before going somewhere for an extended period of time. Given these examples and the success of the Peace Corps and colleges in transitioning people from one home to another (if only temporarily), we think that prisons could learn from these organizations. If prisons could create a checklist for assimilating to life outside of prison, former prison residents would have a better chance of successfully transitioning.

Since Maslow's Hierarchy of Needs model has been recognized as the "foundational checklist" for humans in transition, let's look at a basic checklist for residents leaving prison. While this list may seem excessive and more costly than current discharge checklists, prevention is always cheaper.

Survival Needs

- Legal documents, including a driver's license or state ID card, Social Security card, and birth certificate. In order to get a job, the driver's license and Social Security card are critical. Departments of Corrections could collaborate with state and federal agencies to obtain these documents via the Internet. Prison residents should be able to renew their driver's license while still there. All fines should be removed that impede a resident from getting his or her license.

- Clothes, hygiene products, and first aid supplies to last at least three months, including casual and work clothes, socks and shoes, under-garments, sleepwear, and outerwear—basically everything a person would pack if he or she were going on a three-month trip. A suitcase would also be needed. Prisons could collaborate with local churches or agencies, such as the Salvation Army, in providing a "clothes closet" where residents could shop. Residents leaving prison should be given a list of churches and agencies from which they can find additional clothing and supplies in the town where they are going to live. Additionally, in order to reduce any potential feelings of shame, these support agencies could include a flyer in the resident's planner that assures the resident that he or she is welcome.
- Food vouchers or food stamps to last at least six months to a year, depending on the resident's situation.
- Safe and affordable housing, where the resident can stay for six months to a year. Housing might be with a relative or friend or in a program or the resident can use housing vouchers. The emphasis is on safe and affordable. Many times residents, especially women, can only choose places where they were once victims or where they are more likely to return to substance abuse, because many people in the home or the neighborhood are addicts.
- Health care needs, including Medicaid (or some other type of insur-ance) for at least one year, prescription medicine for at least one month, over-the-counter medications and health supplies (ban-dages, diabetic test strips, and so on) or equipment (eyeglasses, cane, knee braces, and so on) that the resident had been receiving in prison. Many times prisons give the resident a prescription to have filled at a community pharmacy, but without money or insurance the resident is unable to have it filled. For residents with chronic medical and mental health needs, follow-up appointments and transporta-tion to those appointments should be arranged prior to discharge.
- Residents should leave prison with some type of short-term, pre-paid debit card (similar to Social Security disability income) that

provides them with funds to meet basic needs, such as transportation to job interviews, for three to six months depending on individual circumstances.

- Employment or approved Social Security disability income. Prisons should provide ways for residents to seek employment before they leave. We will address this proposal in the next chapter. Residents who are unable to work due to medical or mental health issues should be able to apply for Social Security disability income using an online application system.

Belonging (Social) Needs

- Residents should have opportunities to talk with—either in person or via phone—family, friends, or sponsors who will assist them after they are released to discuss the release plan. Contact should be outside of normal visiting hours and should be used to thoroughly plan the reintegration process to increase the likelihood of success. Discussion topics should include the resident's needs, possible obstacles to success, and the individuals on the reintegration support team that will help with the various needs.
- If the resident has children with whom he or she will have contact after release, arrangements should be made for family counseling in the community to assist the family in the reunification process. The military provides a similar service for military personnel who have been away from their families on lengthy deployments.
- For residents who attend religious services, the resident should have the opportunity to meet with—either by phone or in person—the priest, minister, rabbi, or imam of the house of worship he or she plans to attend. This would ensure that the resident will be welcomed and transportation can be arranged, if necessary.

Self-Esteem Needs

- For some residents, contact with universities or vocational schools should be made prior to the resident's release and appointments made with the enrollment coordinator. Funding, transportation, and other obstacles to success should also be addressed prior to discharge.

• Prisoner residents should be involved in reintegration group therapy prior to discharge, with group therapy continuing at community agencies or parole offices for at least one year after release. Group therapy should focus on increasing self-efficacy, confidence, problem-solving skills, interpersonal relationship skills, and moral reasoning.

Self-Fulfillment Needs

• A discharge planner that not only lists preparation steps, items to obtain, people to contact, and decisions to make but also provides instructions on the importance of maintaining and organizing personal documents and life plans. The planner should include pages for noting planned accomplishments in prison and during the first year out of prison. We will discuss this further in the next chapter.
• A plastic storage bin (about 12″ x 18″) with a sealable lid where prison residents can keep personal papers and items.
• A binder with pocket pages and tabs for important documents.

CONCLUSION

To solve the U.S. incarceration problem, we must focus on ways to improve success and win the game—a whole America with everyone included and flourishing. We need to count ways to score, not penalties. College football teams develop elaborate strategies and practice long hours to win the National Championship. They don't practice to see how many penalty flags will be thrown in each game. Surely we can do the same for offenders who have served their time in prison and want a fresh start when they are released.

CHAPTER 6

Emigrating from the Country Called Prison

The ultimate measure of a man is not where he stands in moments of comfort and convenience, but where he stands at times of challenge and controversy.
Martin Luther King, Jr.

Just like alcoholics who believe they can cure a hangover by drinking more, the current solution of incarcerating more in order to cure crime in America will, in fact, destroy us all in the long run. It has, as we have already noted, created a legion of former citizens who are essentially disenfranchised in their own land at the cost of billions of taxpayer dollars and even more in lost productivity. Of course, these efforts have almost nothing to do with crime control. Most solutions focus on punishment.

A difference exists between our best efforts to punish and/or rehabilitate offenders and our efforts to prevent crime from occurring in the first place. This book is primarily about the ways we punish and habilitate those who end up in the Country Called Prison. However, if we understood better ways to stop crime before it happens, then we could significantly decrease the prison population.

In this chapter, we investigate ways to change the criminal justice system in the long term. Near the end of the chapter we address ways we can prevent crime before it occurs. We believe that both sets of strategies will help us decrease the prison population and emigrate many from the Country Called Prison.

In our proposals to reinvent the criminal justice system, we use theories and models from sociology and macro social work to orchestrate legitimate changes. These are our big ideas, the macro changes that will require legislation, long-term policy and procedure changes, and long-range visions that focus and measure success rather than failure. Our assumptions in writing this chapter rest on our belief that change is essential because the current system of mass incarceration:

1. is economically unsustainable.
2. is in opposition to the dominant values of the United States, namely that all people should have equal opportunity regardless of their race, creed, or social class.
3. has created more problems than it has solved.
4. has created a new nation within the United States, the Country Called Prison, that is populated by millions of marginalized U.S. citizens who are tax-users rather than taxpayers and social contributors.

All social structures have manifest (intended) and latent (unintended) consequences. The manifest consequence of incarceration is to protect us from those we fear. The latent consequence has created this expensive Country Called Prison. Since social systems are designed by people, they can be changed by people. The status quo has evolved over time, and it can change again over time. So how can the system change so that everyone wins?

Social conflict theory teaches us that in every social situation there are winners and losers. To paraphrase what a wise old professor once told John, "If something is functioning in a society, it must be functional for someone." The key question is functional for whom?

Many of the winners of the current system are not bad people. They are merely smart enough to figure out ways to make a buck under the rules of our current society. Politicians win when they run for office on the "tough on crime" mantra. Entrepreneurs win when they build private, for-profit prisons by claiming that they can house dangerous people more cheaply and effectively, all the while turning a profit. Prison staff win when they cash their (albeit meager) paychecks and pay their bills. Each of these groups will resist change because it is in their vested interest to maintain the status quo. If change is to occur, these "winners" must be safeguarded in some way and encouraged to see that their short-term win is really a long-term loss for them and everyone else.

At the same time, those who "lose" are not always eager for change either. Many people who live in dangerous neighborhoods prefer dangerous people to be locked up to rid them from the neighborhood. They know that drug dealers cause problems, so they support locking them up too. In many poor neighborhoods, so many people are in prison that it often may seem more like a rite of passage than a punishment.

John once taught in a community college in a poor area. During class, when he asked if anyone knew someone who had been in prison, almost all of the students raised their hands. Something is not quite right about that. People who are addicted and out of work may see crime as a means of survival and prison as merely the cost of doing business. It is certainly possible that the corner drug dealer may be a motivated guy because he is, at least, working and supporting himself financially.

Taxpayers often protest change as well. Many believe that the only way to stay safe is to fill up prisons with everyone who is nonconforming. In short, many people believe that punishment works, and if crime persists it must be because the punishments are not harsh enough. If your parent or teacher ever punished you harshly, try to remember what you thought about those caregivers immediately after the punishment. As a child of the Baby Boom, John was regularly spanked for misbehavior. As he lay in his room crying, his thoughts toward his parents were never charitable. He never thanked them for punishing him for his own good. He hated them and sometimes thought about running away. When we punish harshly, we risk creating alienated citizens who hate the society from which they come and run away from their social responsibilities.

Of course, punishment is needed in some cases. There are people who do very bad things, and we need to isolate them for everyone's protection. Recently, in a conversation with a friend about this book, John mentioned that he was hopeful it could be used as a blueprint to decrease the prison population. The friend's first reply was, "Won't that hurt public safety?" He was shocked to learn that about half the prison residents in this country are incarcerated for illegal drugs and/or nonviolent offenses. This is an educated, well-read, business owner who regularly votes, and yet he had no idea. We think many Americans are just like him.

This book does not suggest that America stop locking up people society should fear. A few years ago, John was leading a tour group in prison when a serial rapist admitted to him that he "liked raping women" and that if he was ever released "he'd do it again." He is a criminal society should fear. No one questions the logic of locking him up for life.

However, as we have already shown, more than 50% of the incarcerated are not like this man. So why do we lock up people we do not fear? Why do we incarcerate people who have mental health or addiction problems? And, most important, what are the consequences to our society as a whole because we are doing this?

We have already discussed the economy of the prison system, including its hidden costs, in previous chapters. The way the cost of incarceration is calculated is flawed. Prison costs far exceed bars and guards. Taxpayers never see the lost tax revenue when a worker is removed from society. We hide the increased welfare costs that arise when that person's children go into state custody or the spouse and children need food stamps. It is nearly impossible to determine the actual price of a lifetime of lost or decreased income or costs of long-term unemployment of those we release from prison. To thoroughly understand the futility of the current system, we need to look at the real costs.

In the current system, most of the financial incentives seem to fall on the side of incarceration, at least for police, district attorneys, and those who work in the criminal justice system. Full jails and prisons bring in state tax dollars, more jobs for the Departments of Correction, increased funding for district attorney's offices, and other involved departments and agencies. What business doesn't want that? For local police chiefs, sheriffs, and district attorneys, reelection is perhaps an even more powerful force that drives high incarceration rates.

Recently a district attorney running for reelection made the mistake of knocking on John's door. As John recalls the conversation, it went something like this. The DA gave John his pitch, citing his high conviction rate, over 95%, as evidence that he was doing his job. "I'm protecting you by locking up bad guys," he said. John asked,

"What percentage of your convictions were nonviolent offenders?" He did not have an answer. John, then, asked him, "Would you say half would be a fair number?" He replied, "I don't think that many." "What percent do you think?" He replied, "Probably around 30%." Although dubious of his answer, John did not confront it. Instead, he asked: "What do you think about prison diversion programs for that 30%?" The DA replied, "Those are hard to find." "So," John said, "about one-third of the people you send to prison are there because it's easy to send them there?" "Well, not exactly," the DA mumbled. "But prison is paid for by the state, so it doesn't cost us [the local tax-payers] anything and we get these law breakers off our streets." He then quickly excused himself from John's porch.

This conversation with the politician cemented for us the economy of the prison system. District attorneys are elected because they are good at putting people in prison. They may not be good at justice at all. And the costs of their decisions do not come out of their local budgets. If America is going to significantly reduce the population of the Country Called Prison, this detached accountability much change. Below are some proposals for large-scale change of the current criminal justice system in the United States. We realize that almost all of these proposals will require legislative action or, at the very least, a concerted effort on the part of our elected officials. It is our firm belief that, if these proposals are implemented, taxpayers will actually save money and everyone in society will benefit. In the Appendix, implementation strategies and outcomes are identified for each proposal.

PROPOSAL 1: SHIFT THE COSTS OF INCARCERATING NONVIOLENT OFFENDERS TO COMMUNITY STAKEHOLDERS

Imagine a place where people had to directly pay to lock up neighbors they wanted incarcerated. As a result, they might be a little bit more thoughtful about the seriousness of their neighbor's offenses and use other means to correct that behavior before sending them to prison. In essence, this is the core principle of this proposal.

Recall the discussion regarding the district attorney campaigning for reelection. Incarceration is *free* to the communities that decide to send convicted offenders to prison. This helps to make the use of prisons appealing to community stakeholders because they see that costs are transferred to everyone in the state. We suggest that this is flawed thinking because, in effect, the county is using the state's "credit card" to pay for something the county voters want.

We propose a system that directly accounts for the decision to incarcerate. We suggest that the costs of locking up nonviolent offenders be charged to the county from which they came. If a community wants to lock up every pot smoker in the county, that's fine; however, that community would need to pay for it. In this way, it is similar to public education, where property taxes from the local community pay for local public schools. Taxpayers are free to increase their own taxes to build new buildings or remodel old ones to help their community. If they want nice parks, they can tax themselves to build them. If a county believes that being tough on minor crimes is a good idea, then the county should pay for it.

We believe that the cost of incarcerating violent offenders should still be paid for by the state. This will avoid a geographic bias, since violent crimes tend to occur more often in cities. We see incarceration of the violent as a public good, and so it should be paid for by everyone. Violent offenders are really everyone's problem, as murderers, rapists, and child molesters are unlikely to contain their illegal activities within one county.

An important component to this proposal is that the district attorney's office should oversee the budget for the county's use of prison bed-space for nonviolent offenders. This seems most logical, since the district attorney is the one responsible for charging, convicting, and sentencing offenders. While some might say it is the judges who are responsible, they should recall that over 90% of criminal cases in this country are settled through the plea bargaining process (Devers, 2014). District attorney's offices decide the specifics of the plea deal. Therefore, the road to the Country Called Prison starts at the district attorney's office.

Where will the district attorney get the money to pay the bill? Since many currently see prison as "free," we need to modify this perspective. Furthermore, we need to adjust the perspective of people who are most likely to have influence over elected officials. Why did that district attorney knock on John's door? The answer is simple. He always votes. Candidates obtain the voting records of people and only knock on the doors of those likely to vote.

We believe that if we were to attach the county tax for incarceration to property taxes, we would most likely gain the attention of those who vote. Voters then would have some direct say in how their money is used for incarceration of nonviolent offenders. In this way, we could start the emigration from this Country Called Prison.

For this proposal to be successful, there has to be a way for nonviolent offenders to be punished for their criminal behavior without going to prison. We believe that states should fund diversionary programs that will not only act as a judicial restraint but will also provide socialization and treatment to help nonviolent offenders avoid going to the Country Called Prison. These community diversionary programs will likely cut the overall costs of the criminal justice system.

Right now, district attorneys do not really benefit from diverting people from prison. Their conviction rate goes down, and voters might say, "They are soft on crime." If states funded drug treatment and other rehabilitation programs, they could be used by counties looking for free and/or low-cost alternatives to incarceration for nonviolent offenders. By encouraging the use of these alternatives, we believe fewer people will go to prison and recidivism will decrease because more people will remain out of prison. They will stay in the community working, obtaining treatment, becoming more socialized to the American way, and, most important, contributing financially to their community tax base.

We suggest that every district attorney's office should establish a new department based on the principles of social work. This new department will manage the funds, conduct pre-sentence assessments, and advise the court on sentence determination that will provide for a safe community as well as the rehabilitation of offenders. This department will connect offenders with programs in the community that educate, train, and assist both offenders and their families. Services should include programs for substance abuse and addiction, treatment for mental illness, and classes that teach proper socialization, parenting, and interpersonal skills. Furthermore, assistance in learning how to apply for jobs and keep them is equally important. Any jobs lost in the prison industry could easily be shifted into this new department. Its main goal will be to move citizens from the tax-user to the taxpayer category.

The most important part of this proposal is that it must be tax neutral. For every dollar that is passed to the county to pay the bills, the state should cut taxes by the same amount. States that contain exceptionally poor counties may wish to create some form of revenue sharing, much like the so-called robin-hood laws related to school funding. A poor community should not be so worried about spending money on incarceration that the community becomes unsafe. This is another reason that we believe this proposal should only apply to nonviolent offenses. The primary point of this proposal is to hold the people who make the decision to incarcerate accountable for that choice.

State politicians would benefit in many ways from this proposal. First and foremost, they would get the credit for cutting state taxes. Second, they would get credit for giving the power *back to the people*. Undoubtedly, at the local level, county politicians would take the political hit for having to raise property taxes. However, with an increased budget for the district attorney's office, the DA, in particular, would have a number of new political opportunities. A DA candidate running for election would not want to knock on doors and explain why we are safer because of high rates of incarceration. He would knock on doors to tout how much money he has saved the community through the use of state-funded diversion and rehabilitation programs.

Of course, those who win because of the status quo will take some convincing. They would need some short-term financial incentives to expand their scope beyond the razor-wire boundaries of the Country Called Prison and into the untapped market of prison diversion. When diversion programs are created to remove those we are "mad at" out of prison, then criminal justice careers, and all the costs that support those positions, will shift toward rehabilitation programs. We believe that the job loss because of this shift will be small, and businesses supporting the criminal justice system will remain profitably strong. Quite simply, the overhead costs of building and maintaining a prison are quite high, while treatment programs, halfway houses, and other diversion programs have much less infrastructure costs and fewer security demands.

In this proposal, taxpayers win, because in the long run accountability will drive down the costs as cheaper alternatives begin to be used. People who have been convicted of a crime win because they are more likely to be treated as citizens of the United States and not remain disenfranchised within the culture of the Country Called Prison. And, last but not least, communities win because society will not only be safe but enhanced as diversion programs increase the number of taxpayers.

By increasing diversion programs, such as drug court, mental health court, restorative justice programs, drug treatment, group homes, halfway houses, vocational-technical/college programs, and electronic house arrest, we expect a decrease in recidivism, crime, and the total criminal justice budget. More and more people will be able to emigrate from the Country Called Prison back to their country of birth. Tax-users will be turned back into taxpayers and eventually everyone will benefit.

PROPOSAL 2: CREATE A CRIMINAL JUSTICE ACCOUNTING SYSTEM THAT IDENTIFIES TRUE COSTS AND INFORMS THE PUBLIC ON A REGULAR BASIS

As we have discussed, it is extremely difficult to determine the actual costs of incarceration. No state is able to provide a true accounting to the taxpayers of what it really costs to put someone in prison, because determining true costs is nearly impossible. However, we think other options worthy of consideration can help us get a clearer picture.

To account for the overall cost of the decision to incarcerate, we need to charge the prison system for all the actual and collateral costs we can. Currently, if we incarcerate a woman who is the sole custodian of her children and those children go into state custody, the bill for foster care is not paid by the criminal justice system. The same can be said for food stamps, Temporary Assistance for Needy Families (TANF), and housing assistance. This should change.

During the intake process at social service agencies, intake workers can easily assess whether someone is seeking services as a result of a family member becoming involved in the criminal justice system. The intake worker could merely put in a code whereby some department within the system, such as the newly developed county DA's department, is billed for the costs if it is a nonviolent offense. The same idea could apply to a host of common ills that those released from prison face, such as disability costs, halfway house funding, and work-training costs. If all, or most, of the collateral expenditures were accounted for by the criminal justice system, we would have a clearer picture of the true costs of the criminal justice system, especially the correctional component.

Furthermore, if a person who is released from prison has difficulty finding housing and/or employment, those costs should not be borne by a social services agency, as they are now in most states. They should be paid for by the prison system. Here again, this is not to *punish* the system but to provide the taxpayer a more accurate accounting of the costs of incarceration, which also includes probation and parole services. Until taxpayers have a sense of the true costs, how can they assess the value of social policies?

PROPOSAL 3: INCREASE JUDICIAL DISCRETION AND DIVERSIONARY OPTIONS FOR ADULTS AND JUVENILES

Adult Issues

There is a need to increase judicial and jury discretion while reducing plea bargaining and determinate sentencing. Our roots in British common law emphasize the importance of the role of the judge in the judiciary process. In the past, the U.S. system of justice believed that judges were in the best position to make decisions about fairness and sentencing. However, over time, the discretionary role of the judge has declined as scandals and the electoral process have caused us to lose faith in the idea that a judge could be trusted to make good decisions. In today's judicial system, there are three major problem areas: 1) excessive use of plea bargaining, 2) determinate sentences, and 3) jury nullification.

Plea Bargains

The criminal justice system benefits greatly from the plea-bargaining process. However, it is a potentially coercive process. Hank, a former student, was getting a ride to school in a friend's car. His buddy was driving and sped through a school zone. They were pulled over. Upon giving the driver a ticket, the police officer suspected there might be drugs in the car. After a search, he found crack cocaine. The student had no knowledge of the existence of the drug in the car, but it was under his seat. Therefore, he was charged as an accessory to the crime of transporting a dangerous substance.

After a brief preliminary hearing where bail was set at an amount Hank could not afford, he sat for weeks in jail awaiting trial. The day before his scheduled court appearance, a public defender he had never met came to see him. Hank, who had not been found guilty of anything, had been in jail for about fifteen weeks. The lawyer told him, "If you plead guilty, the DA will let you off for time served and you can go home. If you insist on proclaiming your innocence and we go to trial, you are looking at fifteen years if we lose. What do you want to do?" Hank took the plea and left for home. Of course, he left with a criminal record that previously he did not have. This decision derailed his funding for college, his career choices, and his future. Why was the proposed sentence so long? The answer is determinate sentencing laws.

Determinate Sentencing

Determinate sentencing refers to legislated sentences given to judges for specific types of crimes. Both federal and state legislatures have created schemas by which individuals are sentenced. For example, a first-offense cocaine distributor would receive a specific number of years, while a second offense would yield more time. On the surface, this seems both efficient and fair. Judges no longer need to adjudicate; they are merely accountants keeping score of offenses, looking in a book for the punishment and sentencing someone to the required years of imprisonment or probation.

The problem, of course, is that no two cases are the same, and most have mitigating or aggravating circumstances that might influence the determination of fairness in each specific case. Judicial discretion allows judges to evaluate these circumstances and weigh out the relative fairness. Organizations like Families Against Mandatory Minimums (www.famm.org) have lists of individuals who had judges apologize for the unjust sentences they were forced to hand down. Our story about Hank is not an isolated case, and millions of other stories like this one are, in part, responsible for the boom in incarceration.

Jury Nullification

Jury nullification refers to the ability of a jury to nullify a law that they see as unjust. In theory, a jury can find the defendant not guilty even though they believe she or he committed the act for which she or he is on trial. In the United States, judges almost never inform juries that they can do this. Instead, they order the jury to be determiners of fact, not the law. However, jury nullification can protect people from unjust punishment. The student who takes a ride with a drug dealer is not really a person of which we are afraid. However, based on the way the laws are written, he was guilty. Had he gone to trial and jury nullification was a possibility, he may have been set free without a felony record to ruin his life.

Jury nullification can allow the jury to accept the evidence of guilt without the corresponding, life-ruining conviction. Although some may insist that the determination-of-fact rule is best because it prevents bias from entering into legal decisions, the power of the jury to determine the applicability of a law in a specific situation may actually be preferable. A judge seeking reelection may be more inclined to consider the political consequences of a decision instead of justice. Meanwhile, a jury of peers who have no long-term involvement in the criminal justice system may actually be more able to ensure that justice is served.

Juvenile Issues

There is a need to address the rising number of juveniles entering the adult criminal system. From 1983 to 1998, the American prison population grew by 163%; however, for juveniles housed in adult jails, the increase was a staggering 366% (Austin, Johnson, & Gregoriou, 2000). Between 2007 and 2008, the number of prisoners under age 18 grew from 2,283 to 3,650 (Carson & Golinelli, 2013). This trend of incarcerating juveniles seems to be evolving into a regular, rather than exceptional, practice as juveniles held in adult jails today equal 4600.

The question may arise: Are today's teenagers really worse than those a generation ago or is something else causing this significant rise in youthful offenders? One element that seems to be contributing to the increase is the zero-tolerance policies found in most schools These policies require that students be expelled, and often criminalized, for doing things that years ago might not have been that major of an offense. Research has shown that enforcement of the zero-tolerance policy tends to be linked to the most vulnerable and disenfranchised students, often the poor and minorities. These students often end up on the wrong end of a rigid rule (Skiba, 2000).

John recalls a friend who got in a high school brawl over a girl that resulted in a bloody nose and a black eye. Today, in a zero-tolerance school, that same fight would likely result in a report to the police for assault, expulsion from school, and another teen added to a juvenile probation officer's case load. In John's day, nothing happened to his friend, the brawler; he now owns a successful business and is a valued member of society.

As we have pointed out, prison rarely corrects adult criminal behavior; it certainly is not going to correct juvenile delinquency. Youthful prisoners have a significantly increased likelihood of being raped and assaulted while in prison (Austin, Johnson, & Gregoriou, 2000). They also have higher risks of suicide. Unfortunately, most prisons try to avoid these problems by placing juveniles in administrative segregation. This practice borders on cruel and unusual punishment, as teens are locked down 23 hours a day in a single cell just when their psychosocial and moral development is most important for healthy adult functioning. We lock juveniles away, prisonize them in a stagnant, wretched environment, and then wonder why they act immature and irresponsible when they are released from prison years later as adults.

Using a progressive discipline model for juveniles is essential. We should use adult incarceration as the absolute last resort. Throwing away 16-year-olds because they did something we don't like is a sure way to continue to grow the Country Called Prison. We must consider the deeds of teenagers in the context of their psychological and social development. The ability to engage in long-range planning is not common in most teens, and so it should not surprise us that they engage in behaviors that we would prefer they not do. Almost everyone recalls episodes from their teenage years that later in life they look back on, shake their head, and ponder, "What was I thinking?" The same is true for teenagers today, many who have been labeled as criminals.

Diversion programs for teens are much less expensive to operate than for adults because teens usually live with their parents or guardians, do not have children, and do not need to find employment. The "nothing works" backers would support locking them up. However, we believe that policy makers should divert money from prisons to programs that may have an effect on changing their behavior. The costs of doing nothing or keeping the status quo are not just in dollars but in lives. If we could rescue a teen from this detrimental path we would all be better off for generations to come. We must expand the number of diversion programs for teens and adequately fund them so the programs can actually be successful. The earlier we divert citizens from the Country Called Prison, the slower the growth rate of that culture and the less expensive it is for America.

We believe that all these issues are interrelated. As is frequently the case, one solution may actually create a different problem somewhere else. The unintended consequences of massive plea bargaining, limited judicial discretion, and harsh rules for juveniles have been to increase the size of the Country Called Prison. We need to make sure that we develop solutions that focus on reducing its population, not just fix one component of the criminal justice system.

PROPOSAL 4: STOP CRIMINALIZING PEOPLE WITH ADDICTIONS AND MENTAL ILLNESS

Every criminologist we know of admits that the Country Called Prison has grown in large part due to the "war on drugs" and many of our "get-tough-on-crime" policies that began in the 1980s. At the same time, most mental health facilities have been left short of funding and unable to meet the needs of those who are without medical insurance. This often results in the mentally ill and addicted falling through the cracks of America's welfare system to the one place that cannot say no, prison, at a 32% higher cost than treating them in the community (NAMI, 2014).

The tenets of labeling theory apply here. This theory suggests that the labels, or classifications, society puts on things actually create them. For example, if we define a person with a drug habit as *sick,* then we send that person to a hospital to get *well.* If we define that person as *criminal,* off to prison he goes. Generally speaking, we know that about half of the men and women who go to prison are convicted of drug possession. They are not drug dealers or traffickers; they are merely drug users. Our society has decided to try to punish away their drug addiction. This simply will not ever work.

Drug abuse is often linked to another common ailment in prisons, mental illness. The majority of those whom Mary sees who have a diagnosable mental illness usually have a drug problem as well. Frequently, they are referred to as "dually diagnosed." For those involved in the criminal justice system, this will come as no surprise. Many mentally ill people self-medicate with illegal drugs to try to curb the symptoms of their mental illness.

In many states, the prison system is the largest single provider of mental health services. The Bureau of Justice Statistics (Glaze & James, 2006) estimates that 24% of state prisoners and 21% of jail inmates have a history of mental illness; of these, 72% have co-occurring substance abuse disorders (Ditton, 2006). Unquestionably, sending people with mental illnesses to prison does little to help their problems. More often than not it creates an expensive revolving-door problem, as 25% of prison residents with mental health problems have had 3 or more previous incarcerations. So, data suggest that society is, once again, choosing the most expensive and least effective solution to a problem in America.

Over the past 10 years, more and more veterans have become drug criminals. When Mary meets a veteran at the Department of Corrections reception center, he has usually returned from a war zone within the past five years and is suffering from PTSD. In efforts to self-medicate their terrible psychic pain, many war veterans turn to drugs and alcohol. One resident convicted of a fourth DUI told Mary that alcohol was the only thing that kept away the bad dreams. Instead of locking this person up with murderers and rapists, perhaps judges and district attorneys need to "sentence" the offender to take advantage of the services provided by the Veterans' Administration. In fact, judges and district attorneys need to use their discretion to sentence all individuals with mental health and addiction problems to treatment facilities, not prisons. These programs are far more effective in controlling addiction and are cheaper as well.

Legislators also need to refashion the community mental health system so that people can get continuous and effective help. There is a need for court systems and probation and parole offices to create specialized departments to coordinate the services needed by this group of people. There needs to be an increase in and adequate funding for mental health courts and drug courts with processes that focus on treatment, not punishment.

In one of the largest federally funded research studies congressionally mandated, the National Treatment Improvement Evaluation Study (1997) showed that when individuals receive treatment, significant positive changes take place:

- Participants reduced drug use by nearly 50% within a year after completing treatment.
- Participants' use of primary drug declined from 73% to 38% in same time period.
- Addicts' quality of life improved by 53% percent.
- Alcohol- and drug-related medical visits declined.
- Illegal drug sales decreased by 78% in areas that provided adequate drug treatment programs.
- Assaults decreased by 78%.
- Shoplifting declined by nearly 82%.
- The number of individuals who supported themselves through illegal activities declined by 48%.
- Drug treatment programs not only make neighborhoods safe but also save residents money.
- Substance abuse treatment programs helped improve quality of life for everyone in society.

One thing is certain. If we are serious about decreasing crime and drug addiction in this country, as well as helping people with mental illness, then prison is not the answer. It is clear that we cannot punish away addiction. Anyone who ever tried to get a friend to sober up by yelling at them knows it doesn't work. Shifting the perception that addiction and mental illness are public health issues is more likely to benefit our society as a whole, lowering our costs and decreasing crime rates.

PROPOSAL 5: MAKE IT EASY FOR PEOPLE FROM THE COUNTRY CALLED PRISON TO SUCCESSFULLY MIGRATE BACK TO THE UNITED STATES
Stop the Self-Fulfilling Prophecy Brought on by Labeling

Let's consider the labels we use for people leaving prison. We call people who have finished their sentence and returned to society "ex-cons." There is no word in the English language that describes the category of people discharged from prison without the use of some form of a word that denotes criminal, convict, or offender. In other words, offenders are labeled and never forgiven.

The concept of "time-out" as a disciplinary strategy for children works best when parents hug their child after time-out is over to demonstrate forgiveness and unconditional love. In the Amish culture, which uses a form of "adult time-out" called *shunning*, the same thing occurs. After the person completes their allotted time of shunning for their misconduct, the community immediately welcomes the person back into full membership and nothing is said again. Many cultures around the world use this same form of social discipline and forgiveness strategy. Major crimes rarely occur in these cultures.

Labeling theory suggests that people behave as we expect them to. Research has consistently shown that students tend to perform better when teachers expect it (Al-Fadhili & Singh, 2006; Kuklinksy & Weinstein, 2001). This is commonly known as the self-fulfilling prophecy. When we continue to refer to people who have completed their punishment as "criminals," "ex-cons," or "ex-felons," then we should not be surprised that they continue to commit crimes. We label them as unchanged, therefore they don't change.

So, one of the simplest changes that we propose is to stop label-ing people who complete their probation, prison, and/or parole sen-tence. Names have strong connotations. When a person knows your name, they have some power over you. They call for you, and you at least turn your head. When we name someone "ex-con" or "ex-felon," we have kept their previous status tied to their personality. When you describe your friend who was divorced and then remarried to another person, do you refer to her as an "ex-wife" because her first marriage broke up? With people in prison, and those who have left, we do this every day.

Not labeling a group of people is hard. In reality, though, why do we need a label? No one likes to be labeled. Even when we try to change labels to be more positive, such as changing the label "prison guard" to "correctional officer," in the end we still create a euphemism that groups people together indiscriminately. Therefore, any new "politi-cally correct" label we put on a person who has completed his or her punishment will eventually become code for "ex-con." So, if the per-son's name is Bob, we should call him Bob. Let's avoid the self-fulfilling prophecy and think of labels as four-letter words that we shouldn't use. Eliminating labels from policies and procedures manuals is a great place to start.

Automatic Criminal Record Expungement

One of the most important things missing in the American criminal justice system is forgiveness. Once you are convicted, you are perma-nently labeled. You will now live your life trying to run from some type of moniker that identifies you as a criminal.

A few years ago a college student in John's class admitted that he was a registered sex offender. One night at a party he had relieved himself on the lawn of an apartment complex. A passing police officer saw him and arrested him for indecent exposure. After pleading guilty, he was put on the sex offender registry. As he gave his oral report on criminal justice issues, he told the class that he was lucky because his father was an attorney and that they were already working on getting his record expunged.

Expungement usually applies to first-time offenders and literally means that records from earlier criminal activities are sealed. Therefore, the guilty party no longer needs to worry about background checks discovering his or her felonious past. It is, in effect, a legal forgiveness.

An important point to understand is that expungement is a civil action. The plaintiff must ask the court to declare the records sealed, which usually involves lawyers, money, and time. In the case of this student, he didn't have to find the thousands of dollars it would take to hire a lawyer. But what happens if your father isn't a lawyer? How do you get your records expunged?

Most first-time, nonviolent offenders meet the criteria for expungement after a specific amount of time has elapsed. Unfortunately, most lack the knowledge and financial resources to pull this off. Therefore, we suggest that all nonviolent, first-time offenders be given an automatic expungement after a relatively short period of time, perhaps between two and five years. While this proposal would take some legislative action, hopefully in a country that prides itself on second chances, this pride will extend to people from the Country Called Prison.

Eastern societies such as that of Japan practice "reintegrative shaming" (Braithwaite, 1989), which refers to the way the bond can be mended between the offender and the society. Until recently, Western cultures tended to use stigmatizing shame; once you've done something wrong, you can never get away from that negative action. Therefore, the individual stigmatized has no way to escape the past. Over the past 10 years or so, the United States has begun to use a restorative justice model that includes such mending activities as restitution and face-to-face meetings between victim and offender. However, until restorative justice becomes the more traditional way to mend a tear in society, we believe that automatic expungement for nonviolent, first-time offenders can be a way to welcome them back into society. As well as getting on with their lives and feeling less shameful, they will be able to find employment and housing more quickly. Automatic expungement would also reward good behavior and show residents of the Country Called Prison that society wants them back now that they have made positive changes in their lives.

Change Employment Restrictions and Practices

You read previously about Avalon's reentry challenges. Employability is a major obstacle to successful reintegration. As one student with a criminal record put it, "If I admit I've been to prison, they don't hire me. If I lie and they check my records, then they don't hire me either. So I decided to try school." Of course, with a drug offense, many of the loans available to most students were not available to this student. So school for this student didn't last long either.

Over the years, as a social work professor, John has had the following conversation with certain students. A student walks into his office and asks, "Can I be a social worker"? Usually what follows is a confession of a criminal record, often related to drug use. His reply is usually, "Yes, but there are certain agencies that won't hire you." Then a laundry list of agencies from child welfare to nursing homes comes out. It is odd that a 24-year-old recovering methamphetamine addict is treated so differently from a 24-year-old recovering alcoholic. In over 15 years of teaching, John has never been asked by a recovering alcoholic if any employment restrictions applied to him or her.

The simple solution to the employment challenge offenders face would be for businesses to simply delete the criminal history question from the employment application and hire on talent and ability. If businesses are concerned, or are hiring for specific positions for which a criminal history might be a cause for concern, then businesses should run background checks. We understand, though, that businesses are often held accountable for employee activities, and so they feel the need to know the criminal histories of potential employees. We propose a kind of "Good Samaritan" law for businesses, so they can hire people from the Country Called Prison without liability, should an issue arise.

Develop Reintegration Support Services in Prisons

Since nearly 95% of prison residents will leave prison within 10 years of arrival (Hughes & Wilson, 2004), there is a tremendous need to create a support system for these residents when they return to the community. When legal immigrants come to America, support services help them learn English, American customs, and citizenship information so that they can become naturalized American citizens. These same types of acculturation support services are needed for citizens of the Country Called Prison to learn the expectations for becoming prosocial taxpayers.

While many state corrections departments already have some reintegration services, we believe reintegration services should be imperative. Social workers are well aware of the concept of discharge planning. They would never discharge a person in need of oxygen from a hospital unless home medical services were in place prior to discharge. We are proposing the creation of two types of reintegration support services: services that begin in prison and services that are in the community.

We envision prisons having reintegration units where residents live when they are within one or two years of discharge to begin their preparation for leaving prison. These units will be minimally restrictive and be the equivalent of a halfway house. These units should not be "behind the fence." If prison residents can't be trusted to follow rules and regulations, then they should not be leaving prison in the first place. Too often, prisons keep labeling residents as "bad" because of their original crime, rather than seeing the changes they have made in their lives.

When Gloria first came to prison, at age 19, she was full of meanness. She had been convicted of assault and battery of a shop owner when she was high on drugs and robbing the place. Five years later, she had earned her GED and a certificate in horticulture and was the orderly in charge of maintaining the flowerbeds at the entrance of the facility. She was going to discharge in three months, and her case manager, who believed in her, had gotten her a job with a friend who had a landscape business. Gloria now worked to find a place to live so she wouldn't have to return to her terrible neighborhood and possibly get caught up in drugs again. A reintegration unit could help make this kind of success story happen for every nonviolent person leaving prison.

We envision that residents living in the reintegration units would be given preparation planners and would attend classes on employment skills, life skills, interpersonal relationship skills, parenting, marriage, etiquette, life planning, and so on. We hope that the units would function somewhat like a home, with residents sharing in meal preparation, unit cleanliness, and activity planning. Residents would have the opportunity to contact prospective employers. Staff might be able to invite prospective employers to the unit for interviews or they might take residents to interviews at employment agencies or at job sites. Procedures would be in place for finding appropriate housing and obtaining items on the reintegration checklist discussed in the previous chapter. We anticipate that different procedures and programming would be in place for units housing residents under age 50 and those over age 50, since work, family, and aging scenarios would be considerably different.

The creation of reintegration units would not require a great deal of money. Their creation will, however, require a new way of thinking about residents, the purpose of incarceration, and the goal of corrections. Most state correctional departments view their primary goal as protecting the public from dangerous criminals. We agree that the original purpose of prisons was just that, because only the truly dangerous people were locked up. However, times have changed. Private prison corporations would most likely be able to implement reintegration units far more quickly and more effectively than state corrections departments, which tend to be bogged down by bureaucracy and fixed budgets.

As we have pointed out time and again, prisons are full of mostly nonviolent offenders. Yet the goals of prisons have not really changed much. Traditions die hard. We are well aware that most prisons have some type of discharge planning. However, this planning is often focused on the short term. Prisons strive to get the person out the door. The focus is not on helping the resident stay out. Prisons have a tremendous opportunity to reduce recidivism by establishing programs that are designed to help residents leave prison with the best possible chance of success.

Develop Reintegration Support Services in the Community

In the community, the ideal scenario for reintegration support is to create a type of social work division in state correctional departments. The sole purpose of this department would be to create success stories.

To do this, a paradigm shift has to occur away from only punishment of criminals toward assimilation.

Many businesses, agencies, and processes are in place in the community that can provide for the needs that former prisoners and their families have. We don't have to reinvent the wheel; we just need to get people connected with existing processes and services. Medical and mental health hospitals and rehabilitation centers have had social work departments for years that help patients with follow-up care in the community after they discharge. This proposed department would focus on providing services that help former prisoners learn appropriate ways to satisfy their innate human needs. Once again, we use Maslow's Hierarchy of Needs (1954) to discuss the elements that an effective community social work division might contain.

Physiological and safety needs include access to basic survival materials (food, clothing, and shelter), the ability to feel secure, and prospects of obtaining support. People need the proper legal documents to obtain work, rent housing, obtain a car loan, and so on. They need assistance in finding and keeping jobs, which might include coaches who would accompany the person on his or her first day on the job. They need to be able to obtain medical and mental health services immediately upon release. Allowing someone to wait three months to see a psychiatrist is setting that person up to fail. Finally, depending on where the person lives, transportation assistance needs to be made available so they can keep appointments and get to work.

Belongingness and esteem needs include the ability to be accepted and appreciated by others, to have friends, to demonstrate competency, and to gain approval and recognition from others. Former prison residents need to have a support system (not just their family or friends) that is willing and able to assist them for at least three years after release. Just as we have learned from the success of AA and NA (Narcotics Anonymous) meetings led by recovered addicts, former prison residents should be able to attend meetings with other former residents who have successfully reassimilated, others like themselves who have been successful. We need something like an 'offenders' anonymous support group' (without the labeling, of course).

At the same time, former residents should be encouraged to become involved in community groups. Community theater, civic organizations, and churches all provide positive social interaction. To break the cycle of prison, those we release should be encouraged, and perhaps even rewarded, for becoming involved in their communities. Almost every town or city has a volunteer organization of some type. If former prison residents were welcomed to such groups, everyone involved would benefit.

Self-fulfillment needs include the ability of one to reach his or her potential and capabilities as a human being and to help others achieve their potential as well. Satisfying these needs will require long-term strategies through the development of permanency planning and stabilization reform.

One of the most successful reintegration programs around is the Peter Young Housing Industries and Treatment (PYHIT) enterprise (www.pyhit.com) in New York, which provides a full range of services. PYHIT began more than 50 years ago when Father Peter Young realized how socially disenfranchised former prison residents were. He realized that addiction was a disease that needed treatment and that a successful reintegration program must include not only treatment but also housing and employment opportunities. Organizations like PYHIT can be, and should be, implemented in every state if we are going to stop the rising tide of disenfranchised and marginalized people in America.

Avoiding hostile labels, creating automatic expungement of records, reducing the shame of applying for employment, and creating reintegration support services are solutions whose time has come for three reasons. First, and perhaps most important, the nonviolent offender would have a reason, a motivation, to behave properly upon release. Second, odds would be better that former residents would gain meaningful employment, which in the long run would save taxpayers a great deal of money, as well as generate more tax revenue. And, finally, these proposals would help remove some of the unintended consequences of mass incarceration by decreasing the population of the Country Called Prison.

PROPOSAL 6: FOCUS ON MEASURING SUCCESS AND FUND THE MOST EFFECTIVE PROGRAMS

Football and basketball games have rules for the way points are scored and a list of behaviors that are inappropriate, usually referred to as fouls. In all of our years of playing and watching sports, we don't ever recall someone talking passionately about the number of fouls in a game. Instead, people talk about the score because it tells who won. We tend to pay attention to and count what is important.

In the Country Called Prison, we count fouls, not scores. Police count the number of people arrested. District attorneys and judges count convictions. Prisons count how many beds they have filled and at what security level. Probation and parole departments count recidivism.

Therefore, one of the most important things we can do to reduce the population of the Country Called Prison is to change the way we count. In prisons, we should count success, not failure. We should focus on and count prison residents' prosocial behaviors, humanitarian acts, educational and training accomplishments, and so on. We should count prison employees' acts of compassion and kindness, behavior that facilitates positive change in others, and creative and innovative ideas that improve the environment and reduce costs. Goals that address prosocial behavior, social responsibility, and benevolence should be measured and reported in all meetings and operational status reports. When scores are low, analysis and corrective action should be taken.

Manufacturing facilities across the United States display huge banners that identify the number of days without an accident. Prisons need to do the same thing—count the number of days without violence, an incident, or rule infraction. Parole offices should post the number of working clients and perhaps even the total amount of income earned and the total amount of taxes paid.

Many Americans assume that the U.S. prison system is working. They suggest that America is keeping its citizens safe and since only 50% or so return to prison, citizens believe the system must be working. But ask yourself this question. Would you give your retirement fund to a stockbroker who prides himself on only losing 50% of his clients' money? This is essentially the way the U.S. prison system operates.

Under the current system, nothing is more beneficial to the "winners" than recidivism—a fancy word for failure. Recidivism decreases parole officers' caseloads and increases the demand for prison beds without bogging down the court system, because former prisoners are easier to charge and convict for new offenses. For parole violations, the parolee can bypass the court system and go directly to jail.

Prisons benefit from recidivism as well. When former prisoners return to prison, the system gets someone who already understands it. They know what to expect, how to stand in line, how to shut up, and how to follow commands. An added benefit is that they are usually older, which means they are less likely to join a gang and less likely to be violent. Thus, the beds stay full without as much work. The prison system actually gets more money every time someone returns to prison.

When confronted with failure rates, politicians and leaders in the criminal justice system usually put the blame on a new generation of offenders who are "uncontrollable." Their solution to recidivism sees the offender as the problem; thus we must punish longer and more harshly, which leads to more prison beds and more money being thrown away. This reasoning follows the definition of insanity—doing the same thing over and over again and expecting different results. Prison systems have long complained that they cannot be held accountable for results since they cannot control the decisions felons make. Let's think about this a moment. We are both professors. If you took a college class from one of us and half of the students failed, would we, as professors, not have some responsibility for that outcome or would it all be the students' fault?

At all levels of education, we hold teachers accountable for teaching our children, and we have developed ways to count their successes and failures. Although some of these methods of counting are controversial, it doesn't change that we believe that teachers have some responsibility for the success and failure rates of their students. Providers in the criminal justice system need to be held accountable for outcomes.

Clearly, no institution can promise a 100% success rate. However, the current paradigm seems content with high failure rates. For example, in California, of the prisoners released in 1995, 66% returned to prison within three years (Pew Charitable Trust, 2007); of that group, less than half returned for a new offense. Parole revocation accounted for 36% of the returned residents, which means the individual violated the terms of his or her parole without committing a new crime. Of that group, half of the parole revocations were for technical violations, such as missing an appointment, not paying a fine, or failing to report a change of address.

Recently Bill's parole was revoked because he missed a meeting with his parole officer. He had a job interview at the same time and thought getting a job would impress his parole officer and also allow him to catch up on his unpaid child support (another potential rule violation). Not so. The parole officer never bothered to find out the reason he had missed the meeting; the officer merely issued a warrant for his arrest. Bill was sent back to prison without a court hearing.

Quality should be rewarded, especially since several evidenced-based programs with proven success records have been operating for many years, demonstrating that success can be achieved effectively and inexpensively. Prisons (public and private) and programs with high rates of success—creating taxpayers—should get more funding, just as an investor will put more funds into a stock portfolio that is doing well. Prisons and programs with high rates of recidivism won't.

PROPOSAL 7: DECREASE CRIME

If we could reduce the number of crimes committed, we would certainly be able to shrink and eventually eliminate the Country Called Prison. But preventing crime is easier said than done. Here we suggest a few ideas for reducing crime rates. Many social workers and sociologists alike will be familiar with some of these proposals.

There is a difference between punishment and crime control. Punishment is about extracting retribution, while crime control is really about (1) making it more difficult to commit crimes and (2) creating citizens who don't want to commit crimes in the first place. The first is far easier than the latter.

Setting up roadblocks to criminality requires thinking ecologically. Crime occurs within a specific time and in a specific space. It doesn't just randomly occur. Therefore, we can try to eliminate the social settings in which crime is likely to occur.

Marcus Felson (1998) suggests that crime will only occur if three components are in place. We must have (1) a motivated offender who comes into contract with (2) a suitable target in the absence of (3) a capable guardian (see Figure 6.1).

It is difficult to know who is and who is not a motivated offender. When we walk through a mall parking lot, we have no idea if someone is thinking about mugging us. Identifying a motivated offender is difficult if not impossible.

However, the second and third criteria can be controlled. The suitability of a target and the presence of a guardian can have an influence on the likelihood of a criminal act. A large man over 6 feet tall probably has less fear going out late at night than a small woman who is 5 feet tall. The small woman is a more suitable target for people who wish to commit crime.

Another factor in the suitability of a target is its value. At one time, people stole eight-track tapes from cars as a source of easy money. Now eight-track tapes are virtually worthless and are therefore not a suitable target for crime. Who knows what will be a profitable target in 50 years?

The suitability of targets is influenced by what criminologists call "target hardening." When a department store adds a device to clothing so that an alarm goes off if that clothing leaves the store without it being removed, the store lowers the suitability of their clothing to shoplifters. Thieves will simply go to another store that does not use

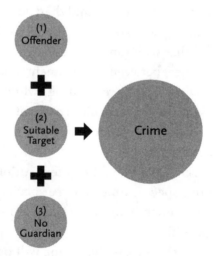

Figure 6.1: Felson's Crime Components.
Source: Felson, 1998.

these kinds of devices. By hardening the target, stores make it less likely that someone will steal from them.

Some people use baby monitors that include video to monitor how babysitters are treating their children. These cameras are even more effective if the babysitter knows they are being watched. The camera hardens the target by providing guardianship to the child. Cameras act as guardians only if they are visible to the motivated criminal. The cameras above cashiers in stores may or may not actually be connected to a monitor somewhere. Nonetheless, they act as guardians to the cash register and force a potential thief to think twice before taking action. In this way, they decrease crime (Felson, 1998).

But no matter how much guardianship is provided or how much a target's suitability is reduced, some people will still commit crime. Very few people attack large groups of people, but it has happened. If a person is truly motivated, nothing will stop him or her. Now we take a brief look at what might be done to reduce a person's motivation to commit a crime.

Although reducing the number of people who want to commit crime appears to be the simplest form of crime control, it is, in fact, difficult to do. Understanding human motivation is never easy. Most of the programs and ideas that we put forth are not perfect protectors against criminality. No program will work 100% of the time, especially when it comes to increasing the number of prosocial citizens. But just because an idea is not perfect does not mean that it is not worth trying.

When you look at what works in reducing criminal motivation, you see that most of the good ideas sound more like social work and less like policing. Social workers know that systems in society interact. The dysfunctional family system interacts with the weak job market, which interacts with substandard schools, which interacts with dangerous housing and a host of other factors to lay the fertile soil from which delinquency and criminality may grow.

In 1998, the National Institute of Justice produced one of the best meta-analysis of crime policies to date (Sherman, Gottfedson, MacKenzie, et al., 1998). Researchers reviewed social programs and criminal justice attempts to decrease criminality and provided a list divided into three groups: 1) what works, 2) what doesn't, and 3) what is promising. Let's look at what works.

Families in high-risk groups because of poverty and other social problems have increased odds of raising a delinquent child. The following programs have shown success in decreasing the odds:

1. Have nurses and other professionals visit homes frequently to work with parents and their infants and preschoolers, thereby decreasing the odds of child abuse. These visits also increase the probability of a healthy childhood, which generally influences positive educational outcomes. Higher educational attainment decreases the likelihood of crime. Home visits also assist at-risk pre-adolescents when those visits are geared toward family therapy and parent training. These visits can focus on needed skills of interaction, which can decrease family tension and increase proper supervision.
2. In schools, social skills training as well as teaching thinking skills have been shown to decrease impulsivity and, therefore, crime. Thus, by enhancing children's intellectual and social development, we decrease the odds they will not engage in crime.
3. Vocational training helps curb recidivism in adults. Using rehabilitation programs for recovering drug addicts is both cheaper and produces better results than does incarcerating them.

While incarceration seems to have a slight influence on crime rates, the other programs suggested are more effective and less expensive. For example, using probation in lieu of incarceration, particularly for first-time offenders, shows significantly lower rates of recidivism and decreases the costs of social control.

If policy makers would consider the costs of crime victimization as well as the costs of incarceration, many of these programs will seem like a bargain. However, when someone suggests that we need more outreach to poor children, the mantra is usually "How can we afford it?" We believe that we are at a point where we "cannot *not*" afford it. Therefore, we need to ask, "How can America keep its citizens safe while significantly reducing the population of the Country Called Prison?" Maintaining the status quo is unsustainable. This Country

Called Prison continues to grow even while incarceration rates are dropping because the reach of those affiliated with the criminal justice system is broad. Something has to change or we will follow in the footsteps of many failed empires that preceded us.

CONCLUSION

This chapter provided some big ideas for your consideration and debate. Stakeholders in the current system are unlikely to immediately embrace these ideas because they make money from today's criminal justice processes. Courageous legislation will need to be passed for any of these changes to go into effect.

One thing is certain. America has built a new nation within its own borders called Prison. It is filled with a variety of people: some who are feared, many who are not. Our proposals are for those whom we do not fear. We want to help these people emigrate from the Country Called Prison and reassimilate them in their country of birth—the United States. Implementing our proposals will go a long way toward decreasing the prison population and freeing us all from this self-imposed drain on our people and resources. We created the current system; therefore, we can change it.

CHAPTER 7
Assimilating the Country Called Prison

The only thing necessary for evil to triumph is for good men to do nothing.

Edmund Burke

In this book, we have considered the mass incarceration epidemic in the United States and its latent consequences. Our intention in writing this book has been to provide readers an opportunity to see the situation in a new light. The scope of the problem is significantly larger than most people realize. Furthermore, many people don't care much about this issue. They see themselves as removed from law break-ers and therefore have no sympathy for them. While understandable, this attitude is built on an assumption that people can be thrown away and the resulting consequences won't eventually affect everyone else. In short, the attitude is built on a theory that somehow we are not all connected. However, if ecological and environmental studies teach us anything, it is that we are intimately connected to all things, including criminals.

In the early chapters, we provided information that uncovered the deep underlying sources from which the incarceration mountain has steadily risen. We believe that in America's attempt to provide a safe environment for its citizens, it inadvertently created a new nation within its borders, a country we call Prison. Not only is the Country Called Prison an expensive solution, it also is not working.

Throughout human history, empires have come and gone. Debates over why various empires have collapsed are too complex for this text, but one thing is true. Each empire did eventually fall, and a part of the reason was that some unforeseen force attacked it. We are concerned that the Country Called Prison could be this force in the United States. Why? Because many have already decided that creating this country within our nation is not only justified but vital to our safety. To suggest that the prison industry has gotten out of control is almost un-American.

We are not the first nation to engage in an activity that eventually hurts it. Consider the history of penal colonies. While they seemed like a good idea, they did not always work out so well. Penal colonies were often on islands or in remote places that were badly in need of labor. The idea was to send the "undesirables" to a far-off place and profit from them. In reality, penal colonies were often little more than slave communities. British attempts to export their undesirables to the Americas and Australia had interesting results.

In each case, the intended consequence was to expand the power of the British Empire while allowing economic gains. To do this, the British encouraged migration of "honorable people" but also transported criminals from the homeland. In the case of the United States and Australia, these troublemakers eventually created their own countries and separated from Great Britain. The plan backfired. Contrary to the plan, the empire did not expand, because each "penal colony" developed its own distinct culture, variations of language, and norms and eventually left the home country. The effort to export British problems and culture created individualistic countries that eventually separated from the empire; the separations were often violent and expensive. With the independence of the colonies, the strength of the empire actually weakened. Thus, the goal to export problems and reap profits eventually brought about weakness for the empire. We believe this is happening today in the United States as more and more taxes are paying for the Country Called Prison, and other important services that citizens need, such as education, public health, and good roads, are abating.

As we write this book, Israel is again at war in the Gaza Strip. This confrontation dominates the news. However, the residents of the Country Called Prison outnumber the residents of Israel by a factor of two. Yet nothing is reported about them. Why?

We believe that the United States has, through deliberate action, disenfranchised millions of its own citizens, citizens who could pay taxes, support local schools, and care for their children. Instead, these disenfranchised citizens are residents of the Country Called Prison. We believe they go unnoticed because most people in America simply are not aware of the extent of the problem. Added to this is the fact that some offenders have done unspeakable things to others; sympathy for inmates is hard to muster. Another complicating factor is that many offenders and inmates come from already disenfranchised groups. As we identified in previous chapters, most inmates are poor and disproportionately come from minority groups. They are often mentally ill and poorly educated. They go unnoticed because these types of people in America generally go unnoticed anyway.

Of equal concern are the nearly 50 million children, many of whom with parents who are or were in prison, who are currently growing up in poverty. These children will add to the problem if we do not do something now.

Among the data and theories we have interwoven anecdotes to illustrate that the people in the Country Called Prison have histories, names, and faces. We hope that you have learned that not everyone in prison is to be feared. Many have simply done things that we prefer they had not done.

The book has shown you that the United States is in the midst of an experiment of mass incarceration. America incarcerates its own citizens at extremely high rates, significantly more than other industrialized nations. The idea that this is somehow justified comes from criminology theories about punishment and its efficacy. When one studies the history of punishment, the data suggests that we have reached a point where we can no longer think of alternatives.

We laugh at the notion that years ago people used the dunking stool (punishment whereby a person was tied to a chair and dunked in water) because they thought it was an effective crime deterrent. For the past 30 years the primary method used to deal with those who commit crime is prison. Yet the data we have presented strongly suggest that prison is now as antiquated as the dunking stool. We hope that this book will inspire others to come up with new ideas. Statistics do not lie. The data clearly show that the policy decisions that have led to the mass incarceration of U.S. citizens, and the unintended creation of the Country Called Prison, must change. We must bring down the incarceration mountain now.

We have suggested that the prison system in the United States has become a new nation within America's borders. We have shown that each element of a nation is present in this new country. Prisons have a unified people, geography, history, language, and culture. Those who enter this nation assimilate to it. As they assimilate, they learn behaviors, language, and skills that are not easily transferred outside the razor-wire fence. Thus, a successful prison resident does not make a successful U.S. citizen.

Of course, many of those we send to prison are set up for failure anyway. As we have shown, criminals frequently have many demographic similarities. Perhaps most important, only a minority of prison residents are violent offenders. This point cannot be overstated. The United States spends billions of dollars each year caring for the basic needs of people at whom we are mad. We do not fear these people. This situation cannot continue. It is a waste of lives and money and is completely unsustainable.

We have shown that deprivation and poverty often coexist with abuse and neglect, which significantly decreases a child's ability to develop healthy adult functioning. The children who are headed for the Country Called Prison often grow up in very different environments with very different psychosocial development processes. We suggest that part of the reason for the continued high rate of recidivism is that convicted offenders lack basic psychological and social strengths in the first place. Also, we continue to base solutions and programs on erroneous assumptions: that the offender doesn't want to change and is the only one at fault.

The root of the problem includes an impeded normal childhood development process, as well as social and cultural components that encourage criminality. Therefore, in order to transform the current culture of the Country Called Prison into a more prosocial one, we propose solutions that focus on restoring offenders' psychosocial development process.

The 1970 Stanford Prison Experiment conducted by Phillip Zimbardo showed the way power can influence people's actions.

We hypothesize that prisons have four different subcultural groups that coexist within the prison system. Inmates, security personnel, administrative staff, and licensed professionals all interact within the Country Called Prison. Each group has its own language, customs and values, power, perception of power, and relationship patterns. The different roles that each of these four groups play create a significant power imbalance that helps foster the predation and coercion so common in today's prisons.

When we consider the issue of release, we look at the experience of Avalon, whose story was detailed in chapter five. We wonder why a person who supposedly wants to stay out of prison finds the task so difficult. Her story illuminates the numerous and unintended obstacles that block the way for successful integration back into America for most former prisoners. We identified several innate human needs that must be met for citizens of the Country Call Prison to immigrate to America. Using Abraham Maslow's Hierarchy of Needs model, we suggest ways to make this happen.

We also proposed some "big-picture" ideas. We believe these proposals would help decrease the size of the Country Called Prison. If you believe that people vote with their pocketbooks, then the first proposal in Chapter Six may be the most important. People need to be informed about the costs to incarcerate, and those costs should be borne by the people who make the decisions. Prison today is a free ride for policy makers. But it is not free for taxpayers. However, the manner by which they pay for prison is so diverse that there is really no way to know how much of any one person's tax bill actually goes to prisons. All social systems are designed by people and, therefore, can be changed by people. To reinvent the criminal justice system, we use theories and models from sociology and macro social work to orchestrate legitimate changes.

The current culture of the Country Called Prison is, in itself, the obstacle to change. In this book, though, we have identified and discussed several dimensions of the culture that directly contribute to the coercive power paradigm. We have proposed ways to shift these elements so they create a cooperative and egalitarian paradigm. Our solutions are based on scientific reasoning; many of them have been successful in other areas, such as the education system.

The mission is simple. We want America to be a place where life, liberty, and the pursuit of happiness is available to everyone. Our new paradigm involves going back to old ideas and adding a few new ones.

One of the founding "old ideas" of the United States is that all people have value and are created equal. Everyone deserves a second chance, and no one should be stigmatized for life because of a minor mistake. Another "old idea" is that we are all in this together—"of the people, by the people and for the people." Therefore, accountability for outcomes should apply to the people who break the law as well as the people managing the prison industrial complex.

We know that we will always need prisons because dangerous people in a society must be contained. We also know that even if all of the proposals mentioned in this book are immediately implemented, the emigration from the Country Called Prison will take many years. Most important, though, we need to stop wondering why people commit crimes. The real question is not "why" but "what." What are we going to do to stop the mass incarceration epidemic and tear down the incarceration mountain that we have already built?

We have to believe that addiction, mental illness, and petty crime cannot be punished away. These are social issues, not criminal issues. We need to work on humanizing prisons so that both residents and employees can develop their potential and offenders can return to the community better off than they were when they entered prison.

We need to provide incentives for people not to return to prison. We need to realize that without legitimate opportunities for success, petty criminals are unlikely to change their behavior. We need to move forward with solutions that provide the public with accurate information as to consequences and costs associated with incarceration. We need to create prisons with programs that help prison residents and prepare them for life outside the razor-wire boundaries. Once they are released, we need to provide a reason for former felons to stay out of prison and provide them with real opportunities for change and a real chance to be successful in America.

During a 30-plus-year incarceration binge, the United States unintentionally built a new nation within itself. The intent was to eliminate crime and drug abuse. Unfortunately, a new country was born out of our good intentions.

This new country we call Prison has its own heritage, culture, politics, and values, which does not assimilate well into American culture. This new nation-state has made it difficult for us to continue evolving as a great nation. If the changes proposed in this book, and more like them, are implemented, we believe we can eliminate the Country Called Prison.

It is hard for many in this country to truly see the situation. It is like being at the bottom of a canyon and trying to look up and see the sky. Large mountains rise around and block the view. Incarceration in the United States is such a mountain. We can tear down this incarceration mountain. The mountain does not have to come down all at once. We only have to move one piece at a time. What piece are you willing to pick up?

Summary of Proposals

CHAPTER THREE

Target Population: Nonviolent Offenders

1 Increase Executive Functioning Skills in Prison Residents

1) Strategies
   a) Use online interactive classroom technology to provide prison residents and community-based offenders with curriculum-based instruction for them to learn life skills, executive functioning skills, and psycho-educational material.
   b) Use self-paced, computer educational programs to allow prison residents and community-based offenders to practice life skills, problem solving skills, organizational skills, emotional reasoning skills, abstract reasoning, and brain exercises.
   c) Allow prison residents to use electronic gaming technology to strengthen prosocial attitudes and decision-making skills.
   d) Develop reward system based on outcome-based assessment criteria for prison residents who demonstrate increased executive functioning skills.
   e) Select and train prison residents serving life and/or 20-plus-year sentences to be facilitators for classroom and computer library services.
2) Outcomes
   a) Increase prosocial problem-solving skills, emotional reasoning, frustration management, planning and organization skills,

and effective interpersonal relationship skills in prison residents and community-based offenders.

b) Decrease prison security issues and medical costs resulting from violence.

c) Decrease need for close supervision in community-based programs.

2 Increase Literacy and General Knowledge and Foster Values to Build Character, Improve Parenting Skills, and Participate in Civic Responsibilities

1) Strategies

a) Use interactive online, classroom technology to provide prison residents and community-based offenders opportunities to prepare and test for their GED, enroll in college courses, and take vocational training and classes in parenting, civic education, and character building.

b) Use self-paced computer educational programs to allow prison residents and community-based offenders to practice their skills in parenting, civic education, moral reasoning, and character building.

c) Provide discussion groups for current events and book clubs at different reading levels and varying interests for prison residents and community-based offenders.

d) Develop reward system based on outcome-based assessment criteria for prison residents and community-based offenders who demonstrate increased skills and complete higher education levels.

e) Select and train prison residents with 20-plus-year sentences as facilitators for classroom and computer library services.

2) Outcomes

a) For prison residents and community-based offenders, increase general knowledge, self-discipline, communication skills, coping skills, interest in community endeavors and safety, and prosocial values.

b) For prison residents and community-based offenders, decrease arguments with staff, noncompliance with rules, contraband, and disruptive behavior in prisons.

3 Modify Prison Environments to Intrinsically Habilitate Delayed Psychosocial Skills

1) Strategies
   a) Assess and separate sociopathic and violent prison residents from nonviolent residents.
   b) Establish housing units based on developmental age groups and length of sentence.
   c) Use discernment in housing assignments for prison residents.
   d) Develop appropriate milieu operational policies and procedures for each unit typology.
   e) Select and train at least two prison resident facilitators who are serving life sentences (per unit) to act as stabilizing mentors and coaches.
2) Outcomes
   a) Increase prison residents' ability to care for themselves and others appropriately.
   b) Increase prison residents' ability to manage their frustration with changes and challenges.
   c) Increase prison residents' accountability and responsibility for their actions.
   d) Decrease inappropriate attention-seeking behavior and manipulation strategies.

CHAPTER FOUR

Target Population: Nonviolent Offenders

1 Modify Prison Environments to Promote Cooperative Behavior and Prosocial American Values

1) Strategies
   a) Increase prosocial behaviors, cooperation, and compassion.
      i) Develop secure ways for prison residents to perform acts of charity and kindness under a supervised structure to prevent manipulation.
      ii) Develop milieu operational procedures that encourage civic and social responsibility based on proven methods used in American school systems.

iii) Allow and encourage, through intrinsic and extrinsic reward systems, both prison residents and employees to follow the five mechanisms of cooperation: direct reciprocity, indirect reciprocity, spatial selection, multilevel selection, and kinship selection.

b) Increase personal pride and self-respect in prison residents.

i) Remove objectifying language from policy and procedures by using words that are affirming of human dignity.

ii) Insist that all people use niceties (please, thank you, excuse me) and greetings that are respectful (such as Mr. Smith or Ms. Jones, rather than someone's last name only).

iii) Allow and encourage (via a reward system) prison residents to do good deeds, engage in acts of good citizenship (such as voluntarily keeping an area clean), make resolutions and follow up on them, and share their prosocial knowledge and experience with others (through mentoring activities).

c) Decrease learned helplessness and institutionalization.

i) Increase opportunities in which prison residents can make choices regarding their living and working environments and their personal lives.

ii) Reduce the need for "indigent" services—find ways to allow residents to earn things they need through legitimate activities.

d) Establish multidisciplinary unit teams.

i) Create unit teams that represent security, case management, social work (mental health, chaplain, and so on), and prison residents that have the power to establish unit rules and procedures that provide structure and social development for the unique needs of each unit, as well as complement the larger organization.

ii) Unit teams should teach and model civic responsibility through unit meetings and democratic processes with prison residents.

e) Increase employees' knowledge and understanding of social science principles.

i) Encourage employees to obtain at least an associate degree in one of the social sciences (psychology, sociology, social work, criminal justice). Reward them when they do.

    ii) Encourage management personnel to obtain a bachelor's degree in social sciences or public administration. Reward them when they do.

   iii) Encourage senior management to obtain a master's degree in criminal justice or public administration. Reward them when they do.

   iv) Expand employee training programs to include information on childhood development, social psychology, mental illness and addictions, diplomacy, mentoring and coaching skills, and egalitarian principles.

    v) Reward staff, both intrinsically and extrinsically, who practice the skills required to shift the coercive culture that currently exists within the criminal justice system to a more cooperative and altruistic one.

2) Outcomes
  a) Increase respect, cooperation, altruism, and civic and egalitarian behavior throughout the prison system.
  b) Decrease coercive and predatory prison milieu

CHAPTER FIVE

Target Population: Prison Residents Discharging

1 Provide Prison Residents Who Are Discharging with the Immediate and Essential Needs to Reenter Society Successfully and with Dignity

1) Strategies
  a) Develop discharge planners for all prison residents six months to one year from release.
  b) Provide prison residents the opportunity to join small discharge planning groups facilitated by prison resident facilitators and/or community volunteers.
  c) Train selected prison residents and community volunteers to become discharge mentors.

d) Provide discharging prison residents with legal documentation (driver's license or state ID card, birth certificate, and Social Security card) prior to release.

e) Provide services for discharging residents to seek employment prior to discharge and services for post-discharge to ensure that all residents capable of working have an adequate job within a month of release.

f) Allow prison residents who will not be able to work due to disability or mental illness to apply for Social Security disability prior to release so that income is available within the first month of release.

g) Plan for discharging residents to have adequate housing, clothing, personal supplies, and medication for at least one year.

h) Schedule appointments for medical/mental health services prior to release.

i) Provide or plan transportation arrangements for discharging residents to seek employment, go to appointments, and attend community activities.

2) Outcomes

a) Increase the reintegration success rate to 90% for 3 years and 80% for 5 years.

b) Decrease the population of the Country Called Prison by 80% within 10 years

CHAPTER SIX

Target Population: Criminal Justice System

1 Shift the Costs of Incarcerating Nonviolent Offenders to Community Stakeholders

1) Strategies

a) Each county pays to incarcerate nonviolent offenders.

b) The county district attorney's office acquires funds to pay for nonviolent offenders' incarceration from real estate taxes.

c) State taxes will fund offender diversionary programs that all counties can use. Programs will be adequately funded and based on successful outcome strategies.

d) Strategies will be a tax-neutral process.
e) Establish within the county district attorney's office a department of social work that will manage the funds, conduct pre-sentence assessments, and determine if the offender will go to a diversionary program or be incarcerated. The department will also produce reports identifying the costs and success rates.

2) Outcomes
   a) Increase in diversion and treatment programs moves offenders from being tax users to taxpayers.
   b) Increase in healthy families.
   c) Decrease in recidivism and costs associated with incarceration.

2 Create a Criminal Justice Accounting System That Identifies True Costs and Informs the Public on a Regular Basis

1) Strategies
   a) Create a statewide computer system that allows tracking of all (or most) of the collateral effects of an offender's conviction.
   b) State and community service agencies (mental health, housing, and so on) that offer services to family members of the convicted person will enter data into the system.
   c) State and community service agencies offering services to community-based convicted offenders and former prisoners will enter data into the system.
   d) The system can be monitored by the Department of Corrections or the state attorney general's office.
   e) Statistical and analytical reports, similar to reports generated by the U.S. Department of Justice, should be compiled at least annually.

2) Outcomes
   a) Gather more data regarding true costs of the criminal justice system for use in social policy decision making and taxpayer knowledge.
   b) Decrease ineffective social policy and justice system reform due to incomplete information.

3 Increase Judicial Discretion and Diversionary Options for Adults and Juveniles

1) Strategies
   a) For adults, decrease use of coercive plea bargaining.
   b) For adults, decrease use of determinate sentencing.
   c) For adults, increase use of jury nullification.
   d) For juveniles, decrease use of zero-tolerance school policies.
   e) For juveniles, increase the use of progressive discipline model that helps juveniles complete school, work, and attend diversionary programs and community activities.
   f) For juveniles, increase diversionary programs with adequate funding and those based on outcome-driven success strategies.
2) Outcomes
   a) Increase treatment and social habilitation programs that transition offenders from a criminal lifestyle to a healthy, civic lifestyle.
   b) Decrease costs of incarceration, recidivism, and crime.

4 Stop Criminalizing People with Addictions and Mental Illness

1) Strategies
   a) Increase treatment programs that prevent criminal behavior, both inpatient and outpatient, for people with mental illness and addictions.
   b) Increase diversionary programs for people with mental illness and addictions who have committed nonviolent crimes.
   c) Increase drug court and mental health courts for offenders who need frequent monitoring. Make the programs practical so that clients can work or attend school.
   d) Create a mental health and addiction recovery system that provides a continuum of care, not stopgap measures.
2) Outcomes
   a) Increase healthy lifestyles for people with mental illness and addictions.
   b) Decrease the number of people with drug addictions.

c) Decrease the higher costs accrued from coping with this group via the criminal justice system.

5 Make It Easy for People from the Country Called Prison to Successfully Migrate Back to the United States

1) Strategies
   a) Stop labeling people who discharge from prison or community-based correctional programs.
   b) Create automatic criminal record expungement.
   c) Increase ways for formerly convicted citizens to obtain adequate employment; decrease employment restrictions and practices.
   d) Develop reintegration support services for citizens convicted of crimes and for former prison residents.
      i) Start reintegration units that specialize in preparing prisoners for successful re-entry.
      ii) Create a corrections department of social work that assists all former prisoners with meeting their basic needs, such as work, housing, food, clothing, treatment, community involvement, and education.
2) Outcomes
   a) Increase success rate for citizens transitioning from a criminal lifestyle to a healthy lifestyle and active participation in American society.
   b) Decrease costs and problems associated with crime and recidivism.

6 Focus on Measuring Success and Fund the Most Effective Programs

1) Strategies
   a) Measure success, not failure, in all criminal justice data analysis and reports.
   b) Develop strategies and measurable goals that focus on improvement, not just decreasing failure.

c) Fund prisons, government agencies, and social service agencies that have a proven success record for transitioning citizens from a criminal lifestyle to a prosocial lifestyle.

2) Outcomes
   a) Increase successful, evidenced-based programs that assist citizens in becoming prosocial, active participants in society.
   b) Decrease spending that does not get results.
   c) Decrease costs and problems associated with crime and recidivism.

BIBLIOGRAPHY

Ainsworth, M., & Bell, S. (1970). Attachment, exploration, and separation: Illustrated by the behavior of one-year-olds in strange situation. *Child Development, 41*, 49–67.

Alexander, K., Holupka, S., & Pallas, A. (1987). Social background and academic determinants of two-year versus four-year college attendance: Evidence from two cohorts a decade apart. *American Journal of Education, 96*, 56–80.

Alexander, M., & West, C. (2012). *New Jim Crow: Mass incarceration in the age of colorblindness.* New York: New Press.

Al-Fadhili, H., & Singh, M. (2006). Teachers' expectancy and efficacy as correlates of school achievement in Delta, Mississippi. *Journal of Personnel Evaluation in Education, 19*, 51–67.

Alston, F. (2010, July). Latch key children. education.com. Retrieved from http://www.education.com/reference/article/Ref_Latch_Key_Children/

American Psychiatric Association. (2013). *The diagnostic and statistical manual of mental disorders* (5th ed.). Washington, DC: American Psychiatric Association.

ASCA. (2010). Staff to inmate ratio survey. American Society of Correctional Administrators. Retrieved from http://www.asca.net/system/assets/attachments/471/Staff_to_Inmate_Ratio_Survey.pdf

Austin, J. (2000). *Juveniles in adult prison and jails.* Washington, DC: Bureau of Justice Assistance.

Austin, J., & Irwin, J. (2001). *It's about time: America's imprisonment binge.* Belmont, CA: Wadsworth/Thomson Learning.

Austin, J., Johnson, K., & Gregoriou, M. (2000). *Juveniles in adult prisons and jails; A national assessment.* Washington, DC: U.S. Department of Justice, Bureau of Justice Assistance.

Bandura, A. (1963). *Social learning and personality development.* New York: Holt, Rinehart, and Winston.

Baumrind, D. (1967). Child-care practices anteceding three patterns of preschool behavior. *Genetic Psychology Monographs, 75*, 43–88.

Baumrind, D. (1991). The influence of parenting style on adolescent competence and substance use. *Journal of Early Adolescence, 11*, 56–95.

Beccaria, C. ([1764] 1963). *Essays on crimes and punishments* (H. Paolucci, Trans.). Indianapolis, IN: Bobbs-Merrill.

Beck, A., Rantala, R., & Rexroat, J. (2013a). *Sexual victimization reported by adult correctional authorities, 2009–2011 (NCJ 243904)*. Washington, DC: U.S. Department of Justice, Bureau of Justice Statistics.

Beck, A., Rantala, R., & Rexroat, J. (2013b). *Survey of sexual violence in adult correctional facilities, 2009–2011 (NCJ 244227)*. Washington, DC: U.S. Department of Justice, Bureau of Justice Statistics.

Bentham, J. ([1789] 1970). *An introduction to the principles of morals and legislation* (J. Burns & H. Hart, Eds.). London: Athlone Publishing.

Blackburn, C., Bonas, S., Spencer, N., et al. (2004). Parental smoking and passive smoking in infants: Fathers matter too. *Health Education Research, 20,* 185–194.

Blomberg, T., & Lucken, K. (2010). *American penology: A history of control* (2nd ed.). Edison, NJ: Transaction Publishers.

Bonczar, T. (2003). *Prevalence of imprisonment in the U.S. population, 1974–2001 (NCJ 197976)*. Washington, DC: U.S. Department of Justice, Bureau of Justice Statistics.

Bonczar, T., & Beck, A. (1997). *Lifetime likelihood of going to state or federal prison.* Washington, DC: U.S Department of Justice, Bureau of Justice Statistics.

Bowlby, J. (1960). Separation anxiety. *International Journal of Psychoanalysis, 41,* 89–113.

Braithwaite, J. (1989). *Crime, shame and reintegration.* New York: Cambridge University Press.

Branden, N. (1994). *The six pillars of self-esteem.* New York: Bantam Books.

Brooks-Gunn, J., Duncan, G., Klebanove, P., & Sealand, N. (1993). Do neighborhoods influence child and adolescent development? *American Journal of Sociology, 99,* 353–395.

Bureau of Labor Statistics (2012). *Occupational outlook handbook; 2012 corrections officers.* Bureau of Labor Statistics. Retrieved from http://www.bls.gov/ooh/protective-service/correctional-officers.htm

Burke, K. (1954). *Permanence and change* (2nd ed.). Berkeley: University of California Press.

Butcher, S., Graham, J. Ben-Porath, Y., et al. (2001). *Minnesota Multiphasic Personality Inventor,* 2nd ed. San Antonio, TX: Pearson.

CA-EDU. (1989). *Characteristics of middle grade students.* California Department of Education. Retrieved from http://pubs.cde.ca.gov/tcsii/documentlibrary/characteristicsmg.aspx

Campbell, D., Levinson, M., & Hess, F. (2012). *Making civics count: Citizenship education for a new generation.* Cambridge, MA: Harvard Education Press.

Carson, E., & Golinelli, D. (2013). *Prisoners in 2012: Trends in admissions and releases, 1991–2012 (NCJ 243920)*. Washington, DC: U.S. Department of Justice, Bureau of Justice Statistics.

Carson, E., & Sabol, W. (2012). *Prisoners in 2011 (NCJ 239808)*. Washington, DC: U.S. Department of Justice, Bureau of Justice Statistics.

Centers for Disease Control and Prevention. (n.d.). *Youth online: High school years*. Centers of Disease Control and Prevention. Retrieved from http://www.samhsa.gov/data/nsduh/2012summnatfinddettables/nationalfindings/nsduhresults2012.htm#ch2.3

Centers for Disease Control and Prevention. (2014, August 11). *2010, United States suicide injury death and rates*. Centers for Disease Control and Prevention. Retrieved from http://webappa.cdc.gov/cgi-bin/broker.exe

Centers for Disease Control and Prevention. (2011). Trends in the prevalence of marijuana, cocaine, and other illegal drug use: National YRBS: 1991–2011. Centers for Disease Control and Prevention. Retrieved from http://www.cdc.gov/healthyyouth/yrbs/pdf/us_drug_trend_yrbs.pdf

Central Intelligence Agency. (2013). *CIA world fact book: Population rankings*. Central Intelligence Agency. Retrieved from www.CIA.gov: http://cia.gov/library/publications/the-world-fact-book/rankorder/2119rank.html

Champion, D., Merlo, A., & Benekos, P. (2013). *The juvenile justice system: Delinquency, processing and the law*. Upper Saddle River, NJ: Pearson.

Chomsky, N. (1975). *Reflections on language*. New York: Pantheon Books.

Christian, S. (1998). *With liberty for some: 500 years of imprisonment in America*. Boston, MA: Northeastern University Press.

Clear, T. (2007). *Imprisoning communities: How mass incarceration makes disadvantaged neighborhoods worse*. New York: Oxford University Press.

Clemmer, D. (1940). *The prison community*. New York: Rinehart.

Code of Hammurabi. (n.d.). Retrieved from http://eawc.evansville.edu/anthology/hammurabi.htm

Collier, J. R., Rosaldo, M., & Yanagisako, S. (1982). Is there a family? In B. Thorne (Ed.), *Rethinking the family: Some feminist questions* (pp. 25–39). Boston: Northeastern University Press.

Cooper, A., Durose, M., & Snyder, H. (2014). *Recidivism of prisoners released in 30 states in 2005: Patterns from 2005 to 2010*. Washington, DC: U.S. Department of Justice, Bureau of Justice Statistics.

Covey, S. (1989). *The 7 habits of highly effective people: Powerful lessons in personal change*. New York: Simon and Schuster.

Davis, A. T. (2008). *The declining number of youth in custody in the juvenile justice system*. Washington, DC: National Council on Crime and Delinquency.

Dawson, P., & Guare, R. (2010). *Executive skills in children and adolescents: A practical guide to assessment and intervention* (2nd ed.). New York: Guilford Press.

Delaney, C., & Kaspin, D. (2011). *Investigating culture; An experiential introduction to anthropology*. Chichester, West Sussex, UK: John Wiley & Sons.

Devers, L. (2014). *Plea and charge bargaining, research summary*. Washington, DC: U.S. Department of Justice, Bureau of Justice Assistance.

Directory of Representatives. (n.d.). Retrieved from www.house.gov: http://www.house.gov/representatives/#state_id

Ditton, P. M. (2006). *Mental health and treatment of inmates and probationers.* Washington, DC: U.S. Department of Justice, Bureau of Justice Statistics.

Dube, S., Felitti, V., Dong, M., et al. (2003). Childhood abuse, neglect, and household dysfunction and the risk of illicit drug use. *Pediatrics, 111,* 564–572.

Durose, M., Cooper, A., & Snyder, H. (2014). *Recidivism of prisoners released in 30 states in 2005: Patterns from 2005 to 2010.* Washington, DC: U.S. Department of Justice, Bureau of Justice Statistics.

Dynarski, S. (2003). Does aid matter? Measuring the effect of student aid on college attendance and completion. *American Economic Review, 93,* 279–288.

Edin, K., & Kefalas, M. (2005). *Promises I can keep: Why poor women put motherhood before marriage.* Berkeley: University of California Press.

Edin, K., & Lein, L. (1997). Welfare, work, and economic survival strategies. *American Sociological Review, 62,* 253–266.

Equal Justice Initiative. (2013). Retrieved from: http://eji.org/childrenprison

Erickson, P., & Erickson, S. (2008). *Crime, punishment, and mental illness.* New Brunswick, NJ: Rutgers University Press.

Erikson, E. H. (1959). *Identity and the life cycle.* New York: International Universities Press.

Farrington, K. (2000). *History of punishment & torture: A journey through the dark side of justice.* London: Hamlyn.

Fay, D., Borrill, C., Amir, Z., Haward, R., & West, M. (2006). Getting the most out of multidisciplinary teams: A multi-sample study of team innovation in health care. *British Psychological Society,* 553–567.

Federal Bureau of Prisons. (n.d.). Retrieved from http://www.bop.gov/about/statistics/statistics_inmate_race.jsp

Federal Bureau of Prisons. (n.d.). Retrieved from http://www.bop.gov/about/statistics/statistics_inmate_ethnicity.jsp

Felson, M. (1998). *Crime and everyday life.* Thousand Oaks, CA: Pine-Forge Press.

Feuerstein, R. E. (1980). *Instrumental enrichment: An intervention program for cognitive modifiability.* Glenview, IL: Scott, Foresman & Co.

Fisher, W., Silver, E., & Wolff, N. (2006). Beyond criminalization: Toward a criminologically informed framework for mental health policy and service research. *Administrative Policy Mental Health and Mental Health Services Research, 33,* 544–547.

Franco, L. J., & Hill, D. (Producer), & Carpenter, J. (Director). (1981). *Escape from New York* [Motion picture]. United States: Goldcrest Films.

Frank, D., Augustyn, M., Knight, W., et al. (2001). Growth, development and behavior in early childhood following prenatal cocaine exposure: A systematic review. *JAMA, 285,* 1613–1625.

Freedmen. (2013). Civil War home. Retrieved from http://www.civilwarhome.com/freedmen.htm

Garfinkel, H. (1956). Conditions of successful degradation ceremonies. *American Journal of Sociology, 61*, 420–424.

Girard, R. (1986). *The scapegoat.* Baltimore, MD: Johns Hopkins University Press.

Glaze, J. E., & James, L. E. (2006). *Mental health problems of prison and jail inmates.* Washington, DC: U.S. Department of Justice, Bureau of Justice Statistics.

Glaze, L., & Parks, E. (2012). *Correctional population in the United States, 2011 (NCJ 239972).* Washington, DC: U.S. Department of Justice, Bureau of Justice Statistics.

Golding, W. (1954). *Lord of the flies.* New York: Perigee Books.

Gorski, T. (2014). *Post incarceration syndrome.* Retrieved from www.tgorski.com: http://www.tgorski.com/criminal_justice/cjs_pics_&_relapse.htm

Gottfredson, M., & Hirschi, T. (1990). *A general theory of crime.* Stanford, CA: Stanford University Press.

Greenspan, S. (1997). *The growth of the mind.* New York: Addison-Wesley.

Guerino, P. H. (2011). *Prisoners in 2010.* Washington, DC: U.S. Department of Justice, Bureau of Justice Statistics.

Hansen, S. (2013). *The executive functioning workbook for teens.* Oakland, CA: Harbinger Publications.

Hare, R. D. (2004). *Psychopathylogy Checklist–Revised,* 2nd ed. North Tonawanda, NH: Multi-Health Systems.

Harlow, C. (2003). *Education and correctional populations (NCJ 195670).* Washington, DC: U.S. Department of Justice, Bureau of Justice Statistics.

Harrison, L. E. (2006). *The central liberal truth: How politics can change a culture and save it from itself.* New York: Oxford University Press.

Haveman, R., & Smeeding, T. (2007). The role of higher education in social mobility. *Opportunity in America, 16*, 125–150.

Hirschi, T. (1969). *Causes of delinquency.* Berkeley: University of California Press.

History of Prisons. www.prisonhistory.net/prison-history/history-of-prisons/ (accessed May 12, 2014).

Hughes, T., & Wilson, J. J. (2004). *Reentry trends in the U.S.* Washington, DC: U.S. Department of Justice, Bureau of Justice Statistics.

Humans Rights Watch. (2006). Retrieved from http://www.hrw.org/news/2006/09/05/us-number-mentally-ill-prisons-quadrupled

Janis, I. (1972). *Victims of groupthink.* New York: Houghton Mifflin.

Jencks, C. (1994). *The homeless.* Cambridge, MA: Harvard University Press.

Johnston, N. (2000). *Forms of constraint: History of prison architecture.* Champaign: University of Illinois Press.

Jones, D., & Glaze, L. (2006). *Mental health problems of prison and jail inmates* *(NCJ 213600).* Washington, DC: U.S. Department of Justice, Bureau of Justice Statistics.

Joos, M. (1967). *The five clocks: A linguistic excursion into the five styles of English usage.* New York: Houghton Mifflin Harcourt.

Jung, C., & Campbell, J. (1976). *The portable Jung, a compilation.* New York: Penguin Books.

Keeshin, B. R., Cronholm, P. F., & Strawn, J. R. (2011). Physiologic changes associated with violence and abuse exposure: An examination of related medical conditions. *Trauma, Violence & Abuse, 13,* 41–56.

Kennedy, R. (2014). *School size matters.* Retrieved from http://privateschool. about.com/od/choosingaschool/qt/sizematters.htm

Kesteren, J. V., Mayhew, P., & Nieuwbeerta, P. (2000). *Criminal victimization in seventeen industrialized countries: Key findings from the 2000 international crime victimization survey.* The Hague: Ministry of Justice, WODC.

Kong, A., & Fitch, E. (2002). Using book clubs to engage culturally and linguistically diverse learners in reading, writing, and talking about books. *Reading Teacher, 56,* 352–362.

Koteskey, R. (2014). *What missionaries ought to know about culture stress.* Missionary Care. Retrieved from http://www.missionarycare.com/brochures/br_culturestress.htm

Kozol, J. (1991). *Savage inequalities: Children in America's schools.* New York: Crown Publishers.

Kuklinksy, M. R., & Weinstein, R. S. (2001). Classroom and developmental differences in a path model of teacher expectancy effects. *Child Development, 72,* 1554–1579.

Lamb, H., & Weinberger, L. (2005). The shift of psychiatric inpatient care from hospitals to jails and prisons. *Journal of the American Academic Psychiatry Law, 33,* 529–534.

Lewis, C. (2006). Treating incarcerated women: Gender matters. *Psychiatric Clinics of North America, 29,* 773–789.

Lickona, T. (1992). *Educating for character: How our schools can teach respect and responsibility.* New York: Bantam Books.

Looman, M. (2010). Establishing parental capability as a legal competency in child maltreatment cases. *Annals of the American Psychotherapy Association, 13,* 45–52.

Looman. M. (2012). Grounded strategies that improve self-efficacy. In K. Trotter (Ed.), *Harnessing the power of equine assisted counseling; Adding animal assisted therapy to your practice* (pp. 253–262). New York: Routledge.

Lyons, L. (2004). *History of punishment: Judicial penalties from ancient times to the present day.* Darby, PA: Diane Publishing.

Marquis, P. (1992). Family dysfunction as a risk factor in the development of antisocial behavior. *Psychological Reports, 71,* 468–470.

Martinson, R. (1974). What works? Questions and answers about prison reform. *Public Interest*, 22–54.

Maslow, A. (1954). *Motivation and personality*. New York: Harper Publishing.

McDonough, P. (2009, October). *TV viewing among kids at an eight-year high*. Nielsenwire. Retrieved from http://blog.nielsen.com/nielsenwire/media_entertainment/tv-viewing-among-kids-at-an-eight-year-high

McRaney, D. (2013). *You are now less dumb*. New York: Gotham Books.

Meisler, A. (1996). Trauma, PTSD and substance abuse. *PTSD Research Quarterly*, 7, 1–6.

Messner, S., & Rosenfield, R. (2008). *Crime and the American dream*. Belmont, CA: Wadsworth.

Milgram, S. (1965). Some conditions of obedience and disobedience to authority. *Human Relations*, 18, 57–76.

Millon, T., Millon, C., Davis, R., & Grossman, S. (2009). *Millon Clinical Multi-axial Inventory*, 3rd ed. San Antonio, TX: Pearson.

Moffitt, T. E., & Caspi, A. (2001). Childhood predictors differentiate life-course-persistent and adolescence-limited antisocial pathways among males and females. *Development and Psychopathology*, 13, 355–375.

Montano-Harmon, M. R. (1991, May). Discourse features of written Mexican Spanish: Current research in contrastive rhetoric and its implications. *Hispania*, 74, 417–425.

Morey, L. (2007). *Personality Assessment Inventory*. Lutz, FL: PAR.

Mruk, C. J. (2006). *Self-esteem research, theory, and practice* (3rd ed.). New York: Springer Publishing.

NAMI. (2014). *CIT toolkit: Criminalization of the mentally ill*. Retrieved from http://www.nami.org/Template.cfm?Section+CIT&Template=/ContentManagement/ContntDisplay.cfm&contentID=57465

National Treatment Improvement Evaluation Study. (1997). Retrieved from http://www.icpsr.umich.edu/files/SAMHDA/NTIES/NTIES-PDF/nties-fnl.pdf

NCCP. (n.d.). National Center for Children in Poverty. Retrieved from http://nccp.org/publication/pub-1074.html

Noonan, M. (2012). *Mortality in local jails and state prisons, 2000–2010; Statistical tables (NCJ 239911)*. Washington, DC: U.S. Department of Justice, Bureau of Justice Statistics.

Nowak, M., & Highfield, R. (2011). *SuperCooperators: Altruism, evolution, and why we need each other to succeed*. New York: Free Press.

Nowak, M., & Sigmund, K. (1998). Evolution of indirect reciprocity by image scoring: The dynamics of indirect reciprocity. *Nature*, 393, 573–577.

Numbers USA. Retrieved from www.numberusa.org

Office of Disease Prevention and Health Promotion (2014, August 9). Retrieved from http://www.health.gov/phfunctions/public.htm

Payne, R. K. (2005). *A framework for understanding poverty*. Highlands, TX: aha! Process, Inc.

Petersilia, J. (2005). Hard time: Ex-offenders returning home after prison. *Corrections Today, 67*, 66–71.

Petersilia, J. (2011). Beyond the prison bubble. *NIJ Journal, 268*, 26–31.

Peterson, C. M. (1995). *Learned helplessness: A theory for the age of personal control*. New York: Oxford University Press.

Pew Charitable Trust. (2007). *When offenders break the rules: Smart responses to parole and probation violations*. Retrieved from http://www.pewtrusts.org/uploadedFiles/wwwpewtrustorg/Reports/sentencing_and_corrections/Condition-Violators-Briefing.pdf

Pew Charitable Trusts. (2013). *Sentencing and corrections; Condition violators briefing*. Retrieved from http://www.pewtrusts.org/uploaded-Files/wwwpewtrustsorg/Reports/sentencing_and_corrections/Condition-Violators-Briefing.pdf

Prins, S. (2011). Does transinstitutionalization explain the overrepresentation of people with serious mental illnesses in the criminal justice system? *Community Mental Health Journal, 47*, 716–722.

Pruitt, D., & AACP. (1999). *Your adolescent: Emotional, behavioral, and cognitive development from early adolescence through the teen years*. New York: Harper Collins.

Reckless, W. (1970). *Containment theory*. New York: John Wiley.

Reiman, J. (1998). *The rich get richer and the poor get prison: Ideology, class and criminal justice*. Boston, MA: Allyn and Bacon.

Rideout, V., Foehr, U., & Roberts, D. (2010, January). *Generation M2: Media in the lives of 8–18 year-olds*. Kaiser Family Foundation. Retrieved from http://www.kff.org/entmedia/upload/8010.pdf

Rodrigues, L., & Lockwood, D. (2011). Leprosy now: Epidemiology, progress, challenges, and research gaps. *Lancet Infectious Diseases, 11*, 464–470.

Roscigno, V., Tomaskovic-Devey, D., & Crowley, M. (2006). Education and the inequalities of place. *Social Forces, 84*, 2121–2145.

Rose, D., & Clear, T. (2001). Incarceration, reentry and social capital: Social networks in the balance. Federal HHS Project: *From prison to home: The effect of incarceration and re-entry on children, families and communities*. Washington, DC: U.S. Department of Health and Human Services.

Ross, J., & Richards, S. (2009). *Beyond bars: Rejoining society after prison*. New York: Penguin Group.

Ross, L. (1977). The intuitive psychologist and his shortcomings: Distortions in the attribution process. In L. Berkowitz (Ed.), *Advances in experimental social psychology* (pp. 173–220). New York: Academic Press.

Ryan, W. (1971). *Blaming the victim*. NY: Pantheon Books.

Samenow, S. (2004). *Inside the criminal mind* (rev. and updated ed.). New York: Crown Publishers.

Schmitt, J. W. (2010). *The high budgetary cost of incarceration.* Washington, DC: Center for Economic Policy and Research.

Schweinhart, L. (2002). *The High/Scope Perry Preschool Study through age 40: Summary, conclusions and frequently asked questions.* High/Scope Educational Research Foundation. Retrieved from http://www.highscope.org/productDetail.asp?intproductID=2164

Scott, C. (2010). *Handbook of correctional mental health* (2nd ed.). Washington, DC: American Psychiatric Publishing.

Seligman, M. (1975). *Helplessness: On depression, development, and death.* San Francisco, CA: W. H. Freeman.

Sherman, L., Gottfedson, D., MacKenzie, D., et al. (1998). *Preventing crime: What works, what doesn't, what's promising.* Washington, DC: U.S. Department of Justice, National Institute of Justice.

Singer, M. (2013). *Prison rape: An American institution.* Santa Barbara, CA: Praeger.

Skiba, R. (2000). *Zero tolerance, zero evidence: An analysis of school disciplinary practice.* Bloomington: Indiana Education Policy Center.

Snyder, M. (2013). *The beginning of the end.* Washington, DC: Author.

Solomon, A. (2012). *In search of a job: Criminal records as barriers to employment.* National Institute of Justice. Retrieved from http://www.nij.gov/journals/270/criminal-records.htm#note1

Stephan, J. (2005). *Census of state and federal correctional facilities.* Retrieved from http://www.bjs.gov/content/pub/pdf/csfcf05.pdf

Stephan, J. (2008). *Census of state and federal correctional facilities, 2005 (NCJ 222182).* Washington, DC: U.S. Department of Justice, Bureau of Justice Statistics.

Storti, C., & Bennhold-Samaan, L. (1997). *Culture matters; The Peace Corps cross-cultural workbook.* Washington, DC: Peace Corps Information Collection and Exchange; T0087.

Substance Abuse and Mental Health Services Administration (SAMHSA). (2012). *Results from the 2012 National Survey on Drug Use and Health: Summary of national findings.* U.S. Department of Health & Human Services. Retrieved from http://www.samhsa.gov/data/nsduh/2012summnatfinddettables/nationalfindings/nsduhresults2012.htm#ch2.3

Sutherland, E. (1947). *Principles of criminology.* New York: Lippincott.

Sykes, G. (1958). *The society of captives: A study of a maximum-security prison.* Princeton, NJ: Princeton University Press.

Sykes, G., & Matza, D. (1957). Techniques of neutralization: A theory of delinquency. *American Sociological Review, 22,* 664–670.

Tarullo, A. (2012). Effects of child maltreatment on the developing brain. In T. LaLiberte & T. Crudo, *Child welfare 360: Using a developmental approach in child welfare practice* (p. 11). Minneapolis, MN: Center for Advanced Studies in Child Welfare, University of Minnesota.

Travis, J. M. (2005). *Families left behind: The hidden costs of incarceration and reentry.* Washington, DC: Urban Institute, Justice Policy Center.

U.S. Census. (n.d.). U.S. Census quick facts. Retrieved from http://quickfacts. census.gov/qfd/states/00000.html

U.S. Census. (n.d.). Popclock. Retrieved from www.census.gov/popclock

U.S. Census. (n.d.). U.S. Census 2010. Retrieved from http://www.census. gov/2010census/

U.S. Census. (2012). *The 2012 statistical abstract: State rankings.* Retrieved from http://www.census.gov/compendia/statab/rankings.html

Visher, C., Debus, S., & Yahner, J. (2008). *Employment after prison: A longitudinal study of releases in three states.* Washington, DC: Urban Institute, Justice Policy Center.

Wakefield, S., & Wildeman, C. (2014). *Children of the prison boom: Mass incarceration and the future of American inequality.* New York: Oxford University Press.

Waldram, J. (2009). Challenges of prison ethnography. *Anthropology News, 50,* 4–5.

Weber, M. (1968). Basic sociological terms. In G. Roth & C. Wittich (Eds.), *Economy and society* (pp. 3–62). Berkeley: University of California Press.

Wedge, C., Saldanka, C., Baldo, M., & Carlee, J. (Directors). (2002). *Ice Age.* USA: 20th Century Fox.

Weikart, D. (1985). An early education project that changed students lives: The Perry school program 20 years later. *Education Digest, 51,* 32–35.

Western, B., & Pettit, B. (2010). Incarceration and social inequality. *Daedalus, 139,* 8–19.

Wilson, W. (1987). *The truly disadvantaged: The inner city, the underclass, and public policy.* Chicago, IL: University of Chicago Press.

Wolfe, M. (2013, July 28). From PTSD to prison: Why veterans become criminals. *U.S. News.*

World Economic Outlook Database. (n.d.). *World economic and financial surveys.* Retrieved from http://www.imf.org/external/pubs/ft/weo/2014/01/weodata/index.aspx

World Prison Brief. (2013). Retrieved from https://www.cia.gov/library/publications/the-world-factbook/rankorder/2119rank.html

Zimbardo, P. (2004). The social psychology of good and evil: Understanding how good people are transformed into perpetrators. In A. G. Miller (Ed.), *The social psychology of good and evil* (pp. 21–50). New York: Guilford Press.

Zukerman, B., Frank, D. A., Hingson, R., et al. (1989). Effects of maternal marijuana and cocaine use on fetal growth. *New England Journal of Medicine, 320,* 762–768.

INDEX

Note: Page numbers in *italics* refer to material found in graphs, charts or maps.

detached accountability, 163
determinate sentencing use, 169–170
deterrence
    components necessary for, 6
    general, 4–5
    specific, 5–6
Differential Association Theory
    (Sutherland), 57
discharged prisoner difficulties (case
    study). *See also* proposals for prisoner
    reentry to society
    adjustment to freedom, 134
    adult self, development of, 152
    change, resistance to, 139–140
    childhood trauma and, 132
    clothing needs, 137
    cognitive dissonance, occurrence of, 139–140
    communication/translation issues,
        145–146
    community support, need for, 153
    coping strategies, 143
    ego-identity, role of, 138
    employment skills, 149
    food stamp/Medicaid, applying for, 148
    housing choices, 138
    ID, lack of legal, 136, 142, 145
    income/employment sources,
        143–145, *144*
    learned helplessness of, 149
    nurturance, role of, 137–138, 139
    parole issues, 143, 149
    poor attachment, results of, 134–135
    pre-release psychotherapy, 132
    problem solving methods/skills, 141, 153
    psychosocial goals, 147–148, 201
    release from prison, 133
    returning home, 137
    role-models, need for, 151
    self-awareness, lack of, 150
    self-efficacy, lack of, 151
    sponsorship of, 149
    suicidal thinking, 150
    work, applying for, 148–149
disenfranchisement, of citizen prisoners,
    xx, 94, 123, 167, 193
dispute mediation, 117
district attorneys, 163–165
diversion programs, 16, 81–82, 163,
    165–168, 172, 204–206
drug abuse, 12, 38, 173, 196. *See also* illegal
    drug use

drug addiction, 51, 133, 173, 175, 188,
    206–207
drug courts, 16
drug offenses/possession
    admissions by ethnic/racial group, 27
    demographic data, 27
    Devon, case study, 76
    ethnic/racial group admissions, 27
    first commitment/parole violations, *30*
    global rates of, *xiv*, xv
    international rate of, *xiv*, xv
    Monique, case study, 105
    new prison commitments by gender, *28*
    Steve, case study, 67
    trafficking, 21
    "War on Drugs," 12
    women vs. men, 29
drug treatment programs, 165, 167, 174,
    182, 205–207
drugs as currency, 49
dungeons, 7, 10
dunking stool, 3

economics
    annual prison budgets, 14
    of prison system, 162–163
Edin, K., 37
education
    increasing literacy through, 82–83, 200
    inmate data on, 38–39
    latchkey children challenges, 60–61
    online education, 83
    for parenting, 83–84, 200
    poverty's impact on, 22, 38
    in prison, 112
    spending on, xvi
egocentricity, of prison residents,
    106–107
ego-identity, role of, 138
Einstein, Albert, 55
electronic gaming technology. *See*
    computer games
electronic media influences, 60
emigrating from Country Called Prison.
    See discharged prisoner difficulties
    (case study); proposals for prisoner
    reentry to society; proposals to
    decrease prison populations
Emotional Development Model
    (Greenspan), 63
empathy, lack of, 73

jury nullification use, 170
labeling, elimination of, 175–176, 207
plea bargaining use, 169
reintegration services in prisons,
    178–180
true cost identification, 167–168, 205
proposals to modify prison environment
    establish multidisciplinary unit
        teams, 128
    increase knowledge of social science
        principles, 128–129
    promote cooperation/compassion, 126,
        201–203
    promote pride/self-respect, 126–127
    reduce learned helplessness, 127
prosocial behavior development theories
    childhood as common element, 59
    Containment Theory, 58
    Differential Association Theory, 57
    General Theory of Crime, 58–59
    Social Bond Theory, 58
prosocial maturity, levels of, 150–151
prosocial skills/values development, 57–59,
    87, 201–203
prostitution, in prison, 122
psychiatric hospitals, 11–12
psychosocial goals, 147–148, 201
public good, debate on, xvi–xvii
public health/public health issues
    crime as, 50–51
    goals of, 71–72, 86
    mass incarceration as, 17
    mental illness as, 175
public order crimes, by ethnic/racial
    group, 27
public welfare, spending growth, xvi
punishment
    Bentham on, 6
    Code of Hammurabi, 1–2
    crime control vs., xix, 185
    in early Greek//Roman societies, 2
    forms/descriptions of, 3
    historical examples, 3
    for illegal drug use, xv
    Judaic-Christian tradition, 6–7
    as logical fit to a crime, 4
    in preliterate societies, 1
punishment, theories of
    deterrence, 4–6
    expiation, 4
    "get tough" laws, 12

in moral reformation, 6
rehabilitation, 10–11
retribution/retaliation, 3–4
warehousing model, 12

racial inequality
    in incarceration, 8–9
    inmate percentages by ethnicity, 8
rape
    global rates per 100,000 people, xiv
    international rate of, xiv
    in prison, 22, 122
razor-wire fences, xviii, 16, 24, 43, 45, 49,
    110, 117, 194, 196
Reagan, Ronald, 12
recidivism
    childhood development and, 194
    cost reduction and, 205–208
    discharge planning and, 180
    diversion programs and, 165, 167
    inmate employment and, 144
    inmate learning and, 118
    Mass Incarceration Mountain, 14, 15
    politicians/leaders and, 184
    probation/parole departments and, 183
    rate of, 78, 131
    reasons for, xviii, xix, 109
    social network focus, 13
    successful program funding and, 185,
        207–208
    vocational training and, 188
reciprocal determinism, in social learning
    theory, 59–60, 59
Reckless, Walter, 58
reducing criminality, interventions
    for, 51–52
reentry strategies. See discharged prisoner
        difficulties (case study); proposals for
        prisoner reentry to society
reform movement, of 1900s, 10
reform schools, 11
refugee camps for freed slaves, 8
regulation
    application to criminals, 65
    in effective parenting, 61–62, 62
rehabilitation programs, 165, 166, 181, 188
rehabilitation theory, 10–11, 12
Reiman, Jeffrey, 36
reinforcement
    of executive functioning skills, 81
    in social learning theory, 59–60, 59, 79